The Imperfect Panacea
American Faith in Education

"Just see wherever we peer into the first tiny springs of the national life, how this true panacea for all the ills of the body politic bubbles forth—education, education, education."
—Andrew Carnegie

"The answer for all our national problems comes down to one single word: education."
—Lyndon B. Johnson

The Imperfect Panacea

American Faith in Education

FOURTH EDITION

Henry J. Perkinson
New York University

Boston, Massachusetts   Burr Ridge, Illinois   Dubuque, Iowa
Madison, Wisconsin   New York, New York   San Francisco, California
St. Louis, Missouri

McGraw-Hill

A Division of The **McGraw·Hill** Companies

This book was developed by Lane Akers, Inc.

This book was set in Palatino by ComCom, Inc.
The editor was Lane Akers;
the production supervisor was Kathryn Porzio.
The cover was designed by Tippit/Woolworth Design.
Project supervision was done by Tage Publishing Service, Inc.
R. R. Donnelley & Sons Company was printer and binder.

This book is printed on acid-free paper.

3 4 5 6 7 8 9 0 DOC DOC 9 0 9 8 7

ISBN 0-07-049371-5

Library of Congress Cataloging-in-Publication Data

Perkinson, Henry J.
    The imperfect panacea: American faith in education / Henry J.
Perkinson. — 4th ed.
        p.   cm.
    Includes bibliographical references and index.
    ISBN 0-07-049371-5
    1. Education—United States—History.   2. Education—Philosophy.
I. Title.
LA209.2.P422   1995
370'.973—dc20   94-40277

http://www.mhhe.com

About the Author

Henry J. Perkinson is Professor of Educational History at New York University. He is the author of *Teachers without Goals/Students without Purposes*; *Learning from Our Mistakes: A Reinterpretation of 20th Century Educational Theories*; and *Getting Better: Television and Moral Progress*. He is Past President of the History of Education Society, and former editor of the *History of Education Quarterly*.

For Audrey

Contents

Preface

Most of my professional life has revolved around the issues dealt with in this book. Since the early 1960s, when I first took up the theme, I have been trying to uncover both the origins and the consequences of America's faith in education. With each successive edition of the book, I have corrected earlier errors and mistakes. Few authors are so fortunate to have such an opportunity, and I am grateful to my editor, Lane Akers, for the chance to do it one more time.

The Imperfect Panacea first appeared at a time when the history of American education was undergoing a remarkable transformation. Educational historians had begun to shake the narrow, parochial, in-house, celebrationist outlook that had long characterized the field. Under the leadership of Bernard Bailyn of Harvard and Lawrence Cremin of Teachers College, a fresh group of historians brought a new rigor and depth to the field. Schools of education prepared better-trained historians of education and history departments turned out historians interested in the American educational history. Historians like Rush Welter, Stanley Schultz, Selwyn Troen, Paul Mattingly, Carl Kaestle, Robert Church, and Marvin Lazerson, have all made contributions that have enriched and improved the history of American education.

At the same time as it was becoming more academically respectable, the new history of education had more relevance to practicing educators—particularly in the domain of educational policy. As they came to look at American education in less pietistic ways, historians of education became critical of American education. Some—especially those who took practicing educators, rather than professional historians, as their primary audience—tried to find out why American schools were failing.

Lawrence Cremin, in his pathbreaking *The Transformation of the School*, laid the blame on the professionalization of schooling, which had cut educators off from the political allies needed to bring about and secure reform in American schools. In his later, monumental, *American Education*, Cremin presented the converse of the same argument, claiming, and demonstrating, that education, if construed more broadly than mere schooling, has been widely successful in America.

One of the most influential explanations of why American schools have failed has come from those scholars who adopt a Marxist, or neo-Marxist, approach to history. Scholars such as Michael Katz, Colin Greer, Samuel Bowles, Herbert Gintis, Clarence Karier, Paul Violas, Joel Spring, and David Nassau, have argued that capitalism lies at the root of the failure: schools necessarily serve the interests of the capitalist class and help to reproduce that inherently unfair system.

Other historians have traced the failure of the schools to the ideologies of those who have promoted and maintained them. According to David Tyack and Carl Kaestle, the ideologies of the educators of the past and present have colored and narrowed their vision, resulting in the creation of rigid, inflexible bureaucratic school systems.

Another popular explanation of school failure has come from Diane Ravitch, who has argued that the intransigence and doctrinnaire outlooks and personalities of too many of the participants has destroyed the give and take of negotiation and compromise necessary to the political world of educational policy making.

In *The Imperfect Panacea*, I originally argued that the failure of the schools followed from the grandiose expectations that Americans had—expectations that the schools can and should solve all of the problems of the society. In subsequent editions, I pointed out that in addition to the problems of racial inequality, urban decay, unemployment, and nationalization, Americans now expected the schools to solve the problems of overpopulation and AIDS via sex education programs, the problem of pollution via environmental education, the drug problem via drug education programs, the automobile safety problem via driver education, discrimination and intolerance via multicultural education, crime via values education . . . on and on.

Since first publishing the book, I have come up with the hypothesis that this faith in education rests on the conception that education is socialization. This notion that education consists of changing people in some predetermined way is what underlies the faith in education to solve our social problems. Once the schools change people, the story goes, the problem of racial inequality, or unemployment, or poverty, or social conflict, would go away. The problems did not go away. The schools failed.

I have devoted a large chunk of my professional work in recent years to formulating an alternative conception of education, which I call a critical approach. However, although I think that the notion that education is socialization is mischievous and corrupting, I do not believe many educators are likely to give it up.

In this fourth (and final) edition, I have added a chapter on the development of the public school in the nineteenth century. I have also integrated the epilogue from the third edition into the body of the text. And I have incorporated what is called cultural theory, as developed by the anthropologist Mary

Douglas, to explain some of the goings on I talk about in the book. In this edition, I have concluded that, besides being an imperfect panacea, public schools are no longer viable institutions in the society we now live in.

In writing this edition, I am indebted to the work of the scholars I have mentioned in the preface, but most of all, I am indebted to the friendly and insightful criticisms of my students at New York University.

Henry J. Perkinson

The Imperfect Panacea

American Faith in Education

PART ONE

American Faith in Education

CHAPTER 1

Americans and Their Schools

I

From the beginning Americans depended on their schools. Alone in the savage wilderness of their new settlements, the earliest colonists had to rely upon schools and schoolteachers far more than they did in Europe. Forced to spend their days securing the basic necessities of life, these pioneer parents had little time to care for their children. Moreover, since their New World lacked the agencies of civilization commonplace in the mother country, parents in the New World feared that their children, if untended, might degenerate into savagery—not an unlikely fate in this strange, wild, and dangerous land.

In the colony of Massachusetts this fear resulted in the 1642 compulsory education law, which made parents legally responsible for the education of their children. The problem, of course, lay not with parents, who, for the most part, wanted to educate their children, but in finding the time and energy to care for them. The colony realized that it needed schools and schoolmasters, and in 1647 Massachusetts adopted a law that required each town to provide them. Thus it happened that the first compulsory education laws of modern times appeared in the least civilized part of the Western world and, in fact, were a product of that very lack of civilization.

Other New England colonies copied the Massachusetts compulsory education laws, and in the Middle Atlantic colonies the settlers similarly relied heavily on schools and schoolmasters. The Quakers, a year after their arrival in Pennsylvania in 1682, asked Enoch Flower to become a schoolmaster in Philadelphia and in the same year adopted a compulsory education law.

The Dutch in New Netherlands never had any laws or statutes concerning compulsory education, but they did establish a number of schools to care for their children. The absence of laws is less surprising than the existence of schools, since the colony was actually not much more than a hunting and trapping preserve, attracting single men in search of fortune and adventure. A few families did come to settle, and these parents also turned to schools and schoolmasters to do what they found impossible to do alone. When the British acquired this colony in the late seventeenth century, much of the wilderness had been tamed. Consequently, the English families who came to New York had little fear for their children and, thus, no great concern for schools or schoolmasters. This helps to explain the colony's frequently noted "policy of indifference toward educational legislation." Yet this indifference to educational legislation should not be taken as an indifference to schools and schooling. The New Yorkers did not have to look to the schools to preserve civilization; civilization was secure. Instead they looked to the schools to perform a different yet no less vital function: to prepare children for the unexpected.

II

Throughout its early history America suffered from a short supply of labor. In the South this led to the introduction of Negro slaves. In the rest of the country it led to a decline in the system of apprenticeship. While in Europe future physicians, lawyers, merchants, bankers, artisans, and craftsmen of all kinds received their training through apprenticeship, in the New World the short supply of labor prevented Americans from becoming specialists. Rather than apprenticing themselves to one master to learn one skill well, colonial Americans had to learn to perform many different tasks. They frequently had to provide their own clothing and shelter, clear the land and plant the crops, tend their animals and care for their children, and nurse the sick and settle disputes. They had to be jacks-of-all-trades; they could not afford to be specialists. To get along, the American had to be, in Daniel Boorstin's words, "an undifferentiated man."

Since Europe had no labor shortage, it could continue to train children for specific jobs, jobs suited to their social status. In Europe each child expected to enter a specific occupation, which could usually be predicted with a fair amount of accuracy, since the social position of his or her family (and frequently his or her position in the family—the eldest son, for example, inherited the father's estate) inevitably determined career opportunities.

But in America a child's future was indeterminate. Even in the cities that were well established by the eighteenth century, the expanding economy and the shifting population combined to produce unlimited and unexpected opportunities for all. The problem, then, was to prepare for the unexpected. Yet how could this be done? In an unfamiliar, unknown land there was no one to learn from.

On the frontier farm, or in the forests, one learned from one's own experience. There were no other guides. But in the settled cities on the Eastern seaboard the case was different, since one found trade and commerce carried on in more or less traditional ways. There, young Americans preparing for the future never knew what business, calling, or profession they might enter. It was to help solve this problem of urban youth that Benjamin Franklin set forth, in his "Idea of the English School, Sketch'd Out for the Consideration of the

Trustees of the Philadelphia Academy," a proposal for a school in Philadelphia, from which youth "will come out . . . fitted for learning *any* Business, calling, or Profession." This proposal to use the school to prepare youths for the unexpected was not a novel one. Throughout the late seventeenth and the eighteenth centuries private "adventure" schools had sprung up in all of the Eastern towns and cities. These schools usually consisted of one teacher, who provided instruction in a great number of "modern subjects": commercial subjects, including arithmetic, accounting, bookkeeping, penmanship, letter writing; pure and applied mathematics, including engineering, surveying, navigation; modern foreign languages, Spanish, French, Portuguese; as well as geography and history.

Franklin's contribution lay in his attempt to establish a permanent school, an academy, which would take the "adventure" out of such schooling. With the academy, he hoped to institutionalize and guarantee the continuation of the kind of instruction heretofore dependent upon the immobility and longevity of the private teachers. Actually the academy, after a few years, strayed from Franklin's original purpose, becoming primarily a Latin grammar school. Franklin then severed his connections with it, asserting that it "was no longer concerned with education for such a country as ours."

Although his own academy was a sore disappointment, others took up Franklin's idea for a permanent school where youths could be prepared for the unexpected. By the end of the century academies had been set up in all parts of the country, offering both modern and traditional subjects. Yet even as the academy idea triumphed, other educational developments took center stage. Once they had gained their independence from Britain, the Americans looked to the schools and the schoolmasters to perform a new function: a political function.

III

As soon as the War for Independence ended, Americans began to talk about the vital relationship between education and government. In the 1790's the American Philosophical Society sponsored a contest to select the best essay on a "system of Liberal Education and Literary Instruction adapted to the genius of government. . . ." Most accepted the claim that, in a republic, the chief end of education is to promote intelligent citizenship. This followed logically from the American negative conception of government, a conception embodied succinctly in the statement, "that government is best that governs least." Fearful of governmental tyranny, the Americans had set up a national government that could be restrained and held in check. To do this they had adopted a variety of institutional devices: a Bill of Rights; a written Constitution that enumerated specific powers; a separation of the three branches of government, with each one having the power to veto, or check, the others; and regular, frequent elections, so that the citizens could peacefully get rid of undesirables in public office. But the proper working of all these institutional devices depended upon an enlightened citizenry, an educated citizenry. No one saw this more clearly than Thomas Jefferson. In a letter to George Washington in 1786 he wrote: "It is an axiom of my mind that our liberty can never be safe but in the hands of the people themselves, and that too of the people with a certain degree of instruction."

Jefferson went on to say that he thought this "is the business of the state to effect, and on a general plan." A few years earlier he had submitted to the Virginia legislature just such a general plan for a statewide system of schools, the famous "Bill for the More General Diffusion of Knowledge." Here we find clearly articulated the new political function expected of the schools: "experience has shown," he wrote, "that even under the best forms [of government], those entrusted with power have, in time, and by slow operations, perverted it into tyranny and it is believed that the most effective means of preventing this would be to illuminate, as far as practicable, the minds of the people at large."

The Federal Constitution makes no mention of education, which meant that it remained among the powers that the Tenth Amendment reserved "to the states respectively, or to the people." During this early national period each state government, in one way or another, did encourage the setting up of schools. Usually this took the form of financial help—anything from the allotment of special tax revenues to state lotteries. Sometimes the state donated grants of land for schools. Most states created a permanent fund to provide school grants.

Encouragement for the creation of schools came from the national government as well. The famous Northwest Ordinance of 1787 required each township in the Northwest Territory to set aside a mile square section of land for educational purposes. This ordinance captured perfectly the sentiment of most Americans when it declared: "Religion, morality, and knowledge being necessary to good government and the happiness of mankind, schools and the means of education should forever be encouraged."

The same Northwest Ordinance provided that each state in the territory must set aside not more than two townships "for the purposes of a seminary of learning." This concern with higher education also had its roots in the political theory of the new nation. In contrast to the political practices of Europe, where governmental power was in the hands of a hereditary aristocracy, the Founding Fathers proclaimed that theirs was a free society, an open society, where positions of power were accessible to all men. They fondly hoped that this openness of their society would allow men of talent to rise to positions of leadership, regardless of their ancestry or their economic status. Rejecting the artificial aristocracies of the Old World, the Americans looked for, as Jefferson put it, "a national aristocracy of talent."

The identification, cultivation, and preparation of these men of talent became the task of the schools. The schools were expected to produce future leaders. Jefferson's plan for the state of Virginia clearly embodied this function of selecting and training leaders. His proposed hierarchical educational system would, he declared, rake the best geniuses "from the rubbish."

Few, other than Jefferson, saw the necessity for an entire system of education, but most did see the need for institutions of higher learning to perform this political function of producing leaders. During this early national period a number of prominent statesmen—including George Washington, James Madison, and John Quincy Adams—publicly proposed the establishment of a national university. Religion and political difficulties prevented its inception. However, throughout the country colleges and universities sprang up. Some were private, usually religious, institutions; others were public or state colleges. By 1799 America had 25 institutions of higher learning. Only twenty-five years earlier there had been but 9. By 1820 the number of colleges had increased to 50.

IV

Where did this American faith in education come from?

Originally I thought, and so argued in the book, that this faith in education was typically American, an outcome of being the first *new* colony in the modern world, and later, the first *new* nation. Lacking established institutions and settled arrangements for dealing with their social, economic, and political problems, Americans, from the beginning, I suggested, turned to their schools to solve them. But I now think otherwise. Americans are not the only people to have faith in education. People in other countries, especially developing countries, share this faith, display this outlook. Where, then, did this faith come from?

I now think that this faith in education emerged as one of the consequences of the invention of the printing press in Europe in the late fifteenth century. The argument that connects the printing press to this faith in education is complex and convoluted. Briefly, I think that the printing press first made mass education possible, and then made it necessary. More important: the printing press helped to create a new concept of education itself, a concept that lies at the heart of the belief that education is a panacea for all of society's ills. Let me briefly elaborate this argument.

The printing press made mass education possible by reproducing books in multiple copies that could be scattered everywhere. Scholars no longer had to consult hand-copied rolls of parchment hidden away in dusty monasteries. The printing press liquified knowledge and sent it coursing throughout the Western world so that everyone who could read had access to it, even children. Moreover, through the printing press, scholars could now reclaim, permanently, the writings of the ancients—the writings of the Greeks and Romans as well as the writings of the early Christians and Jews. The printing press preserved all these writings, preserved them in "typographical fixity," to use Elizabeth Eisenstein's felicitous phrase.

Yet, although the printing press provided the materials—books in multiple copies—that made mass education possible, no one at that time thought it necessary to educate the masses. The masses were laborers, most of them serfs who grew the crops and raised the livestock and processed the foods; others were craftsmen who manufactured and mended the utensils and artifacts used in daily life. No need to educate them. They had no use for reading and writing. Traditionally, only the clergy were literate. They served as clerks for the church and for the secular rulers as well—maintaining records and accounts, writing letters, copying manuscripts and documents. Some secular rulers might have known how to read and write, but it was more important that they know how to use a sword, how to ride a horse, how to joust; these were the arts central to *their* education. But after the printing press made books readily available, some scholars persuaded some of the aristocracy to educate their sons in the liberal arts—the arts that one could learn from a book *(liber)*. These arts were the humanities, the arts that "liberated" one from living the life of a mere animal and enabled one to realize oneself as a human being. So, those who received the new education—which, ironically, consisted of "ancient" books and texts—were not the masses but the children of the aristocracy.

It was not until after the Protestant Reformation that anyone thought it necessary to educate the masses. And here, too, the printing press played a role. Without the printing press, Martin Luther's quarrel with the papacy would have been little noticed and soon forgotten. The printing press rapidly reproduced and transmitted the broadsides and pamphlets of Luther and his supporters through all of Christendom, fanning the fires of discord and discontent within the church. The Protestant Reformation tore the church asunder, splitting it into competing, and sometimes warring, sects. When the conflicts ended and peace ensued, the clergy of each competing sect realized that it was necessary to educate the masses so that they could read the Bible and understand it as they ought. The children of each sect had to be taught which doctrines to embrace and the proper creeds to which they must subscribe.

By this time, many secular rulers concurred with the proposal to educate the masses—but for their own reasons. The princes and kings of Europe had long sought to secure centralized control over their realms. The printing press finally enabled them to do just this by reproducing multiple copies of the various laws, decrees, communiques, rules, documents, and records that the rulers could use to regulate the lives of their subjects and to unify the state. But if they would be rulers of their realms, the kings and princes required loyal, obedient, and industrious subjects. Here, too, then, was a reason for mass education—for the "good of the nation." So, in the sixteenth and seventeenth centuries, both church and secular authorities began to see the necessity for educating the masses. And throughout Europe, fledgling efforts began to take root.

Let me summarize my argument on this point. As I see it, the printing press helped to change the religious and the political arrangements in Europe, as a consequence of which it became necessary to educate the masses, educate them to be loyal and faithful followers.

This education for the masses was actually an alternative to the "true" education provided for the upper classes. The distinction can be summed up by the terms *initiation* and *socialization*. The education provided the children of the upper classes initiated them into the cultural heritage of Western civilization by having them study the best that had been thought and said and done, as contained in the classic texts from Greece and Rome. "Within these two literatures," Erasmus wrote, "are contained all the knowledge which we recognize as of vital importance to mankind." There was no extrinsic purpose to this liberal education; the sole purpose was to help people become human beings. But the education now beginning to be provided to the masses was quite different. First of all, it was briefer: reading and writing (in the vernacular) and religion. But it also had a different purpose—an extrinsic purpose: to make the masses industrious workers, loyal subjects, faithful church members. In short, this education was a process of socialization: the integration of children of the lower classes into the existing society by having them learn the skills, understandings, sentiments, and beliefs to keep it going.

With the emergence of this new kind of education, new metaphors appeared. The traditional education provided for the upper classes had used the metaphor of the teacher as a mentor who initiated the student to the cultural heritage of Western civilization by guiding his or her study of the classical texts. In contrast, people now described the education provided for the lower classes by recourse to the metaphor of the printing press. Here is how Comenius, an influential educator of the seventeenth century, put it: "Instead of paper, we have pupils," Comenius wrote, "pupils whose minds have to be impressed with the symbols of knowledge. Instead of type, we have classbooks and the rest of the apparatus devised to facilitate the operation of teaching. The ink is replaced by the voice of the master since it is this that conveys information to the minds of the listener, while the press is school discipline, which keeps the pupils up to their work and compels them to learn."

In Europe, this concept of education as a process of socialization applied only to the education provided for the lower classes. But in America, which was settled by Europeans *after* the Protestant Reformation, and by Europeans mainly from the lower classes, this kind of education took root and became the only recognized mode of education. Recall Benjamin Franklin's insistence that the study of Latin and Greek literatures was simply not suited "for such a country as ours."

With the socialization concept of education, one must start off by deciding upon the extrinsic purpose of education, what talents, knowledge, beliefs, values, skills, and understandings must be transmitted to children in order to keep society going. Thus, the construction of education as a process of socialization leads logically to the notion that education is a panacea. Americans, from the earliest colonial times, have been the unwitting captives of the concept that education is a process of socialization, a concept that lies at the heart of this enduring faith in education.

In the nineteenth century this faith in education was institutionalized in the public schools, with the consequence that Americans came to believe that the public schools could solve all of society's problems.

CHAPTER 2

The Evolution of the American Public School

By the 1830s, a new social order had emerged in America. Politically, America had become more democratic; economically, it had become industrialized; and most important of all, socially it had become more urban. For it was in the cities that industrialization took place, and in the cities that democratic politics first emerged.

Although the overall increase in urban populations had not been great—by 1830, only 8.8 percent of the people lived in urban areas (defined as cities and towns over 2500), compared to 6.1 percent in 1800. But the accelerating rate of increase had severe social impact: the urban population grew 82 percent between 1820 and 1830, 68 percent the following decade, and almost 100 percent between 1840 and 1850. In 1800, farmers had outnumbered town and city dwellers by fifteen to one; by 1830, that ratio had declined to about ten to one. Between 1790 and 1830, New York's population grew from 33,000 to 200,000, carrying it past Philadelphia, which had grown from 42,000 to 161,000. Baltimore had become the third largest city, with 155,000 inhabitants, compared with Boston's 133,000. During this period, the building of canals had helped create cities west of the Alleghenies, where Pittsburgh, Louisville, and Cincinnati now had populations between 10,000 and 25,000.

Although some took pride and revelled in the spectacular growth of American cities, many viewed this phenomenon with dismay. At the outset of the century, Thomas Jefferson had warned that he viewed "great cities as pestilential to the morals, the health, and the liberties of man." Alexis de Tocqueville, who visited the United States in 1831, confirmed this antiurban animus when he wrote: "I look upon the size of certain American cities, and especially on the nature of their population, as a real danger which threatens the future security of the democratic republics of the new world."

That was the problem: "the nature of the population."

By 1830 many families long settled in the cities had pulled up stakes, and merchants, too, had moved away from their shops to more distant residences. This left once-stable neighborhoods to newcomers, many of whom were unmarried males, who had recently moved to the city from farms and villages, while an ever-increasing number were foreign immigrants who reflected a wide ethnic, linguistic, and religious spectrum. All had been lured to the cities by the thousands of new jobs now available. Each decade saw new business firms appear in the cities: manufacturers and distributors of textiles, books, shoes, leather goods, glass, and iron; exporters of wheat and cotton. But the periodic "panics," "repressions," and "depressions" during the first half of the nineteenth century threw many of the newcomers to the city out of work, making families, and even whole neighborhoods, destitute. People felt less safe venturing into neighborhoods occupied by people different from themselves. For not only had the city become a world of strangers, it was now threatened by social disorder. The new urban dwellers were restless, indifferent, and vulnerable to intemperance, gambling, sexual immorality, profanity, and Sabbath breaking. Such vices had existed in the villages and rural communities of colonial America, but now in the cities, they became magnified and more menacing.

Menacing not only to social life, but to the polity as well: For, since the 1790s, most states had expanded the franchise, and by the 1830s, most adult white males had the right to vote on election day. At the same time, political organizations had arisen in the cities—like Tammany Hall in New York—that drew their strength from the poor, the immigrants, the laboring masses. For the first time, in 1834, a Tammany-backed candidate became mayor. City after city witnessed new and somewhat disreputable political groups emerge to wrest control from the old governing elites. The governing elites grew more and more apprehensive—concerned about their own loss of status, yes, but also fearful about the preservation of American political institutions. After all, the founding fathers had contemplated a republic ruled by men of "enlightened vision and virtuous sentiments." Could the institutions of republican government survive democratization?

The problem, as those apprehensive Americans saw it, was a moral one. The blame for urban decay, social unrest, and political instability lay directly on the licentious, immoral, irresponsible newcomers who now inhabited the cities. They had to be educated, or socialized, to become moral, upright citizens. This meant they had to be transformed into true Christians.

I

In the 1820s and 1830s urban reformers created a number of different voluntary moral control societies to attempt to stem the social decay in the cities. Initially, they tried oral appeals through revival meetings and missions set up in rental storefront, theatres, public halls, and warehouses. Although they met with some success (the missions in New York City attracted some 4000 members by 1832), they failed to convert many into regular churchgoers. Church membership continued to be made up of those from "the middle ranks of life." The unskilled laborers, the destitute, the transients, the immigrants, remained outside the fold.

The urban moral reformers had more impact when they turned to the printed word and set up associations to print and distribute Bibles. The American Bible Society (ABS), founded in New York in 1816, produced and distributed nearly 6 million Bibles by 1849. According to the society's historian, every incoming immigrant in New York City received an ABS Bible. The Philadelphia Bible Society reported that, as a result of citywide distribution of the Bible, "haunts of wickedness" were being abandoned. In Boston, eighty women volunteers in teams of two distributed bibles throughout the city. Yet, contrary to the claims made, some began to realize that distribution of the Bible was not enough: its length, difficult prose, and lack of immediate relevance diminished the intended impact on the urban masses. Emphasis then shifted to Tracts—short missives, written in the vernacular, that could be cheaply printed, easily distributed, and quickly read.

In 1825 tract societies from New York, Philadelphia, Baltimore, and Providence joined together to form the American Tract Society (ATS). The directors of the ATS declared that "short, plain, striking, entertaining, and instructive Tracts" were the most effective means to "lengthen the cords and strengthen the stakes that bind together the body politic." By centralizing both the production and distribution of Tracts, the ATS launched an impressive enterprise. By 1840 the ATS headquarters occupied a new five-story, fifty-six-room building where a crew of thirty printers operated seventeen late-model steam presses, while the binding room housed another hundred employees. By 1950, the ATS had built up a backlist of over 500 titles and produced over 5 million tracts annually. The society sent bulk shipments to Sunday schools, poorhouses, prisons, orphanages, and immigration depots, and to local tract societies in other cities who conducted systematic home-by-home distribution. Volunteers also met incoming ships to start the immigrants' life in the new world with a Tract in hand.

Some Tracts were especially tailored to the immigrants. Typically, they would urge the newcomers to abandon any "vice or impropriety" they might have acquired in the "old world." Usually, it included a warning like: "God has brought you across the Atlantic, but this is not your home. You will remain here but a little while, and then you will take another voyage. The passage will be short; but whether it shall . . . safely conduct you to the realm of never-ending bliss, or . . . cast [you] into a gulf of tumultuous flame without a bottom and without a shore, depends upon the question whether you consecrate . . . your heart and life to Christ."

Other Tracts were geared to young men "thrown upon the open bosom of the city." These contained warnings about playing into the "fatal vortex of licentious dissipation: where one's doom is sealed: Reduced to penury, stript of character, and corrupted by sensuality, they quickly progress from the shop and the brothel to the prison, the gallows, or some other miserable end."

To parents, the Tracts proclaimed the importance of the family, urging them to create the kind of home that would help the children resist the morally corrosive power of the city. "If your children," one Tract said, "prove to be the curse of their country, as well as the torment and ruin of those most intimately related to them, the guilt is yours."

Bibles and Tracts were intended for adults, literate adults. But what about the children? What about the hordes of street urchins who were becoming "pests of the society"? If their families were failing to nurture them properly, then concerned moral reformers would have to do this. Many poor children were already working as apprentices, but they were free on Sundays.

The Sunday school movement had actually begun in England in the late eighteenth century. It crossed the Atlantic to Philadelphia, where the First Day Society was set up to give rudimentary instruction to the "offspring of indigent parents." Sunday schools were nondenominational organizations, initiated and run by lay people, unconnected with any church, although some denominations, like the Methodists, set up their own Sunday schools.

By 1800 Philadelphia Sunday schools enrolled more than 2000 children. Other cities established Sunday school societies, and in 1822 they joined together to form the American Sunday School Union (ASSU). Within 6 years, the ASSU reported that some 350,000 were enrolled in its schools. In a short time, a vast network of Sunday schools existed in the major East Coast urban centers, and many interior cities as well, like Albany, Utica, Pittsburgh, and Cincinnati. Many cities had annual parades and rallies where the students from each school marched, carrying its own flag and singing Sunday school songs. In 1829 one such rally in Battery Park, New York, attracted some 1200 scholars and 5000 teachers and sympathizers.

Sunday schools typically met both in the morning and afternoon. School activities included prayer, hymn singing, and learning to read. The older children read and recited passages from the Bible. Sunday schools consciously and deliberately set out to transform the character of the young—to prepare them for eternity, but also to train them for lives of "respectability and usefulness here on earth." The ASSU forthrightly declared its aims: "to lay in the children's minds the foundation of obedience to their governors in church and state, to make them contented with the situation which providence has appointed for them in the world, to teach them subjugation of their passions, and the avoiding of the company of dissolute and profligate and vicious characters."

Yet as successful as the Sunday school movement was, it could not suffice. Too many children now lived in the cities, and their numbers increased every year. To stem the tide of moral decay and social dissorder, a more extended and more sympathetic education was needed. What about the existing schools?

II

By the 1830s, the cities had a wide variety of different kinds of schools. There were "dame schools," operated by women in their homes. Here small children learned how to read. There were writing schools, where children learned how to write, and English schools that taught reading, spelling, writing, arithmetic, and sometimes geography and history. All these were "private venture schools," usually taught by one person, sometimes a clergyman. Some cities in New England had town schools that were quasi-public; that is, schools supported by taxes, but where parents were charged tuition "rates." But for the most part, these quasi-public town schools were not very good, so those who could afford the modest fees charged sent their children to the private schools. The private schools charged fees within the means of perhaps three-quarters of the population, and a wide variety of families patronized them. In 1837, according to Carl Kaestle, 56 percent of the children in the city of Salem attended private schools.

Edward Everett Hale, son of a Boston newspaper editor, reports that from age two to six he attended Miss Whitney's (dame) school; at six, he entered a "man's" school. At nine, he did enter a city school, the prestigious Boston Latin School. "But," Hale observes, "there was no public school of any lower grade to which my father would have sent me, any more than he would have sent me to jail."

In addition to the town schools and the private venture schools, there were the academies. The academy, in Lawrence Cremin's phrase, was "a characteristically American catch-all school." Highly responsive to the needs of the community, it provided an education beyond the rudiments in a wide variety of subjects: Latin and Greek, as well as applied, mathematics, history, geography, and scientific studies. Many academies had teacher training departments. Some academies prepared students for entrance to college, but for most, the academy prepared them for "life." Academies enrolled students from all social classes and both sexes. A few academies were for females exclusively—sometimes called "female seminaries," such as Troy Seminary, founded by Emma Willard in 1821; Mt. Holyoke Seminary, founded by Mary Lynn in 1836; and Hartford Seminary, founded by Catherine Beecher in 1828. The female academies trained many teachers; they offered academic studies and "ornamental" subjects—embroidery, dancing, painting, music—as well.

The original academies were quasi-private institutions: controlled by private boards of trustees, but publicly supported by funding and annual grants from the state treasuries. During the first half of the nineteenth century, the number of academies increased phenomenally. In 1800, there were 17 academies in Massachusetts, 19 in New York, and 10 in the State of Georgia; by 1830, there were nearly a thousand academies in the United States. Twenty years later, New England alone had that many, the Middle Atlantic states had over 1600, and the Southern states had nearly 2700. All told, by 1850, there were more than 6000 academies in the entire United States, with 260,000 pupils and more than 12,000 teachers.

But what about the poor? What about the children of those one-quarter or more families who could not afford the fees for the private schools or the tuition "rates" charged by the quasi-public town schools? By 1830 most cities had set up schools to give the children of the poor a rudimentary education free of charge. These "monitorial schools," as they were called, had been invented by a British schoolmaster, Joseph Lancaster, who, being too poor to pay for additional teachers, had hit upon the idea of using student monitors in lieu of assistants. An organizational genius, Lancaster soon developed a total educational system by which a single teacher could conduct a school of up to a thousand students.

The fully developed Lancasterian plan was so efficient and so cheap that it spread throughout England and from there to the new world. In 1806 the first monitorial school opened in New York City, under the auspices of the Free School Society.

Monitorial schools in the United States were quasi-private schools controlled by a local voluntary association like the Free School Society of New York. During the first quarter of the century, voluntary associations in Baltimore, Philadelphia, Washington, Providence, and Albany established citywide systems of monitorial schools for the poor who did not belong to any denomination that provided such schooling.

By 1825 the New York Free Society had established eleven monitorial schools and claimed to have educated 20,000 pupils "from the indigent classes."

The highly organized monitorial school had all pupils constantly employed. "Let every child at every moment have something to do and a motive for doing it," was Lancaster's motto. With anywhere from 200 to 1000 students, assembled in one large room, sorted out according to ability, each row, or form, had its own monitor—while the monitors themselves had monitors who conducted the lessons in accord with the elaborate manuals and lesson plans Lancaster had devised.

Each school had eight reading classes, representing specific levels of ability. The first level learned the alphabet, the second learned words and syllables of two letters, the third and fourth learned words and syllables of three and four letters, the fifth class studied reading lessons of one-syllable words, the sixth had two-syllable words, the seventh class studied the Testament, and the eighth the Bible.

In teaching writing, the monitor in charge—the "dictator"—would dictate a letter, or syllable, or word, to the monitor of each form, who would, in turn, repeat it for the pupils in his or her form, who would then write it on their slates. After six "dictations," the pupils would prepare for inspection by placing their hands behind their backs. The class monitors would then inspect the work. Those who completed the work correctly would advance to the head of the class. Reading and arithmetic lessons were taught in a similar fashion.

In reading exercises, a child would read the words printed on a chart or the wall until making a mistake. The next pupil would correct the mistake and change places with the previous reader. The second pupil would read until corrected by the third, and so it went. When a pupil mastered the lessons of the reading class, the monitor would recommend promotion to the next class.

The monitors also managed the school. There were monitors to take attendance, monitors to keep order, monitors to care for equipment. When admitted to a school, a monitor assigned the pupil to class; when he or she was absent, one monitor ascertained the fact and another found out the reason. (The only excuse for absence was sickness; six unexcused absences in a month meant expulsion.) Monitors conducted all examinations and decided upon promotions.

By 1825 monitorial schools had spread from New York City to Pough-keepsie, Hudson, Troy, Schenectady, and Utica. In Connecticut, Hartford, New Haven, and Guilford had monitorial schools. And in Pennsylvania, in addition to Philadelphia, monitorial schools were found in Harrisburg, Pittsburgh, Erie, and Newcastle. In the South, Charleston, Richmond, Alexandria, and Norfolk all had monitorial schools. And in the West, Detroit, Louisville, Lexington, and Cincinnati set up monitorial schools.

Authoritarian and regimented, with a rigid, mechanical approach to teaching, the monitorial schools converted education into a process of rote memorization. But they were efficient. Most children learned to read and write in a few months. And the schools were cheap. The monitorial school, Dewitt Clinton, the first President of the New York Free School Society, explained, was a system that "operates with the same efficiency in education as labor-saving machinery does in the useful arts." Here is Clinton's assessment of a monitorial school: "When I contemplate the habits of order which it forms, the spirit of emulation which it excites, the rapid improvement which it produces, the parity of morals which it inculcates—when I behold the extraordinary union of celerity in instruction and economy of expense—and when I perceive one great assembly of a thousand children under the eye of a single teacher, marching with unexampled rapidity and with perfect discipline to the goal of knowledge, I confess that I recognize in Lancaster the benefactor of the human race. I consider his system as creating a new era in education, as a blessing sent down from heaven to redeem the poor and distressed of this world from the power and domination of ignorance."

The moral reformers who established the monitorial schools wanted to get children out of their "harmful" family environments—the earlier the better. But they soon realized that the mechanistic, militarylike monitorial approach ill-suited very young children. So, to deal with the young, but potentially "disruptive" clients, new voluntary associations created "infant schools." In New York, Philadelphia, Boston, New Haven, Charleston, and elsewhere, infant school societies set up schools for children from 2 to 6 years old. Here, instead of the drill and repetition of the monitorial schools, women teachers created a maternal climate that inculcated proper moral conduct in the young pupils. In some infant schools, they taught reading as well.

In rural America—where most Americans still lived in 1830—the schools had developed along a different path. Outside the cities, most children attended what were called "district" schools. Since all the children in the community attended these schools, where they all followed the same course of study, people also referred to these schools as "common" schools. They were quasi-public schools, publicly controlled by the local community, and publicly supported through a combination of property taxes, fuel contributions, and state aid; but they were not free—parents paid tuition or "rates." (In the rural South until after the Civil War, schools—except for those in North Carolina— were usually private, set up by itinerant schoolmasters who were paid by the parents who chose to send their children.)

One can trace the district school back to the Massachusetts Colony Law of 1647, which required every town of fifty families to establish a town school. Each town or township usually covered a six-square-mile area, so when peo- ple moved beyond walking distance to the school, they balked at paying taxes for the town school and insisted on setting up a school in their own district. As people moved further to the West, the district school concept spread throughout the rural areas of New England and the Middle Atlantic states.

Pedagogical confusion marked the operations of the district schools of the first quarter of the nineteenth century. Enrollments were higher than in the city schools, but the district schools ran only three or four months in the win- ter and three months in the summer. Girls and young children attended in the summer, while the boys worked on the farms. Each school had but one teacher, usually a college student trying to earn money to pay for his or her own tuition. (Local females taught the summer sessions.) The teacher had to teach as many as forty to sixty pupils, who ranged from four to fourteen years of age. Understandably, teachers spent much of their time disciplining them. The Reverend Warren Burton, who attended one such district school in New Hampshire from 1804 to 1817, later described some of the disciplinary tactics one particular teacher employed: "Almost every method was tried that was ever suggested to the brain of a pedagogue. Some were ferruled on the hand; some were whipped with a rod on the back; some were compelled to hold out, at arm's length, the largest book which could be found, or a great leaden ink- stand, till muscle and nerve, bone and marrow, were tortured with the con- tinued exertion. If the arm bent or inclined from the horizontal level, it was forced back again by a knock of the ruler on the elbow." These punishments, Burton adds, usually took place in front of the fireplace or stove, so that "the pitiable culprit was roasted, as well as racked."

In the district school, students supplied their own textbooks—whatever the family happened to have—which they studied (memorized) at their desks (benches) and then recited to the teacher. Since teachers changed annually, there were no records, so students frequently went through the same book more than once. In the 1830s, Theodore Dwight, in a book called *Things as They Are*, described one district school he observed in Connecticut: "the teacher was mending pens for one class, which was sitting idle; hearing another spell; call- ing a covey of small boys to be quiet, who had nothing to do but to make mis- chief; watching a big rogue, who had been placed on a bench in the middle of the room for punishment; and to many little ones, passionately answering questions of 'May I go out?' 'May I go home?' 'Shan't Johnny be still?' 'May I drink?' "

As unorganized and chaotic as they were, the district schools satisfied the communities of rural America. Their children learned to read and write, and learned some arithmetic, and religion, too. The district school taught what the community wanted its children to learn. As the community varied, so did the school: in some communities, teachers taught in foreign languages, and always included the religious exercises preferred by the community. By 1840 the district system had spread west and south to Ohio, Illinois, Indiana, Tennessee, Kentucky, and North Carolina.

III

In the eyes of many would-be reformers of the 1830s, the existing educational arrangements—rural and urban—remained hopelessly inadequate. They realized, however, that the district school system, such as it was, had deep roots and probably could not be changed. However, the quality of education offered in most district schools needed vast improvement. But as to the cities, the reformers insisted that the variegated collection of private and quasi-private schools there had to go. All of the schools—rural and urban—had to be systematized under public control. Each state, some reformers now argued, had to assert control over the schools and establish state systems of education that would provide free education for all.

Earlier, both New York and Maryland had created the office of state superintendent of education but then abolished it. Some states had created ex-officio state superintendents, but these remained largely figureheads. To most Americans, the whole notion of centrally controlled schools ran afoul of the long-standing tradition of local control. Moreover, the notion of free education for all contradicted the equally strong tradition of each family paying for the education of its own children. Only the poor had received education for free up till now. Understandably, then, the states moved cautiously in assuming control over the schools.

Massachusetts became the bellwether in the creation of a state system of schooling. There, in 1837, the legislature created a state board of education, and Governor Everett persuaded Horace Mann, the president of the senate, to accept the position of first secretary of the board, making him, in effect, the state superintendent of the schools of Massachusetts. Shortly after taking office, Mann revealed he was the right person for the post when, with typical unbuttoned enthusiasm and characteristic hyperbole, he wrote in his journal: "Let the common school be expanded to its capabilities, let it be worked with the efficiency of which it is susceptible, and nine-tenths of the crimes in the penal code would become obsolete; the long catalogue of human ills would be abridged; men would walk more safely by day; every pillow would be more inviolable by night; property, life and character held by a stronger tenure; all rational hopes respecting the future brightened."

Yet the appointed head of education in Massachusetts had no legal authority to tell local communities what he wanted them to do, or any funds to induce them to do what he wanted. The legislature refused to increase the state education fund, or to cede any coercive legal powers to the secretary of the board. To carry out his mission, Horace Mann had to rely on his powers of persuasion which were considerable indeed. Traveling the length and breadth of the state on horseback, he gave speech after speech to local communities exhorting them to improve their district schools, encouraging them to raise the funds necessary to carry it out. He sponsored annual conventions and lectured at any opportunity, to any group, who would hear him. In addition, he created, and edited, the biweekly *Common School Journal,* and wrote twelve massive *Annual Reports* that he circulated widely. In every speech and publication, he issued the same message: the schools of Massachusetts could survive and improve only through systematic uniformity—uniform textbooks, a uniform curriculum, uniform teaching methods, uniform management, uniform discipline, and uniformly trained teachers.

Newly appointed school superintendents from other states soon joined Mann in his crusade to systematize the schools. Henry Barnard took up the task in Connecticut, and later Rhode Island; Calvin Wiley in North Carolina; Caleb Mills in Indiana; Samuel Lewis in Ohio; and Robert Breckenridge in Kentucky. These educational reformers drew freely on each other for intellectual and political support. They corresponded regularly, exchanged lectures, and reprinted one another's essays and reports. New York State circulated Mann's *Common School Journal* to its local school districts and reprinted Mann's *Fifth Annual Report* at public expense. Like Mann, these school reformers used their promotional skills to exhort their fellow citizens to establish and support state systems of free public schools. And like Mann, they gave innumerable speeches, sponsored conventions, and edited journals. According to one count, over fifty new periodicals devoted to education debuted between 1825 and 1850.

With the help of other "friends of education," they created state and regional groups and organizations to further the cause of school reform. In New England, there was the American Institute of Instruction; in the West, the Western Literacy Institute and College of Professional Teachers. These associations sponsored meetings, lectures, and conventions; they published letters, addresses, and reports; and they lobbied the state legislatures. Much of their effort went toward the transformation of teaching into a bona fide profession through the creation of teachers institutes and normal schools to train teachers.

Some historians have called these educational reformers conservatives—aristocrats, even; others have pointed out that most of them were members of the Whig party—the party opposed to the Jacksonian Democrats. But rather than characterize their ideology in political, or economic, or social terms, culture or cultural theory seems to capture best what they were about.

Cultural theory as formulated by the anthropologist Mary Douglas is based on the axiom that what matters to most people is their relationships with other people, and other people's relationships with them. According to cultural theory, everyone acts in ways that support one's preferred way of life. Educational reformers like Horace Mann fit into what cultural theorists call a "hierarchical way of life." Hierarchs believe that specialization and division of labor enable people to live together with harmony and effectiveness. Hierarchs support institutionalized authority and insist that the parts are supposed to sacrifice for the whole. This kind of culture had long existed in America, but the hierarchs feared that the moral depravity now found in the cities threatened to corrode it.

Clearly, the school reformer hierarchs of the 1830s and '40s were cut from the same cloth as the urban moral reformers who had earlier set up and run the Sunday schools, and the Bible and Tract societies. Like them, the school reformers saw themselves as "stewards of God" specially chosen to be their brothers' keepers. They, too, concluded that the moral failings of the individual produced social disorder, and that social disorder threatened political stability. The solution, once again, was education, and by education they meant education in Christian moral virtues. This, the school reformers decided, would restore the kind of culture they preferred.

Daniel Webster epitomized this outlook when he described education of the masses as "a wise and liberal system of police, by which property, and life, and the peace of society are secured." As Webster and other hierarchs saw it, popular education inhibits crime and serves as a political safeguard "as well against open violence and overthrow, as against the slow but sure undermining of licentiousness." Fearful of social conflict of any kind, the hierarchs viewed a common course of study for everyone as the path to social harmony. Although it was not a central plank in their platform, the hierarchs usually supported free schooling, since the schools could never be common to all unless they were free. To pull this off, they argued, required the collective imposition of quality standards in every American school.

Two other ideological groups actively promoted school reform during this period. One group, best characterized as what Mary Douglas calls "egalitarians," wanted to use the schools to create a culture where equality of condition was the sole norm regulating human life. The egalitarians, like the hierarchs, worried about social disorder, and they, too, traced it to moral decay. But the moral deficiencies they zeroed in on were selfishness and greed—the selfishness and greed of the few who had created the vast social and economic inequalities that caused the social disorder rampant in the cities.

Whereas the hierarchs stressed the theme of commonality in their support of the public schools, the egalitarians supported the public schools because they were free. They criticized the "charity" education cities and districts then provided for the poor, since, to receive it, a family had to stigmatize itself as paupers. Rather than do this, the egalitarians explained, many poor families simply refused to send their children to school. Public schools, the egalitarians argued, must be free if they were ever to create an equal society. One egalitarian at the Pennsylvania Constitutional Convention in 1837 put it this way: "If the people should be educated at the public expense, only on condition that they are certified and recorded as paupers, they would surely refuse to avail themselves of the offer."

Egalitarians, like James Carter, lambasted the quasi-private academies that had sprung up in his native state of Massachusetts after the War of Independence. Academies, he complained, drew off the children of parents "who can barely afford the expense of tuition," contributing to the decline and decay of the public schools, now attended only by the poor. Egalitarians favored state action over the action of voluntary associations, since voluntary associations always act for their own private interests. Thus, Carter favored the creation of a *state* normal school for training teachers, warning that, "If it not be undertaken by the public and for public purposes, it will be undertaken by individuals for private purposes."

The other ideological group concerned with school reform was one that cultural theory characterizes as "individualists." According to Douglas, self-regulation is the social ideal of individualists: they seek equality of opportunity (not equality of condition) in order to be able to compete and negotiate social arrangements with a minimum of external interference. This is the kind of culture that actually existed in much of America in the 1830s. So, unlike the hierarchs, who wanted schools to restore a declining culture; and unlike the egalitarians, who wanted schools to create a culture that had never existed; the individualists wanted public schools to preserve the existing culture.

Most of the individualists of that time were Democrats who opposed the state subsidies and grants the Whig politicians promoted, because they created monopolies and unfair advantages for some. Yet, although they opposed government support of internal improvements—like canals and railroads—individualists did favor state support for public education. The Committee of Philadelphia Workingmen expressed this in their Report of 1830: "The original element of despotism is a monopoly of talent which consigns the multitude to comparative ignorance, and secures the balance of knowledge on the side of the rich and the rulers. If then the healthy existence of a free government be, as the committee believe, rooted in the will of the American people, it follows as a necessary consequence of a government based upon that will, that this monopoly should be broken up, and that the means of equal knowledge (the only security for equal liberty) should be rendered, by legal provision, the common property of all classes."

But the individualist educational reformers wanted only state support, not state control. As one prominent individualist of the time, Orestes Brownson, wrote: "Nothing desirable in matters of education, beyond what relates to the finances of the schools, comes within the province of the legislature. More than this, the legislature should not attempt; more than this the friends of education should not ask. Let the legislature provide ample funds for the support of as many schools as are needed for the best education possible of all the children of the community, and there let it stop."

Individualists favored local control of schooling, fearful that central control, state control, would destroy freedom. Here is Orestes Brownson: "The selection of teachers, the choice of schools and of books to be read or studied, all that pertains to the methods of teaching and the matters to be taught or learned are best left to the school district. In these matters, the district should be paramount to the state."

In addition to opposing state control of schools, individualists also opposed making education free for all. The education of children, they argued, was the private responsibility of parents. In Rhode Island, one individualist

farmer threatened to shoot Henry Barnard if he ever caught him on his property advocating "such heresy as the partial confiscation of one man's property
to educate another man's child." In the same vein, a member of the Indiana
legislature of 1837 declared that, when he died, he wanted engraved on his
tombstone, "Here lies an enemy to free schools."

What appealed to individualists about public schools was that such
schools would make education universal. They thought it possible to have universal education without having the state control the schools and without providing free tuition to all.

All these ideological groups—hierarchs, egalitarians, and individualists—
favored state-supported public education, although each group stressed a different function of public schooling: the hierarchs insisted that public schools
provide a common curriculum with commonly held high standards; the egalitarians argued that the public schools must be free to all; and the individualists wanted public schools to be open and available to everyone. An astute and
clever reformer like Horace Mann, a hierarch who prized social stability above
all else, was not above appealing to the ideology of the egalitarians, as he did
when he claimed in his 1848 *Annual Report* that education is "the great equalizer of the condition of man." But, in keeping with his basic hierarchical pro-
clivities, he immediately added that education was also "the balance wheel of
the social machinery." And earlier, in 1840—after the Democratic legislature
had threatened to abolish the board of education—he appealed to the ideology of the individualists by pointing out that the common school promoted
individual social mobility, as well as social stability.

IV

As pompous and self-righteous a windbag as Horace Mann may seem to us
today, he knew exactly what needed doing to systematize the schools of Massachusetts. Shortly after taking office, he clearly delineated the task before him:
"In this Commonwealth," he announced in a lecture of 1837, "there are about
three thousand public schools, in all of which the rudiments of knowledge are
taught. These schools, at the present time, are so many distinct, independent
communities; each being governed by its own habits, traditions, and local customs. There is no common, superintending power over them; there is no bond
of brotherhood or family between them. They are strangers and aliens to each
other. The teachers are, as it were, imbedded, each in his own school district;
and they are yet to be excavated and brought together, and to be established,
each as a polished pillar of a holy temple. As the system is now administered,
if any improvement in principles or modes of teaching is discovered by talent
or accident, in one school, instead of being published to the world, it dies with
the discoverer. No means exist for multiplying new truths, or even for preserving old ones."

Not only did he know what had to be done, he devised the strategy for
doing it, a strategy copied by superintendents in other states. The strategy was

to extend, strengthen, and systematize the already-existing district schools. During the early nineteenth century, the district school system had penetrated some cities, where they were called "ward schools" rather than district schools. So, by the 1830s, rural and some urban areas had independent, ungraded schools managed by school trustees or school committees, paid for by public monies and by tuition payments or "rates." Each district, or ward, levied its own taxes and fees, selected and examined its teachers, determined the methods of instruction, monitored attendance, chose the textbooks, and decided on the length of the school term.

Lacking the legal authority to control the school districts, Mann adopted the tactic of shaming them into reforming their schools. Gathering statistics from each district—on enrollments, attendance, textbooks, courses of study, books in school libraries, methods of instruction, discipline, teacher qualifications, length of school terms, and on and on—Mann then published these in his reports, which he scattered everywhere. In this way, he disclosed the chaos rampant in the Massachusetts schools, the lack of uniformity, the absence of standards, the unfair inequalities. To guide the districts along the correct path, he always included recommendations to remedy and correct the inadequacies he had revealed.

To his surprise and dismay, however, his tactics met recalcitrant resistance. So, in addition to making recommendations to the local districts, he prepared numerous education bills that the legislature promptly voted into law. These included a requirement that school committees keep records and make annual reports to the secretary of the state board of education. To sweeten the burden of increased supervisory responsibilities, Mann recommended that committee members receive a salary from the state education fund. Another statute endowed the board with the power to draw up a list of "approved" books to be included in each district school library. (The legislature, at Mann's recommendation, had appropriated funds to support the purchase of such libraries.)

Perhaps the most important legislation passed in these early years was the bill to create state-controlled teacher training institutions. Armed with $10,000 donated by Edmund Dwight, a member of the board of education, Mann secured a matching amount from the legislature. Within a year, the first of three normal schools opened. Governor Everett, speaking at opening ceremonies as ex-officio president of the state board of education, outlined the course of studies future teachers would pursue. First, they would review all that was to be taught in the common school; second, they would learn how to teach; third, they would "practice" teaching in a school under the direction of a principal. But most important, the governor said, were their studies in the government of the school: learning how to exercise a moral influence "most favorable to the improvement of the pupil."

In his *Third Annual Report,* Mann made a plea to the local school committees to create libraries to supplement the instruction provided in the schools. But this plea soon turned into a harangue against the reading habits of the populace. The attempt to impose his personal views as educational dogma sprang, as always, from Mann's morbid fear of social unrest and instability.

He rejected books of history as appropriate fare for children, since they record naught but conflict, plunder, pillage—actions that appeal to the reader's lower instincts. He dismissed all books written in Great Britain for British readers: "Such books do not contain the models according to which the growth of a Republic should be formed." Most of his hostility he reserved for novels, books that appeal to the emotions, not the intellect; strengthening the feelings, they ill-prepare men for their sound duties, where the emotions must be guided by intellect. In the district school libraries, Mann recommended "useful" readings: works of natural history, the biographies "of great and good men," and colonial history—books on "the great subjects of art, of science, of duty."

By 1840 lots of people—especially those I have labeled "individualists"— were fed up with the increasingly powerful state board of education and its autocratic secretary. Not that individualists opposed popular education. Far from it. They simply believed that the people should manage their own common schools. The new Democratic governor, Marcus Morton, put it plainly in his inaugural address of 1840: the towns and district meetings—"those little pure democracies"—should direct and govern the schools without any adventitious supervision from the state. At the suggestion of the new governor, and with the endorsement of the Democratic-controlled legislature, the House Committee on Education soon undertook an assessment of the work of the state board of education.

Within four days, the committee reported out a bill. Praising the board and its secretary (an ominous beginning), the committee declared that the annual reports bore strong testimony to "beneficial influence." Then, conscious of its own temerity, it proposed to kill the board of education. This was not an attack on the common schools—they had existed prior to the board: indeed, adherence to the schools themselves had led to the judgment to abolish the board, since its operations "are incompatible with those principles upon which our common schools have been founded and maintained."

The committee argued that the so-called advisory power of the board had, predictably, become a power of regulation. The board "has a tendency, and a strong tendency, to engross to itself the entire regulation of our common schools." And the legislature had, unfortunately, become "a mere instrument for carrying its plans into execution."

As to the collection and diffusion of information about education—the purported reason for the creation of the board—the committee allowed that this could better be accomplished, as it had been in the past, via the work of voluntary associations of teachers. (Parenthetically, the committee took note of the fact that such associations had appreciably declined since the coming of the board.) At bottom, the committee construed the board as no more than a governmental agency for the aggrandizement of the teaching profession. "Undoubtedly, in all . . . professions great improvements might be made, but it is better to leave them to private industry and free competition, than for the legislature to put them under the superintendence of an official Board."

Then, with political acumen, the committee delivered its harshest blow: the board was trying to mold the Massachusetts system of public instruction after the example of the French and Prussian systems. The committee found the ideal of a uniform, centrally controlled system of education—the European model—incompatible with the traditional system of local authority. Local control—and here it cites Tocqueville—encourages the zeal, interest, and activity of the people themselves in improving their own welfare, whereas centrally dictated reforms deaden such initiative. Most important, a centrally controlled education system is just the first step toward a system of centralization and monopoly of power in the hands of a few—opposed, in every respect, to "the true spirit of our democratical institutions." Unless we speedily check it, the committee concluded, it may "lead to unlooked for and dangerous results."

Then, one by one, the committee blasted the "reforms" Horace Mann had worked so diligently for. The rules and regulations designed to secure "minute and complicated registers of statistics" merely monopolized the teachers' time with paperwork and took them away from teaching. The school districts had gone along with these bureaucratic demands only because their share of the state school fund depended upon such compliance. The project of furnishing a school library for each district "under the sanction of the Board" had led the state into the hateful arena of censorship and the promulgation of "approved" books.

Finally, the committee turned to the normal schools—another project imported from France and Prussia. Such institutions simply were unnecessary; academies and high schools did, and could continue to, furnish an adequate supply of teachers. Good teachers would appear, the committee predicted, not as the result of special training, but as the result of higher salaries. State normal schools represent another attempt to use the government to create a profession of educators. Abolish them and give Mr. Dwight his $10,000 back.

The Report of the House Committee on Education completely shattered Horace Mann. "Political madmen," he called them. Fortunately for him, the attempt to abolish the Board failed in the legislature by a vote of 182 to 245. Four-fifths of the Whigs voted to save the boards, but so did one-third of the Democrats. These were individualists, men like Robert Rantoul, who was the only Democratic member of the board of education. When some Democratic legislators asked Rantoul what he thought about the proposal to abolish the board, he told them the project was a good one "if they wished to abolish education." On March 18 the House rejected the report of the Committee. The board was saved.

But in February 1841 the Democratic opponents to the board again launched an attack in the legislature. This time using financial retrenchment as the argument, the House Committee on Education proposed to transfer the powers and duties of the board of education to the governor and council. (Assuredly, Governor Morton would then promptly remand all power to the town and district school committees—"those little pure democracies.") The committee suggested that the secretary of state assume the work of the secretary of the board of education. To his immense relief, Horace Mann saw the legislature once again turn back the committee—this time with much less debate, but by a much smaller margin of votes.

The impact of the attack—two years running—was not lost on Horace Mann. Never again would he be so imperious in his annual reports. No more would he construe the function of education in such a narrow, hierarchical way as he had in his first three years as secretary. In the 1841 *Annual Report,* Mann devoted thirty-six pages to "showing the effects of education upon the worldly fortunes and estates of men." Presenting arguments, statistics, and testimonials from successful men—and employers—he demonstrated that education led to prosperity. Education "is not only the most honest and honorable, but the surest means of amassing property." He went on to point out the full political and economic significance of universal education: it destroyed the scarcity principle that had so long dominated all societies. Equality of opportunity had never really been possible before, since—sooner or later—a lucky few captured all the wealth of the community. The poor stayed poor, or became poorer, while the rich stayed rich, or became richer. The grandeur of education was that it actually increased the wealth in any society. Education was the sword to cut the Gordian knot that lashed people to a life of scarcity. Education converted consumers into producers. And more: it increased the producer's producing power.

In his monumental twelfth annual report—the last one—Mann ticked off the inventions *educated* men had drawn from "the weight of waters, the velocity of winds, the expansive force of heat and other kindred agencies." Enlisted in the service of man, these powers of nature increased the total wealth of the society. Pointing with pride to his own state, he attributed the unexampled prosperity of the people of Massachusetts to—what else? Education.

By 1850 not only Massachusetts, but most other states as well, had assumed most of the powers of the local districts: school districts in most states could no longer designate the teachers, select the textbooks, or make up the course of study, nor could the local school committees examine and certify the teachers they selected. By this time, too, state laws specified the length of the school term, the tax rate to be levied, and the subjects that must be taught. Moreover, in place of the single-room school, most Americans now attended schools divided into grades, where they were taught by teachers professionally trained in state normal schools, supervised by professional administrators.

Yet it would be too farfetched to attribute the development of state systems of public education entirely to the gallant efforts of school reformers like Horace Mann. To be sure, the school crusaders informed this development with articulated visions of what a public school system could be. But they never had the power to impose their vision on the nation. For one thing, hierarchs like Mann seemed to be a dying breed—aristocrats out of place in the age of Jacksonian democracy. And the egalitarian educational reformers, like James Carter, were then few in number. Most Americans of that time, as Tocqueville observed, were individualists: "They owe nothing to any man; they expect nothing from any man; they acquire the habit of always considering themselves as standing alone; and they are apt to imagine that their whole destiny is in their own hands."

But as we have seen, individualists opposed the centralized control of schools, and they thought families who could afford it should pay for the education of their own children. In short, individualists pretty much favored the existing educational arrangements—they simply wanted more public financial support. So if most Americans were individualists who accepted the existing variegated collection of quasi-public and quasi-private schools, then how can we explain the emergence of state systems of education between 1830 and 1850? Part of the answer has to be anti-Catholicism.

V

America was a Protestant country from the beginning. Those early settlers— Puritans in New England, Anglicans in Virginia—brought with them the fear and hatred of Catholicism that had existed ever since Henry VIII led England away from Rome. Since Catholicism threatened English independence, anti-Catholicism became a patriotic stance. Seventeenth-century England excluded Catholics from the legal profession, from teaching, and from the universities; priests were banished under the threat of death, and all Catholics were supposed to attend the services of the Church of England under threat of fine. Reared in such a climate, those who came to America carried those animosities with them, where, isolated from the liberal winds that later blew through Europe, their anti-Catholic feelings intensified.

Only a handful of Catholics lived in America throughout the colonial period—only 30,000 by 1776, out of a total population of approximately 3 million. Nevertheless, all the colonies at one time or another passed anti-Catholic laws. In keeping with John Cotton's dictum that "it was tolerance that made the world anti-Christian," the Massachusetts General Court decreed that any Jesuit or priest coming within the colony was to be banished, and, if he should return, executed. New Hampshire required all inhabitants to take an oath against the Pope and the doctrines of the Catholic religion. In the eighteenth century, the Virginia House of Burgesses passed laws preventing Catholics from acting as guardians, from serving as witnesses, or from settling in large groups. Only in Rhode Island and Pennsylvania were Catholics safe from persecution; and even Pennsylvania excluded Catholics from office.

Anti-Catholicism declined during the War for Independence, as American and foreign Catholics joined the fight against England. The federal constitution contained no sign of anti-Catholicism. But seven of the new state constitutions specified that all office holders had to be Protestants, and South Carolina established Protestantism as the state religion. By this time, anti-Catholicism in America had become ideological as well as religious. No matter what cultural theory they subscribed to, American Protestants of the early nineteenth century regarded Catholicism as incompatible with the Amer-

ican way of life. American egalitarians rejected Catholicism for its blatant
authoritarianism; American individualists rejected it because it eliminated all
personal independence of thought and action; and while American hierarchs
were untroubled by the principle of institutionalized authority in the Catholic
church, they did not think the church leaders were men of moral virtue. People simply did not think Catholics could be good Americans. Those reared or
educated as Catholics would not possess the moral uprightness the hierarchs
sought, nor would they share the egalitarian sensitivities cherished by the egalitarians, nor would they develop the self-reliance prized by the individualists.
Protestant Americans could not, of course, prevent Catholics from setting up
schools of their own, but they could prevent public support for such schools,
and they could resist any Catholic takeover of the existing common schools.

The increase in immigration that took place after the War of 1812 fueled
the fire of anti-Catholicism. During the 1820s, 100,000 immigrants arrived in
America; in the 1830s, the number rose to 500,000, and to over 1.4 million in
the 1840s. The vast majority came from Ireland and Germany, and most were
Catholics. By 1840 the Catholic church numbered 660,000 souls; in 1850,
1,600,000.

Many of these immigrants were poor; some were criminals, leading some
nativists to accuse the monarchies of Europe of dumping the derelicts of their
countries into America in order to weaken and destroy it. Not only did the
rest of society have to take care of these poverty-stricken and destitute people,
these people corrupted public morality by their intemperance, their brawling,
and their idleness. Those who did actually work took jobs away from native-
born Americans. And as soon as they became naturalized, these immigrants
voted in blocks, under the control and direction of their growing numbers of
priests. By 1850 America had 6 archbishops, 26 bishops and 1,385 priests.

The increase in immigration coincided with a time of ferment among evan-
gelical Protestant sects. During the so-called second awakening, Congrega-
tionalists, Baptists, Methodists, and Presbyterians all went through a period of
reaffirming their Christian commitments. This rekindling of Christian fervor
among Protestants resulted in the building of new churches and the founding
of missionary societies, like the American Home Missionary Society, to convert the Indians, preach to the Negro slaves, and to reclaim those living on the
Western frontier who had fallen away from the Christian life. It also gave birth
to new Protestant societies created specifically to combat Catholicism—like the
New York Protestant Association, set up in 1831 for "the express purpose of
eliciting knowledge respecting the state of popery, particularly on the western
continent." Other organizations, like the Protestant Reformation Society, published and distributed anti-Catholic Tracts, supplied speakers to individual
churches, and sponsored lectures and debates.

The Protestant Crusade generated books, magazines, and newspapers that
spewed forth anti-Catholic diatribes. According to Ray Billington, between
1800 and 1860, there were at least 25 daily, weekly, or bimonthly newspapers,
and 13 monthly or quarterly magazines, opposing Catholicism, while publishers put out more than 200 anti-Catholic books. *The Protestant*, an openly

anti-Catholic weekly, first published in New York in 1830, declared: "The sole objects of this publication are to inculcate Gospel doctrines against Romanish corruptions." In his highly influential book, *A Foreign Conspiracy Against the Liberties of the United States*, Samuel F. B. Morse—the inventor of the telegraph, who was also an artist and sometime professor at New York University— insisted that the despots of Europe were attempting, by the spread of Popery in this country, to subvert its free institutions.

The major arguments in the anti-Catholic press held, one, that Catholicism was not a true religion, since it was not based on the Bible; two, that Popery was irreconcilable with the democratic institutions of the United States; and three, that the moral standards of the Catholic church were totally unacceptable. Novels, confessions, plays, and reports from "escaped" nuns, "defrocked" priests, and "lapsed" Catholics bore witness to these charges and filled in the details. The schoolbooks, too, as Ruth Elson's meticulous examination of nineteenth-century textbooks revealed, universally contained strong anti-Catholic sentiments. Spellers, readers, geographies, and histories depicted Catholicism as a false religion and a positive danger to the state, while at the same time attacking the popish clergy for their hypocracy, immorality, and greed.

The attacks on Catholics did not remain limited to printed pages and platform speeches. Physical attacks on convents and churches, as well as the burning of shanty houses of Irish immigrants, took place in New York, Boston, Philadelphia, and in Charleston, Baltimore, Pittsburgh, and Ellsworth, Maine. Thousands were wounded and hundreds killed in these violent raids.

The culmination of nineteenth-century anti-Catholicism came in the 1850s, when representatives of nativist societies from thirteen states met to form the Know-Nothing Party—a name applied to them because of members' unwillingness to disclose what they stood for. As much a secret society as a full-fledged political party, the Know-Nothings infiltrated both the Democratic and Whig organizations, gaining converts to their quest to bar Catholics from all political offices—local, state, and national. In the elections of 1854 and 1856, the Know-Nothing Party won state and local elections in the Northern and border states. Although they controlled a number of state legislatures and had one hundred of their party in Congress, the Know-Nothings, largely because of legislative inexperience, accomplished little, and with the emergence of the slavery issue—an issue on which they refused to take a stand—the party disappeared.

In the meantime, some of those in the Protestant Crusade had taken up the task of converting Catholics to true Christianity. To this end, the American Bible Society took to distributing Bibles to Catholics, only to be rebuffed by the Catholic clergy, who forbade their members to read or accept Protestant Bibles. In response, the American Bible Society pledged itself to continuous labor until the scriptures were read in every classroom in the nation—a pledge it repeated annually. This set the stage for a showdown with the Catholic church that ultimately led to the abolition of the quasi-private school systems of the cities and the setting up of state public schools.

Recall that, in the Eastern cities, private school societies, with public support from the states' education funds, ran nondenominational schools for the poor. In addition to these free schools, sometimes called "charity schools," various denominations also ran their own free schools for their own poor. In the 1840s, Catholics in city after city petitioned to receive public funds to support their schools. Part of the Catholics' argument, of course, was that the so-called "nondenominational" schools of the various free-school societies were not, from their angle of vision, nondenominational at all—these schools forced students to read the Protestant Bible.

Rather than accede to the Catholics' demand for public support for their schools, city after city cut off all public aid to all church schools, and to the nondenominational free school societies, as well. In place of this arrangement of quasi-private schools, these cities installed public state schools open and free to all. With the cutoff of public funds to private charity school societies, as well as to all other private and denominational schools, many of these institutions went out of business, and the students attending them shifted to the newly established public schools.

These public schools were supposed to be nonsectarian, but they always allowed Bible reading—agreeing with the 1844 declaration of the American Bible Society that the Bible "is a book peculiarly appropriate for use in common schools, and cannot be excluded from them without hazard both to our civil and religious liberties." The Bible used in the public schools was, of course, the King James, or Protestant, Bible, and when Catholic clergy complained about this, they were accused of being opposed to the Bible. In Philadelphia, the objections of Bishop Kenrick to the practice of reading the Protestant Bible to Catholic children in the public schools caused riots that lasted for three days and resulted in the destruction of two churches and thirteen deaths.

Not unsurprisingly, the Catholic bishops of American began to call for the setting up of a system of Catholic schools in each diocese—a separate system of education "for the children of our communion."

In the rest of the nation, the logic of anti-Catholicism took a different course. In 1835 Lyman Beecher, in a widely read book, *A Plea for the West*, amplified the popish plot to overthrow the republic that Samuel Morse had evisaged. The schools, Beecher warned, would play an important part in winning converts to Catholicism, until eventually these converts and the Catholic immigrants would control the nation. Indeed, during the thirties and forties, many Catholic immigrants had moved west, working on the construction of the canals and railroads and then settling in towns along the way.

In rural America, most schools were quasi-public district schools, run by the local communities and paid for through a combination of public funds and tuition fees. So, as the number of Catholic families increased in each community, more and more Catholic children appeared in the district schools. Clearly, the control of the local district schools would ultimately shift to the Catholic parents.

The Protestant response was to convert their district schools. District after district voted to abolish the rate bills, converting their schools to public schools: free to all, totally supported by public funds, and completely under public, not parental, control. These conversions took place slowly. In Connecticut, for example, 776 out of 1624 school districts had free public schools in 1856. By 1860 the number had risen to 846, and by 1867 to 1225. The following year, the state itself acted to abolish rate bills in all of Connecticut.

During the 1850s, state after state abolished rate bills:

1852	Indiana	1868	Connecticut
1853	Ohio	1868	Rhode Island
1855	Illinois	1869	Michigan
1864	Vermont	1871	New Jersey
1867	New York		

At the same time, state after state adopted constitutional provisions against religious teaching in the public schools, and provisions forbidding the diversion of school funds to church or sectarian purposes. The following states adopted such constitutional prohibitions:

States Amending Constitution		Adopted when Admitted	
New Jersey	1844	Wisconsin	1848
Michigan	1850	Oregon	1857
Ohio	1851	Kansas	1859
Indiana	1851	Nevada	1864
Massachusetts	1855	Nebraska	1867
Iowa	1857	Colorado	1876
Mississippi	1868	North Dakota	1889
South Carolina	1868	South Dakota	1889
Arkansas	1868	Montana	1889
Illinois	1870	Washington	1889
Pennsylvania	1872	Idaho	1890
West Virginia	1872	Wyoming	1890
Alabama	1875	Utah	1896
Missouri	1875	Oklahoma	1907
North Carolina	1876	New Mexico	1912
Texas	1876	Arizona	1912
Minnesota	1877		
Georgia	1877		
California	1879		
Louisiana	1879		
Florida	1885		
Delaware	1897		

In 1875 President Ulysses Grant urged Congress to enact a similar prohibition in the form of an amendment to the Federal Constitution. The proposed amendment, sponsored by Senator James Blaine of Maine, passed both houses of Congress but failed to secure the necessary two-thirds vote in the Senate.

Many thought such an amendment unnecessary, since education remained a responsibility of each state, and every state either had, or was about to, constitutionally guarantee that its public schools would remain nonsectarian—i.e., Protestant.

Earlier, at its 1869 annual convention, the National Teacher Association (soon to become the National Education Association) had boldly confirmed that public schools were Protestant institutions when it passed a resolution that stated: "the appropriation of public school funds for the support of sectarian institutions is a violation of the fundamental principles of our American system of education"; and then coupled it with a second resolution that declared: "the Bible should not only be studied, venerated, and honored as a classic for all ages, people and languages . . . but devotionally read, and its precepts included in all the common schools of the land."

VI

By 1860 Americans had decided that schooling was a public good. The quasi-private and quasi-public schools that had grown up in the first quarter of the century had given way to public schools: schools open to all, free to all, publicly supported, and publicly controlled.

Enrollments rose in the public schools, although the percentage of children attending school in 1850 was about the same as it had been in 1790. What happened, according to Kaestle, was that there was a shift from private to public schooling.

Requiring taxpayers to pay for public schools, and denying public money to any private or sectarian school, created a public school monopoly of education. Private schools now became elitist institutions attended only by the wealthy. The only alternative to public schools for the nonwealthy were the parochial schools set up in the cities for Catholic children.

The emergence of a public school monopoly politicized American education. The school reformers of the nineteenth century believed that public schools would be more responsive to the public than private, quasi-private, quasi-public schools ever were. But taking control out of the hands of the parents and trustees and giving it to the "public" simply deposited control into the hands of those with the most political power. Those who possessed political power—the influentials—could now decide what public schools were for.

As those influentials saw it, schools, public schools, were a panacea for all the ills of society: the public schools would solve all of America's social, economic, and political problems. No matter what ideology they might subscribe to, these influentials all shared grandiose expectations of what schools could do. The hierarchs viewed public schools as the panacea to create social stability. Individualists saw them as the panacea to create equal opportunity for all. And egalitarians cast them as the panacea to create an equal society.

PART TWO

The Public School as a Panacea

CHAPTER 3

Racial Inequality and the Schools

I

It was only six months after Appomattox when Francis Wayland, the president of Brown University, told the National Teachers Association that the root of the recent deluge of blood lay "in the fact of a diffused and universal education in the North and a very limited education of the South." "The Civil War," he explained, "had been a war of education and patriotism against ignorance and barbarism." President Wayland was not alone in viewing the recent holocaust in educational terms. Many Northerners shared his belief that the educational backwardness of the South had precipitated the war. This conviction stemmed, not from some idle speculation about the causes of the Civil War, but from a serious concern with the problem of victory: the restoration of the Union. If the War Between the States was looked at in educational terms, then reunion became possible. Education would restore the Union. Education must be diffused throughout the South; black and white alike must be educated. Not to educate them was to court another war.

President Wayland was sounding a clarion call in Chicago when he asked, "Can we not as educators go boldly into Southern states and teach the truth and the whole truth?" Actually, hordes of Yankee teachers had already invaded the South. President Wayland and the National Teachers Association were too late to be bellwethers. The descent had begun while the war was still going on, with teachers pressing hard on the heels of the soldiers.

As early as 1862, the New England Freedmen's Aid Society sent 72 teachers to Port Royal, Virginia. Another organization, the American Missionary Society, founded as an abolitionist society in 1846, remained active during the war by supplying teachers who literally "followed the army." By 1866 this society had 353 teachers in the field. All together, there were at least seventy-nine different philanthropic associations concerned with sending teachers to the South. Some of these societies were strictly denominational, like the Freedmen's Aid Society of the Methodist Episcopal Church, which established fifty-nine schools, sent out 124 teachers, and expended over $60,000 during the first two years of its work. Some of these philanthropic associations were large and impressive, like the American Union Commission with offices in New York, Boston, Philadelphia, Baltimore, and Chicago. Others were small local associations that were short-lived. The great variety and number of different associations sending teachers into the South make it impossible to determine just how many Northern teachers actually went into the South during this period.

The educational work of these various philanthropic associations was frequently carried out in cooperation with the Freedmen's Bureau. Established in 1865 as the Bureau of Refugees, Freedmen, and Abandoned Lands, this federal agency was responsible for the relief of freedmen through medical and hospital service and supplies, through the supervision of labor contracts, through the control of all confiscated or abandoned lands, and, finally, through the establishment of schools. It was this last function of the bureau that was the special concern of its head, General O. O. Howard, who by his own admission devoted more attention to education than to any other branch of his work. The bureau, operating with funds obtained by the sale of confiscated Confederate property, usually set up the schools while the philanthropic associations supplied the teachers. In many instances the bureau supplied its own teachers; frequently these teachers were newly freed blacks, some of whom, unfortunately, were barely able to read and write.

The Freedmen's Bureau did keep records for the teachers under its jurisdiction. According to these records it had 972 teachers in the field in January 1867. By the following year, the number had increased to 2948 teachers. The peak period for the bureau was July 1869, when a total of 9503 white and black teachers were reported in the field.

What was the Southern reaction to this invasion of Yankee schoolteachers bent upon the educational reconstruction of the South? It does not take much imagination to understand that many Southerners saw this educational reconstruction as an attempt to add insult and humiliation to the military defeat. The fact that most of these Northern teachers were women was an additional affront to the Southerner's pride. Nor did the demeanor of the Yankee teachers help matters, since, for the most part, they regarded the Southerners as sinners whom they had come to redeem with "the truth, the whole truth." The white Southerner, therefore, came to regard these Yankee schoolmarms with coolness, perhaps with disdain, and even with contempt. The Southern whites were not concerned with reconstructing themselves, at least not in the way the Northerners meant. The South, after all, had fought for the right to secede from the Union, the right to preserve its way of life. The South had lost, and one could hardly expect the defeated to have the same concerns as the victor. After losing the war, the South had its own concern: the freed slave.

What did freedom mean? One thing was certain: it meant that blacks were no longer the property of the white man. But did it mean that now blacks were to be accepted as people, equal to white people? If this is what freedom meant, then white Southerners saw themselves divested of both their property *and* their status. But more than status was involved in the white Southerner's refusal to associate with former slaves as equals. If the blacks were treated as equal then they might, in many instances, in many areas, dominate white people. And perhaps even greater than fear of black domination was the fear of black retaliation for former injustices. White people were afraid—afraid for their property, their culture, their very life. The Southerner felt that black people must be constrained, must be dominated, must be segregated. To accomplish these ends, the defeated South now began passing laws that imposed the yoke of servility upon the supposedly freed slaves. During the years 1865 and 1866 every Confederate state except Tennessee passed Black Codes limiting the freedman's life with varying degrees of severity. The blacks' right to hold property was restrained, as well as their right to sue and be sued, and to have legal marriages and off spring. Blacks could appear as witness only in cases where one or both parties were black. Blacks who married whites were guilty of a felony. Nowhere were blacks permitted to hold public office, vote, serve on juries, or bear arms. Mississippi authorized "any person" to arrest and return to their employer any black who quit before the expiration of their contracted term of labor. Georgia warned that "all persons strolling about in idleness would be put in chain gangs and contracted out to employers." Thus, within a year following the end of the Civil War blacks became the victims of white supremacy. The term "victim" is deliberately used since the legal tactics to "keep blacks in their place" were often reinforced by extralegal tactics of violence and intimidation. Somewhat ironically, the fact that they were now free, no longer the property of some white man, made blacks more vulnerable to the wanton and indiscriminate violence that was now directed against them by hoodlums from the "superior" race. There was, as John Hope Franklin has said, "an open season on Negroes."

This wave of terror and violence engulfed all who in any way undermined the scheme to keep whites superior. One group suspected of intentions to subvert white supremacy comprised the Yankee schoolteachers. These suspicions arose from the fact that these teachers had tried to impose "mixed schools" on the South, even though at that very moment segregated schools were common throughout the North. The whites refused to send their children to these Yankee "amalgamated" schools, forcing the Yankee schoolteachers to create, although reluctantly, the first de facto segregated schools for black children.

Faced with none but blacks in their classrooms, most of the Yankee teachers set about their job with missionary zeal. "Oh what a privilege to be among them when their morning dawns," wrote one teacher, "to see them personally coming forth from the land of Egypt and the house of bondage." Such enthusiasm evinced by these Yankees for teaching blacks did nothing to allay the suspicions of white Southerners. Yet often they were relieved, and shared the contemptuous amusement of their neighbors, when they found the Yankee schoolmarms—whose enthusiasm frequently outran their pedagogical sagacity—attempting to teach Latin and Greek to the newly freed slaves.

But this contemptuous amusement turned to fury when whites discovered the Yankees teaching the blacks that they were the political and social equals of the whites. Nor were white Southerners pleased to hear that the black child was taught that the Northerners were his or her friends, that the Republican party was his or her benefactor, and that he or she should support his or her friends and benefactors at the ballot box. The Yankees often used ingenious political catechisms to accomplish their blatantly political aims. Here is a sample:

"Now children you don't think white people are any better than you because they have straight hair and white faces?"

"No, Sir."

"No, they are no better, but they are different, they possess great power, they formed this great government, they control this vast country. . . . Now, what makes them different from you?"

"Money!" (unanimous shout).

"Yes, but what enabled them to obtain it? How did they get money?"

"Got it off us, stole it off we all."

Quite obviously the Southern whites were not going to tolerate this kind of education. And even the most tolerant white Southerners took umbrage when they heard former slaves singing "John Brown" or "Marching Through Georgia," songs taught them by the Yankee teachers. Increasingly then, these teachers had difficulty in getting hotel rooms or accommodations of any sort. Many restaurants refused to serve them. They were told not to attend church services. Corner louts hurled pleasantries after them, like "damned Yankee bitch of a nigger teacher." At times schools were burned, teachers flogged or driven out of town, usually after being tarred and feathered. In 1866 the Reverend J. P. Bardwell, American Missionary Association teacher at Grenada, Mississippi, was severely beaten, other teachers threatened, and an officer of the Freedmen's Bureau murdered.

Yet, despite the fact that white Southerners ostracized and sometimes attacked these Yankee teachers, there were some who approved of the education of the freedmen. A few white planters had actually set up schools for their black "hands." The education of black people was not opposed so much as was "outside interference." The Southerners wanted to control and supervise the education of *their* blacks. Some Southern spokesmen for black education during this period argued that the blacks would be made "safer" if they were made "moral and intelligent," that is, if they were educated "Southern style." In addition to predictions that they would be safer (that is, constrained) if they were educated, there were predictions that they would be better workers if educated. Some strategists went so far as to maintain that blacks should vote, *provided that* the white man controlled, through education, their behavior at the ballot box. The rationale here was that the South might regain some of its political power nationally if it increased its number of voters by enfranchising the blacks.

White Southerners' interest in black education, however, was nothing compared with their interest in education for their own race. Education was the instrument for solving their problem. Whereas to the Northerner education had been the key to achieving reunion and reconstruction, to the Southerners white education now became the key to white supremacy.

II

For the first time, the Southern states began to establish statewide systems of public education. Faced as they were at this period with problems of acute poverty and destitution, it is surprising that the state legislatures bothered at all with educational matters. Yet bills setting up systems of education were passed in state after state throughout the South at the same time that laws were passed for the relief of debtors and allocations of money made to buy food for the starving. The rise of the public school system in the South at this difficult time indicates to what extent the freed slaves were considered a threat, for although the Black Codes had imposed legal constraints upon them, making them subordinate to the white man, it was also necessary to ensure that these bonds could not be broken. The justification proffered for the Black Codes was that the blacks were ignorant, therefore not qualified to exercise the duties of citizenship. A corollary to this argument, of course, was that whites were qualified to exercise the duties of citizenship because they were *not* ignorant. So to make this argument viable it became necessary to make plans to ensure the perpetuation of the ignorance of one race and the enlightenment of the other. Education would ensure that each race remained "in its place." All of the bills passed in the Southern states during the immediate post-war period reveal the strategy of constraining the black persons by curtailing their educational opportunities while at the same time providing liberal educational opportunities for whites. Texas set up a public school fund "exclusively for the education of white scholastics." Georgia's plan for the schooling of all from the ages of six to twenty-one was limited to "free white inhabitants." In 1867 Arkansas established a system of free public education "for whites only." In Tennessee the law provided for the maintenance of schools for not less than five months in the year "with separate schools for colored children." The state superintendent of education in Florida declared that the whites "had a deadly hatred to the education . . . of the freedmen." But Florida did make a concession to blacks: If black males would pay a special tax of $1.25 per year, they could have their own public schools.

Secure in the conviction that the Black Codes had established white supremacy and that the educational plans would both perpetuate and justify it, the South now turned to the problem of "outside interference." The primary target was the Freedmen's Bureau. This agency of the federal government was a "curse," an "engine of mischief"; it was *the* symbol of outside interference. In their campaign against the Freedmen's Bureau the white Southerners had the support of the President of the United States, Andrew Johnson. A native of Tennessee, President Johnson, like every self-respecting Southerner, had high regard for States' rights. When Congress passed a bill to extend the life and enlarge the functions of the bureau, he vetoed it. The bill, he declared, was "unnecessary, unwise, and unconstitutional."

Battle lines were now drawn between a President who contended to preserve the rights of the states and a Congress, dominated by so-called Radical Republicans, who contended to preserve the victory of Appomattox. The Radical Republicans were infuriated by the fact that, less than two years after defeat, most of the former Confederate states had established governments staffed exclusively by white men, who for the most part had been former leaders of the Confederacy. Congress's fight with the President culminated in a set of congressional resolutions that were to become the Fourteenth Amendment to the Constitution. This Amendment in effect declared blacks citizens and then prescribed that: "No state shall abridge the privileges or immunities of citizens of the United States; nor shall any state deprive any person of life, liberty, or property, without due process of law; nor deny to any person within its jurisdiction, the equal protection of the laws." A second section penalized a state for withholding the privilege of voting by reducing its representation in Congress. A third section disqualified from office all rebels who had before the war taken the federal oath of office.

An amendment to the constitution has to be ratified by the states. What would the South do? The answer was not long in coming. Before the end of 1866 Texas, South Carolina, Georgia, Florida, North Carolina, Arkansas, and Alabama rejected the Fourteenth Amendment. In the first months of 1867 Virginia, Louisiana, and Mississippi turned it down. In the meantime the Northern states ratified it, led by Connecticut and New Hampshire, both of whom approved it within a month.

The country once again was divided. Once more the Northerners were to champion the cause of the black people against the Southern white. In March 1867 Congress made a dramatic move. After first declaring that there were no legal governments in the South, Congress ordered the South divided into five military districts, each in the charge of a military governor. Under the aegis of these military governors the rebel states were to form new constitutions framed by conventions of delegates elected by male citizens of "twenty-one years of age and upward, of whatever race, color or previous condition." One other stipulation was that the Fourteenth Amendment must be ratified. After the new state constitutions had been ratified by the electorate and approved by Congress, the states would be entitled to representation in Congress.

Once again the South had to bow to the North. Congressional Reconstruction effectively halted the South's attempt to restore white supremacy through Black Codes and discriminatory educational systems—at least for a time.

III

The most revolutionary aspect of Reconstruction was the entry of blacks into the political arena, and at the moment blacks became politically conscious, they focused attention on education. Just as the Yankee philanthropic societies had originally relied upon education to reconstruct the South and restore the Union, and just as the white southerners had tried to use education to perpetuate white supremacy, so now the black people saw education as the panacea for their problems.

The life of a slave under laws enforcing black illiteracy was poor preparation for the Southern black for the responsibilities of citizenship. But education was the key; education could remedy all deficiencies, education could prepare all for effective participation. W. H. Grey, a black delegate to the Arkansas Constitutional Convention, exclaimed: "Give us the right of suffrage; establish a school system that will give us an opportunity to educate our children; leave ajar the door that leads to peace and power; and if by the next generation we do not place ourselves beyond the reach of mortal man, why then take them away from us if not exercised properly." In South Carolina, black delegate A. J. Ransier was more direct: "In proportion to the education of the people, so is their progress in civilization."

In their concern for the education of their race, many blacks sought and secured important educational posts with the Reconstruction governments. In Louisiana, W. C. Brown was Superintendent of Public Instruction from 1872 to 1876. After serving a term as Secretary of State in Florida, Jonathan C. Gibbs, a Dartmouth graduate, became State Superintendent of Public Instruction. During Reconstruction Thomas Cardoza served as Mississippi's Superintendent of Education, while another black, Blanche K. Bruce, served as a county superintendent of schools before being sent to Congress in 1875 as one of that state's senators. From January 1873 to October 1874, J. C. Corbin, who had attended Oberlin, was Superintendent of Education in Arkansas. The post of Assistant Superintendent of Public Instruction in North Carolina was held for a time by James W. Hood.

Most black leaders saw that the responsibilities of citizenship required not only that blacks be educated, but that they be educated together with whites. Segregated schools would stigmatize blacks as second-class citizens, unequal to whites, and thus violate the Fourteenth Amendment. The black leaders also feared that if separate schools were established, black schools would be unequal to the white schools. So at every state constitutional convention held in the South during 1867–1868, the black delegates precipitated acrimonious debates on the "mixed school" question.

Most Southern whites dreaded racially mixed schools, fearful of the consequences of social intermixture. Many also doubted the educability of black people and saw mixed schools as pedagogically unsound. White opposition to mixed schools generated by these doubts and fears increased when it became evident that such schools would be supported almost completely by the white community. The burden of taxation, onerous in itself, became an insult to many whites when it was proposed that their money be used to support mixed schools.

The force of white opposition was so strong that in only two states, South Carolina and Louisiana, were blacks able to secure constitutional guarantees for integrated schools. The black delegates were successful here only because they outnumbered the white delegates. All other state conventions were dominated by white majorities, but under the watchful eye of Congress none of these conventions tried to exclude blacks from public education. Nor did any have the temerity to state explicitly that its publicly supported schools were to be segregated. There was little doubt that the Radical Republican Congress would reject such a restriction. Most states merely stipulated that education be provided for all children. At some conventions they added phrases like "without partiality or distinction," or "without distinction or preference." But such ambiguous phrases would not do, and the burden was shifted to the state assemblies, where the issue of mixed schools was debated anew. Even here some sought to evade responsibility by permitting the local communities to decide. This move, of course, was violently opposed by the white citizens living in "black counties," where they were outnumbered by blacks. In North Carolina the assembly ruled that the public schools of the state were to be segregated. In both Florida and Mississippi, where blacks dominated the state legislatures, the decision went the other way; the legislatures maintained that the constitution be interpreted to support mixed schools.

One weakness of the mixed-school movement lay in the absence of compulsory education laws. In those four states where mixed schools were now required by law, the whites often refused to send their children to school at all. In Louisiana, for example, out of a school population of 253,000 in 1870, only 23,000 were reported to be in schools. In many communities—in Louisiana, South Carolina, Florida, and Mississippi—the laws were openly flouted by the creation of separate all-white schools.

Actually, within a few years the mixed school question all but disappeared as the white conservatives regained power in state after state. The earliest conservative victories occurred in Tennessee and Virginia in 1869, and in North Carolina the following year. Once restored to power, the conservatives in each state passed laws that explicitly provided for segregated schools. By 1875 Reconstruction had unofficially ended through conservative victories in all Southern states, save Louisiana, South Carolina, Florida, and Mississippi. In that year Congress moved to bolster its faltering program of Reconstruction by passing the Civil Rights Act.

In its original form this act included a provision that prohibited segregated public schools. But it was removed before passage, and with its removal the movement for mixed schools collapsed. The man probably most singly responsible for the elimination was the Reverend Barnas Sears, General Agent for the Peabody Fund.

IV

In 1867 the munificent New Englander George Peabody gave the South $1 million. The money was to be used "for encouraging and promoting schools in those portions of our beloved and common country which have suffered from the destructive ravages and not less disastrous consequences of the civil war." The original board of trustees for the fund consisted of such distinguished names as U. S. Grant; Hamilton Fish, Governor of New York; and David Farragut, Tennessee-born Admiral of the United States Navy. Later elected trustees included Rutherford B. Hayes, Grover Cleveland, William McKinley, and Theodore Roosevelt. It is noteworthy that, at all times, one half of the board of trustees were Southerners.

In setting up this fund, Peabody granted the trustees the freedom to decide how the money was to be distributed. The trustees, in turn, delegated most policymaking to their first general agent, the Reverend Barnas Sears.

Barnas Sears had a rich educational background to prepare him for his work with the Peabody Fund. He had succeeded Horace Mann, "The Father of the Common School," as Secretary of the Massachusetts State Board of Education. Before that he had been state superintendent of Normal Schools in Massachusetts. At the time he was asked to become the general agent for the Peabody Fund Barnas Sears was serving as president of Brown University.

The educational fund he administered rarely yielded more than $90,000 a year, occasionally as much as $130,000. As general agent, Sears' strategy was to use this small amount of money to stimulate the South to support its own public schools. To accomplish this end, he decided that all funds should be dispersed on a matching basis. Rather than pay for the entire expense of a school or institute, only a small portion, usually one fourth, was supplied by the fund. This meant that the Peabody money was spread very thinly throughout the South. The largest donation to any state in one year, from 1868 to 1914, was $37,975—to Virginia in 1874.

Two notable consequences followed from this policy of granting money on a matching basis. First, the only localities able to match the grants were usually the larger towns and cities. The indirect discrimination against rural areas was all the more unfortunate, since this is where most of the school-age children lived. Second, and more important, this policy reinforced segregated schooling in the South. Sears condemned mixed schools and refused to aid them, on the grounds that the white people would not support them, hence would not provide funds to match a Peabody grant. In Louisiana he gave no aid to the public schools, giving instead grants to the private white schools. When criticized for this action, Sears replied that he was helping the white children of Louisiana because they were "the most destitute from the fact of their unwillingness to attend mixed schools." He added that "colored children would likewise be given preference, were they in like circumstances."

Not only did he reinforce the principle and practice of segregated education by refusing aid to integrated schools with Peabody's money, but Sears persuaded others against mixed schools. Taking a special trip to Washington in 1873, Sears appeared before the leading members of Congress to plead against the prohibition of segregated schools contained in the Civil Rights Act. He succeeded in convincing them, he later reported, "that the bill would overthrow the state systems of free schools and leave both the blacks and whites . . . destitute of schools altogether."

Undoubtedly the Peabody Fund and its indefatigable first general agent were the catalysts that helped stimulate Southerners to build, support, and control their own public schools. In accomplishing this work, the Peabody Fund had departed from the usual pattern of Northern philanthropy with its paternalistic concern with private, church, or missionary schools. And yet the Peabody Fund in the long run intensified the South's educational problem, for, although at that time the white Southerner would neither support nor attend mixed schools, the alternative of segregated schools increased the financial burden and prevented the South from attaining educational equality with the North for the next seventy-five years.

And what about Southern blacks? What about their vision of education as the key to acceptance? Black people had believed that the condition of subordination of their race was remediable. Once educated like whites, they would be accepted by the whites. But now, before Reconstruction had officially ended, these plans had been undermined by the establishment of segregated schools. With the passage of the Civil Rights Act in 1875 the black's faith in education was visibly shaken, as evidenced by the decline in school enrollment. In Arkansas black enrollment decreased from 73,878 in 1875 to 15,890 in 1876. In Florida it fell from 32,371 in 1875 to 26,052 the following year. Though weakened, the faith of black people in education did not disappear. At root they still believed in its magical power—else what had they to hope for? Even though they had to settle for segregated schools, at least they had schools, schools that were on the whole as good as those for white children. Now concern shifted to the problem of preserving that equality. The conservatives in all of the Southern states had pledged to maintain parity between white and black schools. It was on the strength of this pledge that many blacks actually cast their votes to return the conservatives to power. Would the pledge be honored?

V

When President Hayes removed the last of the federal troops from the South in 1877, Reconstruction was officially over. Segregated schools were by now a fact of life in the South, but although the black people attended separate schools and separate churches (here by choice), they were not totally segregated from the white man's world. Tolerance and acceptance of blacks were widespread in many areas of public life in the South. There was neither segregation nor separation on trains or streetcars, or at the polls, in the courts and legislatures, on the police force, or in the militia. A black newspaperman from Boston reported from Columbia, South Carolina, in 1885 that he felt about as safe there as in Providence, Rhode Island. Throughout the South, he reported, "I can ride in first class cars on the railroads and in the streets. I can go into saloons and get refreshments even as in New York. I can stop in and drink a glass of soda and be more politely waited upon than in some parts of New England."

It is true, of course, that the blacks at this time were held subordinate to whites and frequently exploited by them. But white supremacy did not, then, mean the degradation of blacks—they were not ostracized, they were not disenfranchised, they were not totally segregated.

The position blacks held in the South during this period was largely due to the white conservatives. Since their coming to power marked the end of Reconstruction, this first generation of conservatives liked to be called the "Redeemers." They were neither Negrophobes nor Negrophiles. Descendants of the antebellum slaveholders, they preached an aristocratic philosophy of paternalism and noblesse oblige. As Governor Thomas G. Jones of Alabama bluntly put it: "The Negro race is under us. He is in our power. We are his custodians . . . we should extend to him as far as possible all the civil rights that will fit him to be a decent and self-respecting, law-abiding, and intelligent citizen. . . . If we do not lift them up, they will drag us down."

But the power of the conservatives was not to go unchallenged. The Civil War had done more than emancipate the black slave; it had emancipated the whites of the lower economic class. Small farmers and tradesmen, from the hill country and beyond, fought against this return to the power structure of antebellum days. During the war and its aftermath they had tasted power for the first time. They did not intend to again be the charges, or the victims, of the aristocracy.

There was one sure way for the lower-class whites to guarantee themselves freedom and autonomy. The key, once more, was education. Free, universal education would make them the equal of the aristocratic conservatives. The laws had been passed; in many cases the schools had been built and the teachers hired. They need only take advantage of what already existed. The increase in school enrollments tells the story. In 1880 there were 1,053,025 white children enrolled in the public schools. In the next fifteen years, from 1880 to 1895, white school enrollment more than doubled.

	White Enrollment	Black Enrollment
1880	1,053,025	714,884
1885	1,378,926	835,053
1890	1,864,214	1,026,947
1895	2,176,464	1,142,500

Increased school enrollment was only half the educational picture. The other half—the half that brings into perspective the power struggle between the two white economic classes—is the sorry condition of financial support, for despite the increased educational responsibility, we find all states spending less for education. In Alabama $523,799 was spent for education in 1875 but only $375,645 in 1880. Louisiana's expenditure decreased from $699,655 in 1875 to $486,320. In South Carolina it went from $426,640 to $324,679. Over this five-year period the South's educational expenditures decreased approximately 21 percent, while enrollment had increased 33 percent.

Part of the explanation for this reduction in expenditures for education at the very time school enrollment was increasing lies in the fact that the aristocrats in power had no personal interest in the public schools. Traditionally they had educated their children in private schools, and this continued to be the case until the mid-eighties. Public schools for the masses, therefore, did not have widespread support among the class in power. William L. Royall, the editor of the Richmond *Commonwealth*, wrote in 1880 that education beyond the barest rudiments was "imported here by a gang of carpetbaggers." He added that taxation to support such education was socialistic. It should be provided, he felt, "for pauper children only, as before the war." The Governor of Virginia, F. W. M. Holliday, agreed, explaining that the public schools were "a luxury . . . to be paid for like any other luxury, by the people who wish their benefits."

The conservatives' lack of support for the public schools was not due solely to their own selfish interests. They had regained power after Reconstruction partly by pledging themselves to a program of financial retrenchment. They promised to "spend nothing unless absolutely necessary." These Redeemers had adopted retrenchment to counter both the extravagance of the Reconstruction government and the depression that had gripped the South ever since the panic of 1873. During the first decade of "home rule," cheap government became widely accepted as the criterion of good government. As Governor George F. Drew of Florida said to his legislature in 1877, "that government will be the most highly esteemed that gives the greatest protection to the taxpayer."

Retrenchment meant reduced salaries for all state officials. It also meant a curtailment in all state services, and the first service to suffer was public education. Actually, the Redeemers did more than reduce education expenditures—they put a strait jacket on them. Fearful that blacks or carpetbaggers might regain political power, the conservatives set up checks against the possible misuse of such power. They did this by adopting constitutional prohibitions against local taxation for schools, by placing constitutional limitations upon the state legislatures with regard to the rate of taxation that they could levy for school purposes, and by limiting the amount of money that could be appropriated for the support of public schools. So determined were the conservatives to guard against black and carpetbagger power, they fashioned "change proof" state constitutions, thereby making it almost impossible for the lower economic classes among the whites to change the constitutions to extend support for free schools.

The small farmers, sparked by the newly formed Grange and later by the Farmers Alliance, continued to agitate for the extension of public schools. They clamored for local taxation; they wanted an increase in the state fund. In both these demands they were constricted by the state constitutions and opposed by the planter aristocrats from the lowlands. In desperation the small farmers turned to the matter of distribution of state funds. They wanted to divert some of the money intended for black education to the white schools. But this demand for abolishing the system of distribution according to per capita school population was also vetoed by the conservatives, who continued to honor their pledge that they would maintain the schools of the black children on an equality with those of white children.

Yet as long as blacks had no *real* political power, diversion of school funds from black to white children was inevitable—despite all pledges. In fact the conservatives themselves became the leaders in this strategy of diversion. By the mid-eighties many of the upper-class planters were beginning to send their children to the public schools. Since these aristocrats lived in "black counties," that is, counties where blacks outnumbered whites, it was possible, as Horace Mann Bond has shown, "to divert some part of the per capita funds intended for Negro education to the improvement of the schools for white children *without altering the per capita distribution given by the state to each county.*" This strategy was first adopted in Mississippi with the help of a teaching certificate law of 1886 that permitted separate salary scales for the two races. From 1877 to 1885 the average monthly salaries of teachers of both races in Mississippi had been identical. With the passage of the certificate law black salaries began to fall, white salaries to rise. In 1886 the monthly average for white teachers was $31.37, for black teachers $27.40. By 1895 white teachers were earning $33.04 per month, black teachers $21.46.

This strategy of diverting funds to white schools was feasible only in the "black counties," since in the "white counties" where the whites were more than a majority, there could be little financial gain to the white schools if a part of the per capita fund for black education was diverted. This caused many of the small farmers of the white counties to grow increasingly bitter over what they took to be an unjust situation. In their own counties they paid most, if not all, the taxes, but their schools were inferior to those for whites in the "black counties." Since the money spent for black education was held to be the reason for the superiority of the white schools in the "black counties," *and* the reason for inferior schools for whites in the "white counties," some whites now began to question the feasibility of black education. Demagogues seized upon the issue and went before their constituents to argue against the education of blacks at public expense, or at least in favor of the division of the school fund on the basis of the tax paid by the two races. Here they were always opposed by the white leaders of the "black counties," who had a vested interest in the continuation of the equitable allocation of state funds for black education—such funds being used in part to improve their own white schools.

The culmination of this struggle between the white economic classes, in which the blacks were used as pawns, came in the nineties with the rise of Populism. The Populist movement in the South articulated the resentment of the small farmer against the old aristocracy. In this political battle the Populists attempted to win the allegiance of blacks. Appealing to the kinship of common grievances, Tom Watson told the blacks that "the colored tenant is in the same boat with the white tenant, the colored laborer with the white laborer." Blacks were promised that, "if you stand up for your rights and for your manhood, if you stand shoulder to shoulder with us in this fight," the People's party will "wipe out the color line and put every man on his citizenship irrespective of color." Actually, with the Populists racial integration went further than it ever had with the conservatives. Blacks served with Southern whites as members of state, district, and county executive committees of the party; they served on campaign committees and were delegates to national conventions. Black and white candidates had places on official party tickets. Audiences of both races heard black and white campaigners speaking from the same platform. According to C. Vann Woodward, "The Negroes responded with more enthusiasm and hope than to any other political movement." And he adds, "it is altogether probable that during the brief Populist upheaval of the nineties Negroes and whites achieved a greater comity of mind and harmony of political purpose than ever before or since in the South." This precarious experiment in interracial harmony, handicapped by suspicion and prejudice, surprised everyone by the good will and cooperation it generated between the races—for a time.

The honeymoon ended when the Populists' bid for political power failed. By using every means at their disposal—including fraud, intimidation, bribery, violence, and terror—the conservatives won the election of 1896. This defeat generated such dismay among the Populists that a scapegoat had to be found to explain away the failure. One was ready at hand: blacks. Alliance with them, white Populists claimed, had alarmed many in the South who would have voted for their cause but did not because they feared "Negro domination." Blacks were blamed for the political fiasco, and the biracial partnership was dissolved.

The outlook for blacks was dim indeed, for not only the Populists but the conservatives as well had now abandoned entirely the black cause. In battling for their political lives, the conservatives had forsaken the stance of paternalistic protector of black people and had moved into the camp of the Negrophobes. Alarmed by the success the Populists were obtaining with their appeal to the black voter, the conservatives had raised the cry of "Negro Domination." Now that they had won their election—in part through the support of extremists—the conservatives saw no reason to go back on their militant platform of white supremacy. All the more so because this platform could now be used to build a rapprochement with the white Populists.

Repudiated by their sometime friends in the South, black people by this time found few friendly voices in the North. For a variety of reasons the commitment of many Northern liberals to racial equality had been considerably exhausted. Some liberals who had started out with a highly romanticized concept of blacks experienced disenchantment with the freedom. Others extended the economic and political doctrine of laissez faire to this area: according to this view the "Negro problem" was the South's problem and could best be solved by the South, without "outside interference." Still other liberals, in response to the political turmoils of the recent past, deplored sectional animosities, for example, those between the North and the South, and identified those who exploited them as reactionaries and demagogues. Drawn toward the cause of sectional reconciliation, the liberals came to see blacks as the symbol of sectional strife. Thus, for a variety of reasons, Northern liberals gave up their role of protector of black people, and some even went so far as to begin mouthing the shibboleth of white supremacy.

As white supremacy gradually became "the American way," the highest court in the land proceeded to give it legal sanctions. As early as 1877 the United States Supreme Court had ruled that a state could not *prohibit* segregation on a common carrier. The Court in 1890 ruled that a state could constitutionally *require* segregation on carriers. In 1896 in *Plessy v. Ferguson* the

Court declared that "legislation is powerless to eradicate racial instincts." In this decision it provided the justification for segregation by its enunciation of the doctrine of "separate but equal." Two years later in *Williams v. Mississippi* the Court approved the Mississippi plan for depriving black people of the vote, completing in the words of Woodward "the opening of the legal road to proscription, segregation, and disfranchisement."

All the stops were out. Blacks were now an approved object of aggression. The way was clear for a capitulation to racism. It had been cleared by the sanctions of the federal courts, by the Northern liberals eager to conciliate the South, by Southern conservatives who had abandoned their policy of protector of black people in their struggle against the Populist, and finally by the Populists in their mood of disillusionment with their former black allies.

The first step was the total disfranchisement of blacks. The first state to disfranchise on a racial basis and evade the restrictions of the federal constitution was Mississippi. Other Southern states followed. The plan was to set up certain barriers, such as property or literacy qualifications, or payment of a poll tax, then cut certain loopholes "through which only white men could squeeze." The loopholes to accommodate the underprivileged whites were the "understanding clause," the "grandfather clause," and the "good character clause."

Some idea of the effectiveness of disfranchisement can be had from a comparison of the number of black voters in Louisiana in 1896, when there were 130,334, and in 1904, when there were 1,342. The literacy, property, and poll tax qualifications had done their work well. In 1896 black registrants were a majority in twenty-six parishes—by 1900 in none.

In conjunction with the device of disfranchisement, the policies of segregation and discrimination were extended by the adoption of a great number of Jim-Crow laws. Separation of the races on all public carriers—trains, streetcars, steamboats—became the law throughout the South. Signs bearing the legends "White Only" or "Colored" appeared over the portals of theaters, boarding houses, waiting rooms, and toilets, over ticket windows and water fountains.

Disfranchised, segregated, and ostracized, black people were held to be incapable of self-government, unworthy of the franchise, and impossible to educate beyond the rudiments. The rudiments cost little, and little indeed was spent for black education. In 1907 Mississippi spent $5.02 per child for the education of white children; for black children the figure was $1.10. In some counties of Mississippi ("black counties"), as much as $30 to $38 was spent for each white child while expenditures for black children ranged from 27 cents to a dollar. In Alabama by 1909 there was a 514.8 percent excess of white expenditures over black expenditures per capita; in other words, for every dollar of public school funds allotted to a black child in 1909, $6.14 was received by a white child. Everywhere there was the contemptuous rejection of black education as something that would make them unfit for work. Even those who devoted time and effort to black education were pessimistic about their educability. A professor from the University of Virginia said in 1900 that "the Negro race is essentially a race of peasant farmers and laborers. . . . As a source of cheap labor for a warm climate he is beyond competition; everywhere else he is a foreordained failure."

And black people—what was their role in this oppression? The resistance of the blacks themselves long ceased to be a deterrent to white aggression. And by the nineties, when the "new South" was beginning to emerge, a black leader came forward to preach a philosophy that tended to undermine black resistance and helped smooth the path to proscription. Once more education was to be the answer to black people's problems. But the new spokesman for his people declared that blacks required a different kind of education from that given to whites. The education of the Negro, said Booker T. Washington, "should make the Negro humble, simple, and of service to the community."

VI

Born a slave in Virginia in 1856, Booker T. Washington knew poverty intimately. His bed as a child was a heap of old rags on a dirt floor. When the Civil War ended young Booker was taken by his mother to Malden, West Virginia, where his stepfather worked in a salt furnace. Their new cabin, he tells us, was worse than the one he had lived in as a slave. Home was in the midst of a cluster of cabins jammed close together with no sanitary regulations, so that "the filth about the cabin was often intolerable." Blacks and whites—"the poorest and most ignorant and degenerate white people"—lived crowded together with much drinking, gambling, quarreling, and fighting. Washington, though only a child, went to work with his stepfather in one of the salt furnaces. While working by day, young Washington attended school at night, where, with the help of a succession of itinerant black teachers and his own determination, he learned to read and write. He continued his night schooling when he left the salt furnace to work in a local coal mine, and even later when he left the mine to become a servant in the home of the mine owner. Mrs. Viola Ruffner, wife of the mine owner, was a "Yankee woman" from Vermont with a reputation for being very strict with her servants. But Washington reported that the lessons he learned in the home of Mrs. Ruffner were "as valuable . . . as any education I have ever gotten anywhere since." He got along with her because he quickly learned what she wanted: "first of all she wanted everything kept clean about her . . . she wanted things done promptly and systematically, and . . . at the bottom of everything she wanted absolute honesty and frankness."

Despite his success at Mrs. Ruffner's, Washington wanted to go to Hampton Institute, a school for blacks he had heard about while working in the mine. So in 1872, at the age of sixteen, he left Malden to make the 500-mile trip to Virginia. He had $1.50 in his pocket, and when he arrived at Hampton, his ragged condition almost kept him from being admitted to the school. He was finally given an entrance examination: sweeping the recitation room.

I swept the recitation room three times. Then I got a dusting-cloth and I dusted it four times. All the woodwork around the walls, every bench, table and desk, I went over four times with my dusting-cloth. Besides, every piece of furniture had been moved and every closet and corner in the room had been thoroughly cleaned. I had the feeling that in a large measure my future depended upon the impression I made upon the teacher in the cleaning of that room. When I was through, I reported to the head teacher. She was a "Yankee" woman who knew just where to look for dirt. She went into the room and inspected the floor and the closets; then she took her handkerchief and rubbed it on the woodwork about the walls, and over the table and benches. When she was unable to find one bit of dirt on the floor, or a particle of dust on any of the furniture, she quietly remarked, "I guess you will do to enter this institution."

Hampton Institute had been founded by General Samuel Chapman Armstrong shortly after the war. Armstrong was convinced that the only hope for the future of the South "lay in a vigorous attempt to lift the colored race by a practical education that would fit them for life." The instruction given at Hampton consisted of manual training. But this education of the hands of the blacks was not intended merely to increase their wage-earning capacity. Manual training, in the mind of General Armstrong, was not just economically desirable; he saw in labor, in physical work, a spiritual force—"a force that promoted fidelity, honesty, accuracy, persistence, and intelligence." A practical education, as he conceived it, disciplined the mind and formed character and at the same time made people economically efficient.

At Hampton, General Armstrong taught selected black students to respect labor, especially skilled labor, and to appreciate the values such work had in the formation of character. If education was to be effective for life, he counseled, it must be like the conduct of life itself, "both alert and patient, beginning where the *pupil was*, and creating character rather than comfort, goodness rather than goods." In keeping with his conception of education as character training, Armstrong insisted that education must be "won rather than given." And once he had an education, the black person was to perform some useful service, some task that the world wanted. Education "must inspire the will to serve rather than the will to get; it must be a struggle, not for life alone, but for the lives of others."

In his autobiography, Washington says that, of the two greatest benefits he received from Hampton Institute, the first was "contact with a great man, General S. C. Armstrong . . . the rarest, strongest, and most beautiful character that it has ever been my privilege to meet." The second benefit was to learn what education was expected to do for an individual; that is, he "not only learned that it was not a disgrace to labor, but learned to love labor, not alone for its financial value, but for labor's own sake and the independence and self-reliance which the ability to do something which the world wants done brings."

After graduating from Hampton Institute in 1875, Washington returned to his home in Malden, to teach in the same school he had attended just a few years before. In 1878 to further his education he enrolled in Wayland Seminary in Washington, D.C. The year he spent in the capital confirmed Washington in the beliefs and ideas he had already distilled from his earlier experiences. At this school he found that the students, in most cases, had more money, were better dressed, and in some cases were more brilliant mentally, than the students at Hampton. But he also found that the Seminary students were less self-dependent and seemed to give more attention to outward appearances. The crucial difference, he noted, was that "they did not appear to me to be beginning at the bottom, on a real solid foundation, to the extent that they were at Hampton." In a significant afterthought he added that "they were not as much inclined as the Hampton students to go into the county districts of the South, where there was little comfort, to take up work for our people." In Washington, D.C., he also met scores of black people who had held government positions during the Reconstruction period. Unemployed and often impoverished, this class of people greatly alarmed Washington by the attention they paid to keeping up appearances and by their seeming dependence upon the government "for every conceivable thing." Once again he was confirmed in his belief that black people must build upon a solid foundation—a foundation in education, industry, and property.

After his year at Wayland Seminary, Washington returned to Hampton Institute as an instructor. He first served there as a house father to a group of Indian students who were brought to Hampton as an experiment. Later he was put in charge of the new night-school program that was started for deserving students. Then in the spring of 1881, Washington took up the career that was to be his life's work. Upon the recommendation of General Armstrong he was offered the job of starting a normal school for black teachers that was to be established in Tuskegee, Alabama.

Most of the month of June, Washington spent traveling through Alabama, visiting with the black families of the state. Talking with them and living with them convinced him more than ever of "the wisdom of the system that General Armstrong had inaugurated at Hampton." Washington had learned well the general's dictum that education must begin where the pupil was. To take the children of such people as he had been among for a month, Washington thought, and give them each day a few hours of mere book education, "would be almost a waste of time." The new head of Tuskegee Normal Institute had no high regard for book learning—not for his people, not at that time. He revealed that one of the "saddest things" he saw during that month of travel "was a young man, who had attended some high school, sitting down in a one-room cabin, with grease on his clothing, filth all around him, and weeds in the yard and garden, engaged in studying French Grammar."

The Tuskegee students, he noted, came from homes where they had no opportunity to learn how to care for their bodies. He wanted to teach these students how to bathe, how to care for their teeth. (Washington was convinced that "there were few single agencies of civilization that are more far reaching than the toothbrush.") He wanted to teach them what to eat, and how to eat it properly, how to care for their clothing and their rooms. Aside from this he wanted to give them "such a practical knowledge of some one industry, together with the spirit of industry, thrift and economy, that they would be sure of knowing how to make a living after they had left." Finally, since 85 percent of the black people in the Gulf states depended upon agriculture for their livelihood, he wanted his graduates "to return to the plantation districts and show the people there how to put new energy and new ideas into farming, as well as into the intellectual and moral and religious life of the people."

At Tuskegee, Washington attempted to apply the doctrines of General Armstrong beyond the walls of Hampton Institute, to apply those doctrines to all black people. As Washington saw it, the black person had one basic problem: to win the respect of the whites. The solution to this problem was simple: practice thrift, industry, and honesty, and the white man would respect you. Washington's personal success—from his job as servant boy in the home of Mrs. Ruffner to his position as the principal of Tuskegee Institute—attested to the efficacy of those virtues. Black people, he taught, should buy homes and farms, establish themselves in even the humblest of occupations. Through their good works as members of the community they would win over the whites.

Booker T. Washington accepted and strongly believed in a society of merit. He was convinced that the black had to earn acceptance into the larger American society. He was equally convinced that blacks could win such acceptance. Education—"Tuskegee style"—was the key to acceptance. Once the black community had been infused with the Protestant ethic of thrift, industry, and honesty, acceptance would come.

With the help of his students, of Northern white philanthropists, and his own drive to succeed, Washington made Tuskegee a showplace for black education. In 1893 he delivered a memorial address at Hampton Institute in honor of the late General Armstrong. On this occasion he pointed out how Tuskegee Institute had been founded on the belief that blacks must be helped to help themselves, a lesson Washington indicated he had learned from the general himself. Washington took this opportunity to recount proudly the achievements of Tuskegee Institute:

> Eleven years ago Tuskegee was one of hundreds of similar villages scattered through the Gulf States. Today it is the lighthouse for that section. Eleven years ago there were 30 students and one teacher; now there are 600 students and 38 teachers; then scarcely a dollar and not a foot of land; now 1,400 acres of land, 20 buildings, and real and personal property worth $180,000; then one blind horse; now 260 head of livestock. Then the plantation where the Tuskegee Institute stood had known nought but the labor forced by lash; today there are 19 industries kept in motion by 600 as happy hearts as can be found in America; then some feared that the Negro youth would be ashamed to work for his education, but these students have made and laid into the buildings with their own hands 2,000,000 bricks, and of 20 buildings, 17 have been built and furnished by the students themselves (*Selected Speeches*).

Over the years Booker T. Washington became known nationally. In 1884 in an address he gave to the National Education Association he said, "the whole future of the Negro rested largely upon the question as to whether or not he should make himself, through his skill, intelligence and character, of such undeniable value to the community in which he lived that the community could not dispense with his presence." The following year Washington was elected president of the Alabama State Teachers Association. The apex of his career came in 1895, when he delivered the opening address at the Cotton State Exposition in Georgia. The invitation to deliver the speech, as well as the warm reception given him, signified white recognition of him as the spokesman for his race. In his first declaration as that spokesman Washington told the white Southerners in his audience that the Negro did not want social equality, that he did not need social equality with the whites. Nor did he want, or need, political or civil equality. To the black people in his audience, Washington emphasized the necessity of co-operation with their white friends. Black education, he proclaimed, should be devoted to the practical education of earning a living. To both whites and blacks Washington preached conciliation and harmony between the races. Holding up his hand, with his fingers wide apart, he exclaimed, "in all things purely social we can be as separate as the fingers, yet one as the hand in all things essential to mutual progress."

The response of the white Southerners to this speech was electric. When he finished speaking, Washington found that Governor R. F. Bullock had rushed across the stage and was shaking his hand. The handshaking, back-thumping, and hearty congratulations were such that Washington had difficulty getting out of the building. Papers in all parts of the United States published the address in full, and for months afterwards there were complimentary editorial references to it. The editor of the *Atlanta Constitution* wrote, in part: "I do not exaggerate when I say that Professor Booker T. Washington's address yesterday was one of the most notable speeches, both as to character and as to the warmth of its reception, ever delivered to a southern audience. The address was a revelation. The whole speech is a platform upon which blacks and whites can stand with full justice to each other." A few days after the Atlanta address Washington received a congratulatory message from Grover Cleveland, the President of the United States.

Perhaps the most poignant comment of all came from a reporter of the *New York World,* who noted that at the end of the speech "most of the Negroes in the audience were crying, perhaps without knowing just why." Among black people, after an initial burst of enthusiasm, there gradually began to grow the suspicion that they had been sold out. The Atlanta address soon came to be referred to as the "Atlanta Compromise." Actually, the speech at Atlanta was no departure from Washington's earlier doctrine. From the earliest he had preached to his fellow blacks: "Make yourself useful to the South; be honest, be thrifty; cultivate the white man's friendliness; above all, educate your children and prepare them for the future." Nor did Washington abrogate social, political, or civil equality at Atlanta. What he said was that such equality "must be the result of a severe and constant struggle." The words and sentiments expressed at Atlanta in 1895 were not new. What was new was the acceptance by a white audience of these as the words and sentiments of the black race. But most important of all to the black people was the fact that this speech, in its enthusiastic endorsement by the white Southerner, occurred at the very moment black people were being disfranchised, segregated, and deprived of their social, civil, and political rights.

Washington accepted completely the reigning ideology of individualism. His whole educational program was grounded in the assumption that America was a society of merit. If black people acquired certain habits, the habits of free people, which would enable them to become independent and self-sufficient—both in their inner life and in their work—then they would increasingly gain civil equality. What Washington did not count on was the political debacle which induced the Southern conservatives to desert blacks in order to subordinate class conflict among whites. Once this took place, Washington's program was undermined. No matter how honest, thrifty, and industrious they might become, the black people were destined to be proscribed, segregated, and disfranchised. America, for them, was no longer a society of merit.

In spite of the empirical reality confronting him, Washington continued to believe. In 1900 he wrote: "I am conscious of the fact that mere connection with what is known as a superior race will not permanently carry an individual to reward unless he has individual worth, and mere connection with what is regarded as an inferior race will not finally hold an individual back if he possess intrinsic, individual merit." This belief was shared by many of his people. When in 1913 black people celebrated their fiftieth year of emancipation, many saw the celebrations and expositions commemorating a half century's progress as testimonials to the teachings of Washington. The statistics for the "year of jubilee" were impressive; in 1913 there were 138,557 Negro farm owners and 550,000 Negro homeowners. In 1900 Washington had organized the Negro Business League. By 1913 there were 38,000 Negro business enterprises, and Washington could point with pride to these self-made black capitalists as the heroes of their race—success had come to them through their industry, their thrift, their honesty. The total wealth of American Negroes was estimated at $700,000,000. Perhaps most impressive of all was the reduction of Negro illiteracy. In 1845 over 90 percent of the Negroes were illiterate; by 1913 this figure had been reduced to 30 percent.

At the very moment Washington was receiving testimonials, the voices of his critics were becoming more strident. The educational gains were laudable, they admitted, but where was the educated black elite, the "talented tenth" necessary to lead the masses to social, political, and civil equality? Washington's level of aspiration had been too low. William E. B. Du Bois poured vitriolic scorn on Washington's educational program in a speech at Hampton Institute: "Take the eyes of the millions off the stars and fasten them in the soil and if their young men will dream dreams, let them be dreams of corn bread and molasses."

And the material gains of the black people? This idea too was praiseworthy, the critics admitted, but look at the price that had to be paid. Washington, they insisted, had sold the human dignity of the black person for a few crumbs of material wealth. The need was not for material wealth, but for justice—political, civil, and social justice.

VII

The man who emerged as the leader of these critics was William E. B. Du Bois. Du Bois, however, never retained that mantle with the tenacity of his predecessor. In fact, Du Bois successively alienated white liberals and blacks during his life time.

It would be difficult to imagine two men more strikingly different than William E. B. Du Bois and Booker T. Washington. Even the conditions surrounding their birth and early lives were markedly different. Washington was born a slave in West Virginia; Du Bois was born a free man in the town of Great Barrington, Massachusetts, a community in which the color line was so faint that, for all practical purposes, Du Bois grew up in an integrated community. Unlike Washington, who never knew who his father was, Du Bois could trace his family back to the period of the American Revolution. The wretched poverty of Washington's youth was matched by the genteel poverty of Du Bois's childhood. Perhaps the most glaring contrast between the two men was their educational background. Washington's formal schooling was on a catch-as-catch-can basis until he entered Hampton Institute at the age of 16. Du Bois had received one of the finest educations of any man of his period; he had taken the classical course in high school, after which he spent three years at Fisk University, going then to Harvard University, where he received a Doctor of Philosophy degree. He finished his studies with 2 years at the University of Berlin. As might be expected, the personalities of these two men were a study in contrasts. Washington's warm, outgoing ways prompted someone once to describe him as looking like a farmer dressed up in his Sunday clothes. But this "Sunday clothes farmer" was a master diplomat, a born leader, with the knack of pleasing everybody. The cold, austere, even haughty countenance of Du Bois was reminiscent of a Spanish aristocrat, an image reinforced by his Vandyke beard. For his first job at Wilberforce College in Ohio, Du Bois arrived on the scene bedecked in a silk hat, gloves, spats, and swinging a cane. Nobody looked less like a farmer! If Washington was the diplomat who pleased everybody, Du Bois became the critic who alienated everybody.

From the years 1894 to 1910 Du Bois was an academician, teaching first at Wilberforce and then at Atlanta University. The relationship between the two men was cordial at first, but gradually tension developed. In 1902 Du Bois published a book, *The Souls of Black Folk*, containing an essay on Booker T. Washington. He called Washington the most distinguished Southerner since Jefferson Davis. But, he went on: "Washington asked the Negro to give up, at least for the present, three things: political power, insistence on civil rights, and higher education of Negro youth." Then Du Bois posed the question: "As a result of this tender of the palm branch, what has been the return?" The return, according to Du Bois, was threefold: blacks had been disfranchised; they had been allocated a distinct status of civil inferiority; and aid to institutions of higher education had been steadily withdrawn. It should be noted that Du Bois did not attribute these developments directly to Washington's teachings, but he said, "his propaganda has, without a shadow of a doubt, helped their speedier accomplishment." So at this point in time there was not an outright repudiation of Washington, but the lines were clearly drawn, as can be seen in the following quote:

> So far as Mr. Washington preaches Thrift, Patience and Industrial Training for the Masses, we must hold up his hands and strive with him, rejoicing in his honors and glorying in the strength of the Joshua called of God and of man to lead the headless host. But, so far as Mr. Washington apologizes for injustice, North, or South, does not rightly value the privilege and duty of voting, belittles the emasculating effects of caste distinction, and opposes the higher training and ambition of our brighter minds, so far as he, the South, or the Nation does this—we must unceasingly and firmly oppose them.

No one who read those words could help but conclude that black people now had another brilliant, articulate spokesman, one more forceful, more aggressive, more militant than Booker T. Washington. The difference between the two leaders was one of emphasis. Du Bois represented the new exclusive concern of black people with their rights. What was missing was Washington's concern with the community. An industrious, honest, thrifty community was a prerequisite, he taught, to the granting of those rights. Du Bois and his followers vigorously rejected the notion that black people had to win their rights and denied that these rights were granted only to those who merited them. "By every civilized and peaceful method," Du Bois wrote, "we must strive for the rights which the world accords to men, clinging unwaveringly to those great words which the sons of the Fathers would fain forget: 'We hold these truths to be self-evident: That all men are created equal; that they are endowed by their creator with certain inalienable rights; that among these are life, liberty and the pursuit of happiness.' "

In 1910 Du Bois left Atlanta University and went to New York to become Director of Research for the recently formed National Association for the Advancement of Colored People (NAACP), and editor of its magazine, *Crisis*. For the next fifty years the role of leader was taken over by this organization. The cult of personality disappeared. Du Bois himself was overshadowed by the organization. He left it once in 1934 after he advocated racial separation, abandoning the association's goal of an integrated society. He later returned but embraced socialism, which led to his second and final break with the NAACP in 1948. From that time until his death in 1963 Du Bois moved further to the left and "aligned his hope with the world forces that he saw fighting for peace and for the working class."

VIII

For Booker T. Washington, who had been born a slave, the problem of black people was to gain acceptance by the whites, especially the Southern whites. He saw education—black education—as the solution to this problem. Through education blacks could acquire the kind of personal virtues and create the kind of community that would win the white people's acceptance. For William E. B. Du Bois, born a free man, it was degrading to seek the white people's acceptance. Blacks had a soul, and in America they supposedly had rights, rights that they shared with the whites. The problem of the black people, therefore, was not to win white people's acceptance. It was to destroy white people's discrimination.

Once Du Bois had rejected Washington's approach, one would expect him to reject Washington's faith in the power of education. But the American faith in the power of education is long-abiding. Du Bois, with that naïve snobbery of the intellectual, placed his faith in higher education, reasoning that his fellow white Americans could not deny equal rights to an educated elite, even though they be black. Then seeing his dream of an integrated America shattered against the adamant wall of white prejudice, Du Bois abandoned the ideology of individualism and took up the ideology of egalitarianism: he now believed that only a society of total equality could secure justice for black people. But most blacks still subscribed to individualism and retained faith in the power of education, focussing their hopes on the NAACP. Once blacks had a good education then discrimination against them would evaporate. The integrated society would be at hand.

Since the objective was the elimination of white discrimination, the NAACP inevitably adopted the approach of legalism. And since the key to integration was education, the major legal battles against discrimination were all attempts to secure educational opportunities—equal to those given to whites. Finally, since the leaders of the association shared Du Bois's original belief in the power of an educated black elite to lead the masses in securing their rights, the NAACP directed its legal assaults against discrimination in higher education. Not until the 1950's did the NAACP fight against segregation in the public schools.

In placing its money on the power of an educated elite, the NAACP concerned itself with a minority and showed little worry about the masses. Moreover, in choosing the way of legalism, the NAACP inevitably centered on the Southern states, largely ignoring the increasing numbers of black people living in the de facto ghettos of the North. These ghettos in time became infected with all the social ills of the twentieth century. Booker T. Washington's vision of a strong, healthy, black community remained a vision, and as the quality and standard of living within the ghettos declined, white fears increased. The fear of contagion reinforced the determination of many whites to keep strong the walls of segregation. Thus, at the very period the NAACP was winning legal victories for black people, white prejudice against them was mounting. And as these legal victories became more spectacular, the danger of black disenchantment increased—disenchantment that could, and did, lead to despair and finally to violence.

May 17, 1954, was heralded—at the time—as the day the walls came tumbling down. On that day a unanimous Supreme Court declared, in the case of *Brown v. Topeka Board of Education,* that segregated public schools were unconstitutional. White Southerners greeted the decision with shock, some with fury.

The *Washington Post* labeled May 17th as "Black Monday." Black people, expectedly, hailed the decision with jubilation. True, the actual desegregation of the public schools in the South would have to await a further order of the Supreme Court, which was not to come for another whole year. However, the great day was at hand, the integrated society was here—or soon would be.

The following year, in May 1955, the Supreme Court ordered the racial desegregation of all public schools "with all deliberate speed." However, when the schools opened in September for a new school year, nothing happened. Segregation in the South continued as if the Court had never spoken. Confusion and disenchantment rose among black people. In December of that year these feelings gathered momentum and found expression in Montgomery, Alabama, setting off what Louis Lomax called the "Negro Revolt."

In that Montgomery bus strike the American blacks found a new national leader in the Reverend Martin Luther King. Here was the first black leader to reject schooling as the panacea for the problem of his people. Discrimination continued to be the problem, but the weapon was different. Nonviolent demonstrations were mounted against white discrimination. Yet, although he expressed no great faith in the power of the schools, Martin Luther King did bear witness to the power of education. In point of fact, the whole nonviolent movement was an experiment in educating, an attempt to educate white people about the extent of discrimination existing in America and to reveal it as a moral evil. Even the Reverend King's claim for "the redemptive power of unmerited suffering," when stripped of its religious connotations, is revealed as an educational slogan.

But not all American blacks followed the lead of Martin Luther King. He had abandoned the unlimited faith in black schooling for a belief in the education of the "minds and hearts" of white Americans. Once "educated," these white Americans would help usher in a truly integrated society. Not so, said some. Integration, they declared, will never come. These Black Nationalists urged that black people accept, indeed welcome, a segregated America. Rather than beg whites for an integrated society on their terms, the energies of the blacks should be directed to securing a strong, vigorous, healthy community. Here was a pursuit not unlike that of Booker T. Washington, but lacking his expected payoff of integration into the larger American society. Here too was an educational task. The creation of a strong, vigorous, healthy community required schooling. But the Black Nationalists rejected the schools—the whites' schools—in favor of various informal educational agencies within the ghettos.

Finally there were other black leaders in the sixties, such as A. Philip Randolph and James Farmer, who had an egalitarian vision of the future of American society. Like Washington these leaders wanted an integrated society, but they rejected merit as a prerequisite for integration. From these leaders came demands for job quotas, for preferential hiring of blacks, for preferential admission to educational institutions, for special or compensatory educational programs, and demands for racially balanced schools. These leaders and their followers were interested in results; they wanted an integrated society; and they wanted it immediately. No longer could they, nor would they, wait for the white community to decide that the black merited full admission into American life.

Convinced that the schools were not *the* agency of change, most black leaders saw the school as one of the many institutions in American society that needed to be changed, for they realized that, instead of integrating black and white children, the schools now actually reinforced the patterns of segregation. In the South "tokenism" in the schools had thwarted the legalistic approach to integration. By admitting a few selected, compliant black pupils to an all-white school while keeping all other black children in their "own" schools, Southern communities could comply with the law prohibiting segregated schools. Twelve years after the Brown decision, less than 10 percent of black schoolchildren in the South attended schools with whites. So through a "token" compliance with the law, many Southern communities actually used the "desegregated" schools to stymie integration.

In other sections of the country discrimination in housing had created racially segregated residential areas. The children living in these black ghettos attended neighborhood schools within the ghettos. In these de facto segregated schools the black children inevitably received an education inferior to that provided in what black people now derided as the "lily-white" schools. What frustrated many was the fact that attempts to break through the barrier of segregation frequently turned the school systems into a battleground that accelerated racial tensions and intensified segregation. As blacks became more militant and more successful in penetrating into the heretofore all-white schools, a tipping point was reached that drove white families out of the community to someplace where the racial balance in the schools was more to their liking. Sometimes white parents removed their children from the public schools and put them into private schools. In some instances the white parents stayed in the community and kept their children in the "racially balanced" schools. But here, more often than not, the schools underwent some significant changes, the principal one usually being the introduction of a "multitrack" system. This system separates children into groups on the basis of what is called "learning ability," which, in effect, separates the children along racial lines. Thus, an ostensibly integrated school on closer examination often proved to be a "cover-up" of a highly segregated educational program.

Yet by the mid-sixties some black leaders had second thoughts about integrated schools. By then it was clear that mixing together lower-class black children with middle-class whites in the schoolroom did not hasten the day of the integrated society. In those schools that had created a racial balance, the results showed that the lower-class black students were not stimulated by being in classrooms with middle-class white children of high aspirations. In fact, as Charles Silberman has pointed out, the black students "seemed to give up trying at all." For the white children the integrated classroom created derogatory racial stereotypes, when there had been none before. The children discovered that the black children in their classes were "not as bright, clean, honest, or well behaved as they."

In the light of these results some black leaders saw that rather than integrated schools, what was *presently* needed was compensatory education for the children in the black schools. Only after their schooling placed them on a level with the white child could both profit from an integrated school. Only then would integrated schools lead to an integrated society. Compensatory education for black children meant prekindergarten instruction as well as supplemental aid and attention throughout their entire school careers.

Once again the schools were called upon to usher in the integrated society. Would they fulfill the promise this time? History had made one thing clear: since emancipation the school had played a central role in the dreams and the frustrations of the American black people. While holding out the promise of an integrated society, the American schools had in fact functioned as a barrier against it.

CHAPTER 4

The City and the Schools

I

In 1860, when there were 31 million people in the United States, less than one fifth lived in cities. Fifty years later the population had increased to 92 million and by then well over two fifths lived in cities. During this 50-year period New York City increased its population fourfold to approach a total of 5 million. The population of Philadelphia tripled during the same period, reaching a million and a half by 1910. Chicago, "the wonder of the West," boasted over 2 million inhabitants in 1910. And in that year St. Louis, Detroit, Cleveland, and Baltimore each claimed a half million or more. America was rapidly becoming an urban society.

Most of these urban dwellers were newcomers. Displaced by the ever-increasing mechanization of agriculture, many farmers and sons of farmers came to the city in search of the wealth, the prestige, and the new lifestyles obtainable through the industrial and commercial jobs that the city now offered. The lure of the city drained the countryside so that, by 1890, over 40 percent of the nation's rural townships showed a drop in population.

The shift from the farm to the city was not limited to America. The same forces of mechanization on the farm and improved transportation displaced the agricultural workers in the Old World. But not all European cities could absorb the dislocated farmers. In the cities of Germany and Scandinavia rapid industrialization did create new employment for those displaced from the land. And in Great Britain many erstwhile farmers were diverted to the dominions and colonies—to Canada, to Australia, and to South Africa. But in other nations, especially those in southern and eastern Europe, emigration held the only solution to the problem of rural displacement—emigration to the United States. The exodus to America of displaced farmers from Austria-Hungary, from Italy, and from other southern and eastern European countries was augmented by the addition of thousands of Jews who fled from persecution in Russia during the last quarter of the nineteenth century.

Originally, these "new immigrants" moved west with the frontier, following the path taken by those who had emigrated to America before the Civil War. The railroad companies, anxious to settle the West with potential customers, sent agents to Europe. There they assembled, organized, and herded the immigrants from their native homes all the way to Kansas, or Idaho, or Nebraska. But during the 1880s the westward movement halted. By then the unsold farm lands were beginning to disappear, and cheap land was almost gone. Simultaneously the farmers' income had dropped to a new low, which further dissuaded newcomers from taking up the plow. The new immigrants now sought a livelihood in the mines, in the mills, and in the factories that had mushroomed throughout America during and since the war. It was to the cities that the immigrants now came.

More than five sixths of the Russian-born immigrants—mostly Jews—settled in urban communities. Three quarters of the immigrants from Italy and Hungary congregated in the cities. There, these "new immigrants" joined and were joined by the Irish, who, as Mawdlyn Jones has noted, "from the earliest had showed a marked aversion to a rural existence in America." By 1890 a fourth of the people of Philadelphia and a third of the Bostonians were of alien birth. In greater New York in 1900 four out of five residents were foreign born, or of foreign parentage. In Chicago the foreign-born exceeded the city's total population of a decade earlier. By 1910 there were well over nine and one-half million foreign born in American cities, together with over twelve million natives of foreign or mixed parentage.

II

The move to the city created problems for the emigrant family. On the farm, or in the village, the family was integrated. Each member had a job, or specific tasks. The entire family, which usually included an aunt or an uncle, as well as some cousins, functioned as an economic unit. Now, in the city, that unity of the family disappeared. In the city the individual, not the family, was the economic unit. The father, usually the older children, and frequently the mother worked outside the home. They worked for an unknown employer, together with unfriendly, impersonal people, at some strange, unfamiliar job that lacked meaning because it seemed totally unconnected with the work of anyone else.

Under these conditions the extended family could not hold together. The responsibilities and the duties of the uncles and aunts, of the cousins and the nephews, lacked clear definitions in this new environment. Gradually the family was reduced to parents and their children. And the city transformed them, too. On the farm the father had been the head of the household enterprise, but now, in the city, he usually was not the sole, or sometimes even the main, provider. When employed, he often worked at some menial task that degraded him in his own and his family's eyes. Nor were the women spared. The move to the city upset their routines, changed their roles. The daily tasks required to tend a family and supply its needs seemed infinitely more complex and confusing than on the land. Whether through ignorance and poverty, or through neglect, the crowded family quarters were often disorderly, the food poor or poorly prepared.

For these people the rise of the city represented a radical break with the past. Urbanization meant more than moving from the country to the city, from work on the land to work in the factory. Urbanization involved basic changes in thinking and behavior as well as changes in social values. The migration, the change in occupation, the shifting of status and roles all inflicted substantial damage on newcomers. Shorn of the shelter of familiar institutions, they suffered a loss of identity. Unprotected and isolated, they became prone to personal deterioration. High rates of mortality, suicide, alcoholism, and insanity showed that, in Oscar Handlin's words, "men raised in one environment could not safely shift to another without substantial damage to themselves."

Yet the decay of traditional institutions was at the same time a release from traditional restraints. To be unsheltered was at the same time to be liberated. So where some succumbed as victims of the city, many newcomers triumphed for the very reasons others failed: the city offered freedom, the opportunity to grow. Many, but not all, grew in the hard testing-ground of the city. To them the slums, the grinding competition, the junglelike complexity, constituted a challenge, not a defeat. And in this race to succeed, the children had a built-in advantage. Born in the city, or brought there as infants, the younger children never experienced the bonds of a preurban existence. And for the older children the move to the city signaled the release from traditional restraints. To the children then, if not always to the parents, America, urban America, was the promised land. Instead of the normlessness their parents felt, the children discovered new norms, new *urban* patterns of behavior; instead of alienation, the children developed new attachments in and to the city, uncovered new meanings in the urban way of life; instead of the powerlessness their parents felt, the children hacked out new paths to success, new ways to achieve their goals.

The eagerness and ease with which the young people grasped America contrasted dramatically with the fumbling, hesitant steps of the adults. The gap between generations grew to undreamed-of proportions. On the farm, in the village, the parents had been models for the children. But in this strange new environment, how could the parents guide them, how could the parents protect them from the physical, the social, the moral dangers of the city? Uprooted, unprotected, and isolated, the newcomers no longer possessed adequate norms of behavior. The city had shattered the traditional patterns of life routines, the traditional unfolding of life sequences. Unable to fulfill their traditional role as behavioral models for their children, many parents felt that their children were growing up like savages in the city wilderness. Something had to be done. The children had to be trained; they had to be civilized.

III

As the newcomers from rural America and from Europe moved into the cities, many middle- and upper-class citizens moved out. This flight of the upper classes was not caused so much by the influx of newcomers as by the industrialization within the city that brought railroad yards, factories, mills, and commercial establishments of all types into or adjacent to what had been quiet, residential neighborhoods. The city became unlivable for the middle and upper classes. Their abandoned houses were soon stocked with newcomers, overstocked, since shrewd realtors cut up the houses into one- or two-room apartments. Not only the houses but the cellars and the stables became residences for the homeless immigrants. In time the supply of homes gave out and new living quarters were constructed, tenements, usually built side by side and back to back so that there was little light or air.

Crowded into the small rooms and dank hallways with inadequate sanitation and almost no ventilation, many fell victim to tuberculosis, typhoid, diphtheria, scarlet fever. Not only disease but drunkenness, crime, and immorality flourished under such conditions.

Confronted with the deterioration of their cities, many native urban Americans placed the blame on the newcomers. The immigrants had produced the filth, the vermin, the diseases now found in the cities. The moral inadequacies of the newcomers had generated the slums that were now laying waste to urban life. Their great tendency to vagrancy and crime, their undemocratic backgrounds, and their lack of understanding of American institutions made them a menace to the city, if not to the nation itself. The newcomers were intemperate, illiterate and ignorant; they lived in filth and wallowed in corruption. But what was most frightening of all: they were breeding! Their kids were everywhere, especially in the streets, where they not only got into mischief but frequently committed serious crimes. These "street Arabs" should not be in the streets threatening the life, limb, and property of law-abiding citizens. The schoolroom was where these young hoodlums belonged. It was scandalous that many of these "future citizens" could hardly speak English, let alone read or write it. They needed to be civilized and Americanized—"socialized" was the word frequently used. Education was the only means to save American society from the threat posed by the urban masses. The "battle against the slums," as Jacob Riis termed it, "would be fought out, in, and around the public school."

The children of the newcomers were a problem in another way. Many of them entered the labor market, where they worked for low wages. By this they either depressed the salaries of all workers, or worse yet, they displaced some adult from a job. Something had to be done. Some said there ought to be a law to keep them out of the ranks of labor. School is where they belonged, and there ought to be a law to keep them in school.

Earlier, in the 1830s and 1840s similar demographic changes had brought forth an increase in hierarchical sentiments among native-born Americans. Now, once again, this ideological outlook gained adherents, and, once again, it led to state-imposed education laws.

For their own sake and for the good of society the younger generation had to be constrained. The very stability of democratic society depended upon their being adjusted to the American way of life. Such adjustment required a long period of careful training. Therefore, in order to preserve American democracy the city children had to be institutionalized, had to be compelled to attend school.

IV

Before the Civil War most Americans viewed the very idea of compulsory education with alarm. In accord with the ideology of individualism that had dominated the antebellum period, most Americans took the doctrine of limited government seriously. They insisted that the state had no right to interfere between parent and child. The parent, alone, had the right to determine what the child should do, including deciding whether or not he or she attended school. It is true that the staunchest opponents of compulsory education—both before and after the Civil War—were employers who feared the loss of their child laborers. Nevertheless, American opinion was such that only the state of Massachusetts passed a compulsory attendance law before the Civil War. Even this meager law—compulsory school attendance of every child between eight and fourteen for at least twelve weeks each year, six weeks to be consecutive—proved ineffectual. An agent of the State Board of Education observed as late as 1861 that "compulsion should be used with caution and only as a last resort."

Only after the Civil War, when the rise of the cities created fears for the stability of society, and drew more people to the ideology of hierarchy, do we find any widespread effort to secure effective compulsory education laws. Four years after the passage of the 1874 compulsory education law in New York the state superintendent reported that the law was effectively enforced in only New York City and Brooklyn. The same urban character of compulsory education is evident in the first law of Maryland, which applied only to Baltimore and populous Allegheny county. In Missouri school attendance was made compulsory from eight to fourteen only in cities with a population over 500,000.

City children, especially the children of the newcomers, had generated both compassion and fear. They were unkempt, uncared for, and untutored. They were in need of help. But they were also a threat, a threat to the workingman, a threat to social customs, mores, and institutions, a threat to the future of American democracy. Partly from fear and partly from compassion, thirty-one states enacted some form of compulsory education law by 1900. These laws soon transformed American urban education.

V

Compulsory education laws exploded school enrollments. The number of 5-to 18-year-olds enrolled in school rose from 6½ million in 1870 to 15½ million by 1880, a rise from 57 percent to over 72 percent of the age group. By 1916 the public schools enrolled 20 million pupils. Compulsory education laws not only brought more children to the schools but kept them there for longer periods of time: the average length of a school term rose from 132 days in 1870 to 144 days in 1900, reaching 157 by 1915.

One might expect American schools to be buried by this avalanche of children. Indeed in the cities additional buildings and even floors of buildings had to be rented for use as schools. As late as 1888 one heard complaints about these rented facilities, which were "unfit" and a "discredit" to the school system. As rapidly as funds could be secured, sites were purchased and proper school buildings erected. And just as the challenge of inundation spawned new school buildings, so it created an educational profession, for once the American people seriously began to provide mass education, the problems of maintaining schools became so complex that educational experts had to be found and hired to run the schools.

Before the Civil War most urban schools were run by politically appointed trustees of each ward or district, who levied school taxes, built and maintained schoolhouses, and hired the teachers. The economic and social inequalities among the various districts within each city made for glaring educational inequalities. Moreover, the way the politicians handled building contracts and hired teachers led to accusations of graft and corruption. Most cities also had a citywide board of education, but these city boards were large, contentious, and inefficient, since they were made up of representatives from every ward or district in the ever-growing city.

The hierarchical ideology that now propelled educational reform, not unexpectedly, prescribed more centralization of urban schools. Arguing that they wanted "to get politics out of education," and "eliminate educational inequalities," the hierarchical reformers in many cities asked the state legislatures to pass laws that enabled them to abolish the district system and create in its place a small, manageable board for the entire city. Chicago abolished its districts as early as 1857; Philadelphia had districts until 1905, when it reduced the city board from 115 to 24. The members of these new, small boards no longer represented a particular section of the city. They were sometimes elected at large by the people, as in Boston and St. Louis; sometimes appointed by the mayor, as in Chicago and New York; or even, as in Philadelphia, appointed by the courts.

Once the control of urban education had been centralized in the hands of city boards, these representatives of the public turned much of the power over to a new breed of educational expert, the city superintendent. Although professional school administration starts at this point, the city superintendent was actually not a new employee. Both Buffalo, New York, and Louisville, Ken-

tucky, had city superintendents as early as 1837. But not until the last decades
of the century did the city superintendent become an executive instead of a
clerk. In 1895 the U.S. Commissioner of Education could report that the city
superintendent retained responsibility for the mechanical elements of curator-
ship, purchasing supplies, keeping records, and supervising construction of
buildings, but that his primary role was that of educational expert: he directed
the course of study, taught methods of instruction, served as counselor and
advisor to the school board, and fashioned and shaped the educational thought
of the community.

These combined duties of supervision and administration proved bur-
densome for many a city superintendent so that he too had to turn many tasks
over to a bevy of specialists. To enforce compulsory education laws, he usually appointed an attendance officer who not only apprehended truant children, but frequently directed the taking of the school census. In addition to
truant officers the policing of the city required a vast amount of paper work:
age certificates, school certificates, working papers, and employment tickets
had to be designed, filled in, and issued. To handle the myriad of forms and
affidavits the superintendent acquired a number of assistant superintendents,
replete with clerical staffs.

Inevitably, city school systems became bureaucratized. People of all ideological persuasions viewed this as a felicitous development: hierarchs, especially those who were educational administrators, valued the order and stability bureaucracy guaranteed; individualists, especially those who were
teachers, prized bureaucracy because it eliminated favoritism and special privileges; and eqalitarians, especially if they were minority parents, believed that
bureaucracy made the school system more accountable and responsive to
complaints about unequal treatment.

Increasingly superintendents became preoccupied with money. School-
keeping was becoming big business. For the country as a whole the value of
school property rose from $130 million in 1870 to $1,567 million in 1915, and
per pupil expenditure rose from $9.17 a year to $32.53. To manage and control the burgeoning finances, most city boards insisted upon appointing a business manager. Finally, to supervise the expanding host of personnel the superintendent came to rely upon special supervisors and principals.

The greatest increase in personnel came in the teaching corps, which
tripled in size during this period, rising from 200,515 in 1870 to 604,301 in 1915.
Yet more significant than the mere increase in their numbers was the fact that,
in the cities, teaching became a profession. In the cities "schoolkeepers"
became "schoolteachers." Only later did "schoolteachers" become "educators."

VI

Specialization is the essence of professionalization, and teachers first found the
opportunity to specialize in the city schools. Long before the Civil War, teachers in the cities had been able to divide their students into separate classes. But

one teacher continued to teach all classes, sometimes assisted by ushers who heard recitations, frequently in the same room with the teacher, while the teacher was hearing the recitation of another class. Horace Mann in his seventh annual report to the Massachusetts Board of Education in 1844 complained that the teacher had too many duties. He supposed that the "perfect school" would be one in which a teacher had "charge of but one class, having talent and resources sufficient properly to engage and occupy its attention." Mann insisted that Massachusetts could have "this mode of dividing and classifying scholars in all our large towns"—were it not for "that *vis inertiae* of the mind which continues in the beaten track because it has not vigor enough to turn aside from it." A few years later John D. Philbrick organized the Quincy school after the model described by Mann in the seventh annual report. This so-called "graded-school plan" soon spread throughout the country, and by the end of the war most cities and large towns had schools of this type.

In the older, ungraded school teachers had spent much of their time trying to maintain order, hearing the recitations of one group, or class, at a time. In the new graded school teachers attended to all students at the same time since they had but one class or grade and so could teach all the students the same material at the same time. The power of the graded school to reduce problems of discipline became one of its most attractive features. William Torrey Harris, onetime superintendent of schools in St. Louis (1868–1880) and later U.S. Commissioner of Education (1889–1906), reported that "it was not uncommon for over 100 cases of corporal punishment to take place in one day" in a St. Louis ungraded school containing about 500 pupils. After the introduction of graded schools Harris claimed that discipline cases dropped in two years from 500 cases per week to 3 cases per week.

Those (male) educators who promoted graded schools claimed that the division of labor and the presence of a male principal in such schools would enable women to handle their jobs more efficiently and to control the older boys. And since women teachers could be hired more cheaply than men, more and more cost-conscious city boards of education speedily adopted the graded school plan. By 1905, 98 percent of the elementary school teachers, and 62 percent of the secondary school teachers, were women. At the same point in time 38 percent of the elementary school principals and 94 percent of the secondary school principals were men.

The graded school stimulated student effort, since all students were expected to complete school by the systematic progression through grades. Lack of effort resulted in being "left down" with the next, younger class. The graded school, for the first time, permitted systematic work. Harris saw the graded school "perfecting the habit of moving in concert with others." He insisted that the graded school in the city was "a stronger moral force than the rural school because of its superior training in the social habits [of] . . . regularity, punctuality, orderly, concerted action and self restraint."

The basis of the graded school was teacher specialization. For the first time the schoolmaster could become a teaching specialist, a specialist in teaching the same material to all the pupils of his or her class or grade. There was a danger of teaching the same material to all, of course, and as early as 1872, E. E. White complained at the NEA convention of "lock step," mechanical education that geared instruction to average students, thus handicapping the bright and the slow learners. This criticism of the graded school was acknowledged by Harris and others, including Charles W. Eliot, president of Harvard University. But the obvious answer to such criticism, as they pointed out, was more specialization. Thus, we find certain teachers with classes composed only of superior students, while others taught only slow learners. In some urban schools, teachers became specialists in one subject. This departmentalization usually took place in the high schools, but a number of cities, beginning with San Francisco in 1887, tried it in the elementary schools. In 1904 New York City introduced the departmental plan in 130 elementary schools. The following year a reporter in the NEA *Proceedings* announced that the teachers were unanimously in favor of the plan, adding that "the age of the Jack-of-all-trades has passed in our vocations and professions."

In most urban schools teachers who were specialists soon acquired special classrooms—for music, for drawing, for physical culture, for domestic science, and for manual training. Frequently in the lower schools there were expression rooms, storytelling rooms, and dramatization rooms.

One of the most remarkable urban developments in teacher specialization was the creation of special city schools and classes for exceptional children. In 1869 Boston instituted the first city school for the education of the deaf. By 1916 seventy-one cities maintained similar schools. New York City established the first public city school for the blind in 1909. By 1916 ten cities had created similar schools. Providence became the first school system to provide special training for the "backward" child when it organized three schools for special discipline and instruction in 1893. Boston in 1899, and Philadelphia in 1901, took steps to segregate the "mentally deficient" from regular classes. By 1916, some 118 American cities had organized school classes for the segregation and training of "retarded" children.

Although this instruction of exceptional children was but one of the many different forms of specialization taking place in education, these teachers decided to appropriate the term "special education." At the NEA convention in 1901 the Department of Deaf and Dumb, Blind, and Feeble-Minded renamed itself the Department of Special Education—"relating to children demanding special means of instruction."

VII

The floodtide of children rushing and being pushed into the city schools did more than create the graded school, for if the graded school offered the schoolmaster the opportunity to become a teaching specialist, then he or she had somehow to learn that specialty. Up until 1860 only 12 state-supported teacher-training institutions, called normal schools, had been established. After the Civil War the cities for the first time began setting up their own normal schools. By 1871 twelve cities had them, and by the end of the century just about every city had one.

Most of these city normal schools were high schools where future teachers received both a general education and professional training. In San Francisco such a program led to a separate postgraduate department of the high school for the professional training of teachers. Many of the city school systems eventually followed St. Louis in developing a full-fledged separate school for the training of teachers.

In these urban normal schools future teachers learned the general method of instruction called "object teaching." Imported into the United States in 1861 by Edward Sheldon, superintendent of schools in the city of Oswego, New York, object teaching had first been developed in England by Charles Mayo and his sister Elizabeth. They, in turn, owed their theories to the famous Swiss educator, Pestalozzi.

Pestalozzi had urged the teacher to begin with the experiences of children, their observations, their ideas. Beginning here, the teacher could proceed by means of carefully graded oral instruction to systematic and organized knowledge. In the system developed by the Mayos the textbook was subordinated to oral instruction so that, instead of hearing recitations, the teacher directed the learning activity by presenting objects to the children and asking them questions about their observations. "What is this?" begins a typical "model" lesson in Elizabeth Mayo's *Manual.* The lesson continues: "A piece of bark. All look at it. Where do we find bark? On trees. On what part of trees? Look and see. (The teacher brings in a piece of the stem of a tree on which the bark still remains.) On the outside. Repeat together—'Bark is the outer part of the stems of trees.' " And so on until the end of the lesson, when the teacher sums up: "Now repeat all you have said. 'Bark is the outside covering of the stems of trees: it is brown: we cannot see through it: it is rough, dull, dry, hard and fibrous.' "

At the Oswego Normal School teachers were taught how to select lesson materials and arrange them, how to frame questions, and how to conduct the learning exercises. Object teaching soon spread rapidly throughout the country, becoming the main fare of most normal schools. Prior to the Civil War American travelers had described the ideas of Pestalozzi in books and reports, but Pestalozzian principles had "remained largely a matter of lectures and books among the initiated few." Now, after the war, when the rapid growth of the graded school freed the urban schoolmaster to teach, object teaching became *the* method of instruction taught to future teachers.

In the nineties the monopoly of Pestalozzi in America was challenged by a fiery band of educational theorists, who called themselves "Herbartians." Disciples of the German philosopher and educator Johann Friedrich Herbart (1776–1841), these American reformers claimed to have the final answer to the problem of effective instruction. Herbart, they said, provided the basis for a science of education: education henceforth must be grounded in psychology— the science of the mind.

As Herbart saw it, the teacher's job was to cause the growth of ideas in the mind of the child. Since this required conformity to psychological laws, education depended upon the science of psychology. Pestalozzi had stressed sense perception, and his disciples upheld the doctrine of instruction by object lessons. Herbart, on the other hand, argued that, rather than sense perception, teachers must attend to apperception, which he took to be a combination of memory and perception. Rather than having pupils see, hear, and handle things, he told teachers to bring their pupils to recognize things and understand them. For this to occur, the pupils had to see the significance, the usefulness, the applicability of what was taught. And this meant that the ideas had to be properly assimilated; they had to be related to the past experience of the pupil. Herbart's disciples worked out the five formal steps in the process of instruction. First the teacher prepared the mind of the child for the ideas about to be presented, then presented them. In the third step, the teacher had the student associate or assimilate these ideas with older ideas. Then came the fourth step, generalization. The final step was application or exercise in using the acquired knowledge.

In their efforts to spread their gospel, the Herbartians were indefatigable. In 1889 Charles De Garmo published the first American textbook based upon the pedagogy of Herbart, *The Essentials of Method: A Discussion of the Essential Form of Right Methods in Teaching.* During the next ten years ten more books written or translated by Herbart's American disciples appeared. These textbooks rapidly became the mainstay of most normal schools, as they strove to improve the effectiveness of instruction. At the NEA meeting in July 1895 the Herbartians were in such force that they inaugurated the Herbart Society for the Scientific Study of Teaching, with Charles De Garmo as president.

Yet despite the flurry of textbooks, articles, and yearbooks produced by his American disciples, enthusiasm for Herbart in America was short-lived. Before the end of the century speakers critical of his pedagogical ideas began to dominate the programs of the meetings of the Herbart Society. Finally in 1902 the Society itself changed its name to the National Society for the Scientific Study of Education.

VIII

The fall from grace of Herbart and the Herbartians was due to the simple fact that they had too narrow a concept of the role of the teacher. This is evident in the change in name of the society, from "the scientific study of teaching" to "the scientific study of education." The Herbartians failed to see the teacher as an educator at the very moment that urban Americans were rejecting "teachers" in favor of "educators."

Recall that the rise of the city had generated a crisis in the minds of most American adults. Whether they were newcomers or oldtimers, they saw the younger generation growing up in a world they never knew—a different world. To them the children of the city seemed a different species. Many adults felt themselves witness to a kind of degeneration. As the tide of immigration from rural America and from Europe to the teeming cities of the New World rose higher and higher in the first years of the twentieth century, the fears of inundation and nostalgia for the simpler, more civilized past grew apace.

Many now redoubled the demand that the schools combat the ills of urbanization. The stick of compulsory education laws had been taken up to drive the young savages into the schools. These laws had spawned a profession of schoolteachers and a profession of school administrators as well as a science of education. But this was not enough. True, the cities now had better buildings, better-trained teachers, and more effective instruction than could be found in rural America. But the improvement of effective instruction seemed to many to be patently ineffective in curing the ills of the city, for, no matter how improved the instruction in the city schools, many students remained uninterested in what was being taught. Many dropped out of school after a year or two. One study made of the schools in St. Louis concluded that the primary cause for pupil withdrawal was "a lack of interest on the part of the pupil"; the second cause was "a lack on the part of the parents of a just appreciation of the education now offered." Obviously the schools could not successfully combat the ills of the city if they could not keep their pupils. Many now began to argue for changes in the content of instruction.

Herbart had not tampered with the traditional curriculum, although he had urged teachers to make that curriculum more meaningful to students. He himself, for example, had proven to his own satisfaction that the *Odyssey* became more meaningful to his students when taught in Greek rather than in translation. He never questioned the teaching of the *Odyssey* itself.

At the fourth annual meeting of the Herbart Society in 1898, M. G. Brumbaugh, professor of history from the University of Pennsylvania, decried the narrow outlook of the Herbartians. History, he insisted, "should be so presented as to arouse the social sense of the child." That same year Spencer Trotter of Swarthmore, in a speech entitled "The Social Function of Geography," told the members of the Herbart Society that the end of the study of geography was "to develop a social intelligence and, consequently, a social disposition."

The following year, at the fifth annual meeting, I. W. Howerth delivered a major revisionist talk entitled "The Social Aims in Education." Reflecting both a holistic and organic conception of society, Howerth warned that the two great dangers of an urbanized society were the atomization of the individual and the retardation of social progress. To prevent these twin evils, Howerth insisted that the aim of education should be "The adaptation of the individual to the prosecution and enjoyment of a social life, the elimination of anti social feeling, and the development of sympathetic emotions." In this way education will "modify and accelerate social evolution." For, he pointed out, "so long as certain classes or certain individuals refuse to recognize their natural relations to society, so long will they tend to retard the advance of society toward its ultimate goal." Howerth summed up this new aim of education in the term "socialization." He took pains to point out that socialization went beyond, and indeed was unlike, "preparation for social life." The Herbartians themselves admitted "preparation for social life" as an aim of education and argued that Herbart's goal of developing many-sided interests in the child was the best preparation for social life. But for Howerth, rather than preparation for social living, socialization meant "a reorganization of the school so as to give all its activity a social value and in such a way that it will reflect and organize the fundamental principles of community life."

Here at last was a response to assuage the fears and nurse the nostalgia of urban Americans. Here at last was a theory of education that could combat the ills of the city by doing battle with urbanization itself. According to this theory the city schools were to do no less than recapture the community of the remembered past. What appealed to many was that this movement to recapture the past was not reactionary but progressive, since, according to the theory, the progress of society itself necessitated the restoration of community. As the primary agency of socialization the school would restore the community and thereby guarantee the very progress of society.

IX

I. W. Howerth taught at the University of Chicago, and in his talk he had referred generously and respectfully to his colleague, John Dewey, head of the unified Department of Philosophy, Psychology, and Pedagogy. With John Dewey the pleas for restoration of community rested on more than a hankering for the past. Without community, the bigness of the city, its variety, and its toleration shattered the individual, leaving him or her undisciplined, dislocated, and alienated. But Dewey thought that the restoration of community could transform these same conditions so that they would promote the growth of the individual and the growth of society itself. Here we find the man who first articulated those holistic and organic conceptions of society that uncovered the twin evils of urbanization: individual atomization and social retardation. Here, too, we find the man first to prescribe the restoration of community as the cure for these ills. And it was Dewey who gave this restoration job to the schools.

As early as 1896 Dewey had set up the Laboratory School at the University of Chicago, a school he described as "a cooperative society on a small scale." The expressed aim of his school was the "ability of individuals to live in cooperative integration with others." In the same year that Howerth delivered his address to the Herbart Society, John Dewey published his epoch-making book, *The School and Society.* In this book the Vermont-bred philosopher insisted that city youths lacked the educational experiences common in preurban America. Growing up in rural America children had had a direct contact with reality, hence an understanding of the world in which they lived, a far better understanding than did the city child of the present. On the farm, or in the small village, unlike the city, Dewey wrote, "the entire industrial process stood revealed," from the production on the farm of the raw materials "till the finished product was actually put to use." If the family did not itself produce all the necessities of life, then it obtained the flour, the lumber, the wool, from "shops in the immediate neighborhood, shops open to investigation and often the center of neighborhood congregation."

Not only did rural children have this direct contact with reality, but almost always, Dewey pointed out, they had a share in the work; they had their chores, duties, responsibilities. The performance of these necessary tasks built character and developed discipline. The child acquired habits of order and industry, accepted responsibility, learned to cooperate with others. But in the city the child had few if any chores or duties, and the nonperformance of them rarely produced dire consequences. The city child did not participate in securing the necessities of life, so whatever chores he or she had were a burden, a drudgery, something to be avoided. The city child did not learn to cooperate with others, rejected responsibility, and rarely acquired the habits of order and industry. In rural America "the educative forces of the domestic spinning and weaving, of the sawmill, the gristmill, the copper shop and the blacksmith forge were continually operative," Dewey explained. But in the city the child grew up unable to grasp the meaning of the phenomena he or she encountered daily. The significance of events—of rain, of the change of seasons—escaped him or her. The logical interconnectedness of things was gone. The complexity of the city had cut the child off from reality, stunted character development, and hindered the growth of cognitive processes. The city had atomized the child.

Now, Dewey argued, the city school had to become a truly educative institution. In the past the school had provided "schooling" while the society itself had "educated" children, educated them in the very process of their growing up. Since urban society no longer educated, the school must assume this role, must abandon the aim of teaching "set lessons" and strive instead to develop the "spirit of social cooperation and community life."

In the Laboratory School at the University of Chicago, the children engaged in the basic activities, activities that provided man's fundamental needs. In this school the children spent most of their time in play and work activities: gardening, weaving, making things in wood and metals. Through these activities, the children, in effect, grew through or recapitulated the history of man's attempt to secure food, clothing, and shelter. As children advanced, they discovered "how the sciences gradually grew out from useful occupations: physics out of the use of tools and machines, chemistry out of the professions of dyeing, cooking, metal smelting, etc." In this mode of schooling the child became "familiar with many aspects of knowledge in relation to living." Here the artificiality of the traditional curriculum was overcome by revealing to the child the social uses of knowledge.

By transforming the school into a place where the children engaged in "real life activities," Dewey expected to do more than overcome the alienation of the child from the curriculum. In this school the children engaged in joint activity to solve shared problems. They learned cooperation and self-discipline. This school was a community, and in it the child learned the values of community and how to function together with others in a community. Once the school became a community, then, Dewey insisted, it would serve as a model for the larger society; the school would be "the best guarantee of a larger society which is worthy, lovely and harmonious."

X

In charging the schools with such an awesome responsibility, Dewey had concocted a new role for the teacher. The aim of socialization, to use Howerth's term, meant that henceforth the teacher was to be an educator, not a mere schoolteacher. The job of socializing the young went beyond the adding or dropping of courses and subjects according to their social relevancy. Now, in a most significant sense, the educator "taught children, not subjects." It was at this point that the specialization in teaching, which had flourished in the urban environment, began to peter out. Instead of a specialist responsible for one small segment of the child's education, each teacher now was responsible for the "whole child."

Forged in the face of advancing hordes of pupils brought to the school door by compulsory education laws, specialization—after creating superior urban school systems—was now to be undermined by the theory of socialization. Yet who can deny that this new aim of education had been implicit in the early reactions to the ills of urbanization? To cure these ills Americans had turned to their schools, so if the traditional schooling did not do the job, then, indeed, the schools must be transformed.

This transformation of the city schools did not stop with the expansion of the responsibility of the teacher, who now taught, or socialized, the whole child. This transformation soon extended the functions of the school itself. Once again John Dewey helped to show the way.

In 1902 Dewey gave a talk at the NEA convention entitled "The School as a Social Center," in which he pointed out that the schoolhouse must become "a center of full and adequate social service"; it must be brought "completely into the current of social life." In his talk Dewey confined himself to the philosophy of the school as a social center, but he stated that he felt that the philosophical aspect of the matter was not the "urgent" or "important" one. "The pressing thing, the significant thing," he said, "is really to make the school a social center. . . ." A few years later, in 1911, the yearbook of the National Society for the Study of Education enthusiastically presented a composite picture of the transformed American schoolhouse. This yearbook, entitled "The City School as a Community Center," revealed that the schools in city after city had taken on new tasks, new functions. Here one found described the public lecture series in Cleveland, the vacation playgrounds in Newark, the organized athletics in New York, the home and school associations in Philadelphia, and the widely acclaimed Civic and Social Center in Rochester.

The city of Rochester in 1907 had hired Edward Ward to conduct an experiment in the community use of schoolhouses. Ward established social centers that not only contained recreational and industrial training facilities but also served as "a citizens' council chamber," a place in which to develop the citizens' capacity for intelligent government. The social center, in Ward's words, was "just to be the restoration of its true place in social life of that most American of all institutions, the Public School Center, in order that through this extended use of the school building might be developed, in the midst of our complex life, the community interest, the neighborly spirit, the democracy that we knew *before we came to the city.*"

XI

Describing the American city in 1921, Lord Bryce said that the inhabitants "were not members of a community but an aggregation of human atoms, like grains of desert sand, which the wind sweeps hither and thither." The quest for community remained unfulfilled. And so long as the newcomers, themselves uprooted and considered a menace by the natives, continued to pour into the city, the battle against atomization seemed hopeless.

During the first decade of the century over $8\frac{1}{2}$ million immigrants came to America. Another 4 million arrived between 1910 and 1914. The First World War practically stopped all immigration. Moreover, the war aroused antialien sentiments along with fears of allegedly unassimilated "hyphenated-Americans." The bitterness and hatred toward the foreign born was more evident among rural Americans, who had little direct contact with the foreigners. These forces were powerful enough, however, to get Congress to pass an immigration restriction law over President Wilson's veto. Four years later the first Immigrant Quota Act passed, and it was followed in 1924 by a second, more restrictive quota system. Actually, immigration had never risen to the million-a-year rate of the prewar years, although by the twenties it rose to well above a half million a year. But after 1924, the Quota Act drastically reduced the numbers coming to America.

Perhaps now the schools could overcome the atomization of urban life. Perhaps now they could recapture the community. But this, of course, did not happen. Within a few years the city schools confronted a new problem, a catastrophe that displaced all earlier anxieties about the ills of urbanization. In the thirties, the American school took on one of its most awesome responsibilities: the Depression. The Depression of the thirties was the worst in American history. More than an economic crisis this disaster all but shattered the abiding American faith in social progress. Could the schools restore that faith? Some argued that the schools not only could, but that they must, go even further and create a new social order. The schools, these people argued, must reconstruct society itself.

The Depression further reduced migration to the city, from home and abroad, so urbanization did diminish as a problem during this period. More to the point, however, is the fact that the ills caused by the Depression cut across all geographic lines. The traditional distinctions between urban problems and rural problems were lost in the suffering shared by all. So it happened that people stopped talking about city schools and rural schools. American educators now talked in terms of *the American* school and its role in American society.

Concerned more with social progress and less with human atomization, schoolmen now needed a school different from Dewey's Laboratory School, different from Ward's social centers. They called their new kind of school the "community school." In this school, improvement of the community or improvement of community living became the primary function. The carrying out of this function required more than infusing schoolchildren with the "spirit of social cooperation and community life," as Dewey had tried to do in the Chicago Laboratory School. And it required more than transforming the school into a place for communal activities as Ward had done in Rochester. Unlike their predecessors in the first decades of the century, those in the thirties who spoke about this new community school assumed that the community existed. With them the quest for community gave way to requests for community service.

First of all, according to its advocates, the community school accepted the total community as the educative agency. Following Dewey they distinguished "schooling" from "education" and opted for the latter. Dewey, in his Laboratory School, had tried to substitute "education" for "schooling" by transforming the school into an "embryonic community active with types of occupations that reflect the life of the larger society." But these new educators of the thirties abandoned the attempt to turn the school into a community. They said education must take place through actual participation in the larger society itself. The students in a community school discovered that the walls were down. They went outside the school to study the needs and problems of their own community. In fact, they made proposals to meet the needs and solve the problems they found. Students engaged in these "worthwhile projects" made surveys of the local industries, stores, and markets; they investigated the educational facilities, the public welfare agencies, the recreational opportunities, and the public utilities; they probed the systems of transportation and communication. The government itself came under their scrutiny, as did the local customs, mores, and peculiarities. Once they identified the problems and ascertained the needs, the students made recommendations.

In Flint, Michigan, for example, the students made a traffic survey and devised a safety program. They also made a housing survey, exploring the matters of home ownership and population density. Emily R. Kickhafer, supervisor of social studies in the Flint public schools, supplied the students with a questionnaire to facilitate the analysis. The questionnaire contained questions like: "What can a local community do to guide housing?" "How may public opinion toward building be molded?" "How is it going to be possible to get out of the jam in which housing finds itself?"

The concept of the total community as the educative agency, in addition to implying that the students could and should be educated through "projects" in the community, also implied that all members of the community were educators. In other words, just as the school no longer was the sole agency of instruction, so the teacher was no longer the sole educator. Convinced that "adults and children have common purposes," the directors of the community schools secured the cooperation of the adults in the community, who then actively participated in these projects in cooperation with the children. When, in 1938, Paul Misner, director of community education, drew up a program of "areas of experience" for the entire educational system of Glencoe, Illinois, he included planned, cooperative experiences for pupils and adults throughout the entire program. At the primary levels (ages six to eight) parents and lay citizens cooperated in taking excursions to farms, dairies, the post office, the telegraph office, the railway station, the fire house, the police station, and stores. In addition Misner scheduled "cooperative activities in which adults and children plan teas, bird sanctuaries, community programs, etc." At the secondary level adults cooperated in a variety of projects, including studies of municipal government "to determine how it can best serve the needs of the community." In this program of planned "areas of experience" adult involvement continued through the college years.

It was the hope of the directors of the community schools that, through participation in these projects, the youth would develop into citizens who would participate intelligently and efficiently in community enterprises. In this way the growth and development of all members of the community would lead directly to the improvement of the community itself.

Educators continued to endorse the community school after the Second World War and on into the fifties. In 1953 the National Society for the Study of Education (NSSE) devoted its yearbook to the topic "The Community School." But by the fifties, as the articles in the yearbook reveal, the message had begun to pale; the proposals now sounded like the slogans of an era long past. In 1953 it was strange to hear an educator say that "the role of education is seen to be more than intellectual training." In the fifties it no longer seemed fitting to regard the school "as an agency for helping to give direction to community growth and development."

Already dissatisfied with the schools, parents were in no mood to tolerate these notions of the so-called "community school." American education was undergoing a "searching reappraisal." In 1953, the same year of the fifty-second NSSE yearbook, a rash of books appeared that pungently criticized the teachers, the schools, and the entire system. The titles reveal both the tone and the thrust: *Quackery in the Public Schools, Educational Wastelands, The Conflict in Education, Let's Talk Sense About Our Schools.*

Arthur Bestor, a history professor, who wrote *Educational Wastelands,* lambasted the "educators," making the term one of contempt. "The school makes itself ridiculous," he wrote, "whenever it undertakes to deal directly with 'real life problems' instead of indirectly through the development of generalized intellectual powers." He insisted that "genuine education" is "intellectual training." Many agreed. And who could take "educators" who endorsed the community schools seriously after Bestor reminded everyone that "the men who drafted our constitution were not trained for the task by 'field trips' to the mayor's office and the county jail."

Before the decade ended, the community school had been ridiculed out of existence. When intellectuals complained about American schools in the thirties, no one had listened. But by the fifties the intellectual in America had come to enjoy more acceptance. Now, according to Richard Hofstadter, the life of the intellect "took on a more and more positive meaning." The leaders of business, of government, of the military all discovered a need for the services of the intellectual, the expert. The Russian sputnik in 1957 merely reinforced this need. And the community school? Had it improved community living throughout America? Probably no more than the predepression urban schools had succeeded in their quest to restore the village community.

XII

In the early sixties Americans once again distinguished urban education from the rest of American education. Urban education, and the problems of education in the city, now seemed worthy of special attention. But by the sixties most educators had abandoned the quest for community; most had given up the notion that the primary function of the urban school was to combat urbanization. Now most accepted urbanization as a fact of twentieth-century life. The community had been eclipsed. Educators, lacking both a memory and a dream of a stable society, were less and less concerned with socialization.

Like their colleagues at the turn of the century, the urban educators of the early sixties took their pedagogical cues from parents. And by this time the dispersal of political power in urban America had given voice to parents who were hip. They did not seek the restoration of a community few of them had ever known. They might not themselves be models of what they wanted their children to become, but they knew what was needed to make good. And to make good meant to break out of the city. The city for the majority of its inhabitants was no longer the promised land. The city had become the land of bondage. The schools offered a way out. This deterioration of the city can be explained largely in terms of the patterns of mobility that formed in the forties and fifties.

Residential mobility played a significant role in this pattern. After both the Second World War and the Korean conflict, the largess of the federal government provided veterans with no-money-down mortgages that allowed many city dwellers to purchase the home they had never dared to dream of before. Moreover, the general wave of prosperity during and after the war prompted many other city families to buy a home of their own. The housing boom created to meet this demand took place outside the city, where the land cost less and the building restrictions were more relaxed.

Not all city dwellers moved to the suburbs. But not all of those who remained in the city did so voluntarily. Racial discrimination kept the nonwhite family—ex-GI or not—out of the suburbs. At the same time a widening stream of Southern blacks poured into the Northern cities. In New York City, for example, the special census of 1957 revealed an increase since 1950 of some

320,000 nonwhites. This increase, together with a decrease of some 416,000 whites, greatly raised the percentage of nonwhites living within the city. In the decade 1950–1960 New York City lost about 1,300,000 middle-class whites, a number exceeding the population of Cleveland, Ohio. It gained 800,000 blacks and Puerto Ricans. New York's population shift was more dramatic than that of any other city, but it was typical of what occurred in other major cities during this period. By 1960, 75 percent of the blacks in the United States were urban dwellers. Outside the South, over 90 percent lived in cities.

In all cities discriminatory housing restrictions forced the nonwhite population to remain within the walls of their ghettos, and the congestion brought on by these restrictions caused the rapid deterioration of living conditions within the ghetto. Expectedly, there was a decline in civic mindedness, a loss of civic conscience. Moreover, the apathy, the ineptitude, and the inaction of city governments reinforced the diminished civic mindedness of the nonwhites. The city fathers now took their cues from the whites remaining within the city. These were the very rich and the very poor, the very old and the not very ambitious. To all of them—either because they had so much to lose, or because they had so little—change was a threat. They all viewed the rumblings within the ghetto with fear and anger. The political moves made by city governments inevitably reflected these emotions.

In some cases the city fathers did try to do something constructive to prevent the rumbling ghetto from exploding. But municipal efforts at urban renewal, hampered by insufficient funds, proved inadequate. Part of the financial plight of the cities, of course, was due to the flight to the suburbs. Once they located in suburbs, new homeowners began to spend their money there. Stores and shops in the cities closed down and moved to the greener fields outside the city limits. And when the city fathers tried to recoup their lost revenue by raising taxes on real estate, or by levying a sales tax, they only made matters worse, for rather than pay the increased taxes, more people fled from the city. As a result properties within the city fell into the hands of speculators, who, to avoid tax hikes, allowed the property to deteriorate while they increased their own revenue by raising the rent—or the number of tenants. Gradually the city succumbed to what was called urban blight.

Most analyses of the decline of the city attribute importance to the postwar patterns of occupational mobility as well as to the patterns of residential mobility. During this period the traditional patterns of occupational mobility disappeared.

Traditionally newcomers to the city began on the lowest rung of the occupational ladder, as unskilled workers. Then in different ways, and with varying degrees of success, they worked their way up that ladder. Some did it by becoming entrepreneurs, usually catering to the specific needs and wants of their own group. Often they succeeded, following the traditional pattern from pushcart vender to grocer, to wholesaler or distributor, or from skilled worker to subcontractor, to manufacturer. Sometimes newcomers remained in an unskilled or semiskilled job their entire working life, projecting their hopes and aspirations onto their children. For them they worked, scrimped, and saved so that they could go to school and advance up the occupational ladder into clerical, managerial, even professional positions.

In the forties and fifties the principal newcomers to the cities came from the Western Hemisphere, not from Europe. As mentioned above, thousands of blacks from the South and Puerto Ricans settled in the northeastern cities—in Philadelphia, in Newark, in New York. Southern blacks and Appalachian whites migrated to the cities of the Midwest—to Detroit, to Cincinnati, to Cleveland, to Chicago. Blacks, Mexican-Americans, and Native Americans flocked to Western cities—to Los Angeles, to Oakland, to Phoenix.

These newcomers shared one thing with earlier migrants to the city—they were desperately poor. But they soon found that the traditional path of occupational mobility used by their predecessors was closed to them.

On the one hand, bigness had squelched entrepreneurship as a way of rising. Supermarkets, department stores, discount houses, chain stores, suburban shopping centers—all made it difficult, if not impossible, for the poor newcomer to start out in business for himself. And the father who tried to stick to his unskilled job in order to send his children to school soon discovered that he was expendable; his work could better be done by a machine. Nor could he easily find a semiskilled job, since most of the large manufacturing plants had moved out of the cities. The poor city dweller found himself cut off from these jobs because the inadequacies, or the high cost, of public transportation prohibited him from commuting from his home to the plant.

The loss of job opportunities within the city forced many to "go on welfare." This enforced idleness frequently sapped all initiative from the workingman, and the spectacle had a deleterious impact on the aspirations of the young. Why bother trying if you cannot get a job? Often the city youth, particularly if black, already suffered from the absence of a father in the home—someone to imitate, to prove oneself to, perhaps to fight against. Black youths in the city frequently lacked someone to encourage their efforts, to applaud their triumphs; they had no one to protect them or solace them when they failed. As a result, often they drew back from trying.

Technological change, uninhibited technological change, had reduced job opportunities for newcomers to the city. James B. Conant commented in a study in the early sixties that, in the slum area of a large city containing 125,000 people, mostly black, roughly 70 percent of the boys and girls aged 16 to 21 were out of school and unemployed. Throughout the nation in 1961 only 50 percent of black men (compared with two-thirds of white men) worked steadily at full-time jobs. By 1963, although blacks comprised only 10 percent of the labor force, they accounted for 20 percent of total unemployment, and nearly 30 percent of long-term unemployment, that is, unemployment lasting 27 weeks or longer.

In the sixties no one denied the fact that all cities contained great numbers of unemployed nonwhites. But there was deep disagreement about the significance of this massive unemployment. Many whites took this to mean that blacks had no desire to work; they had come to the city in order to get the welfare benefits available there. If blacks really wanted to work, the argument went, they would get up and get a job; they lacked initiative and wanted something for nothing.

This demeaning interpretation of black unemployment, rarely openly voiced by public officials or expressed in the press, was nonetheless widespread among all classes of whites, urban and nonurban as well. This white man's interpretation, usually snidely implied, infuriated urban blacks. As they saw it, the widespread unemployment was due to racial discrimination. Blacks, and Puerto Ricans, Mexicans, and Native Americans, just never were hired or promoted to certain jobs. Some commentators have called this the concept of "place." Often an unconscious prejudice on the part of those who hired and promoted kept minority groups out of the better jobs; it also destroyed their aspirations for those jobs.

Urban blacks, convinced that it was white prejudice that kept them out of work, found themselves pushed to the breaking point when taunted by the same white accusations of laziness and lack of initiative. This was the "social dynamite" that exploded in major cities during the decade of the sixties, when racial riots amounting almost to insurrections rocked New York City, Rochester, Cleveland, Chicago, and, worst of all, Los Angeles and Detroit.

By the mid-sixties the federal government and many state governments had laws prohibiting discriminatory hiring practices. The machinery to administer these laws often remained weak, but blacks and other minority groups now began to penetrate into new occupations, especially government jobs and jobs with firms that catered to mass consumers. But the passage of these fair employment laws had a dramatic impact on the interpretations and understanding of the patterns of occupational mobility. Now many came to the conclusion that the crucial obstacle to black employment and occupational mobility was neither white racial discrimination nor lack of initiative. Attempts to implement these fair employment practices revealed that the years of discrimination had taken their toll. Not expecting ever to get more than a menial job, black youths had not prepared themselves for entry into "white man's occupations." Time and time again stories were told of firms who found it impossible to find qualified blacks to fill better jobs. Black youths were unprepared, unqualified, and unready for these jobs. Here was a new obstacle to occupational mobility.

The American answer to this problem, obviously, was education. The schools would prepare young black people for the better, available jobs. The schools would qualify them for movement up the occupational ladder, ready them for entry into what was once the white world of work. In the sixties the urban schoolmasters heeded this cry for career preparation. The more ambitious parents demanded that the schools, from kindergarten through high school, prepare *their* children for admission to college. The less ambitious insisted that the schools teach *their* children some marketable skills.

The new concern with the occupational power of schooling let loose a flood of troubles for urban educators. Blacks, and members of other minority groups, complained loudly and angrily about the unequal educational provisions they had previously accepted. These parents pointed out that the schools that served their children had the oldest, most dilapidated equipment and facilities, the most incompetent teachers, the most watered-down, irrelevant educational programs.

Urban educators responded with projects and programs that stressed academic studies and emphasized vocational preparation. At a 1962 federal conference on "The Impact of Urbanization on Education" those attending concluded that "Every teacher, then, is in essence a vocational educator." In line with this career orientation urban educators spent considerable time, energy, and money on programs of counseling and guidance.

Once the city schools had narrowed their function to instruction in academic and vocational subjects, much attention focused on the matter of the efficiency and efficacy of that instruction. This produced the so-called "revolution in teaching," a revolution in instructional techniques. In the perspective of history this was almost a "missed revolution." Some 60 years earlier, as we saw, the demands for socialization had undermined the advances made in the urban schools' instructional practices. Those advances had resulted from the increased specialization in the city schools. The revolution in teaching of the sixties signaled a return to specialization.

Schools of education now could not keep up with the urban school systems' demands for more and more specialists. Reading, art, and music specialists became commonplace in the urban elementary schools. In addition to the expansion of subject matter specialization, there were specialists in types of pupils: teachers of disturbed children; teachers of "culturally deprived" or slum children; teachers of fast learners and of slow learners. In the sixties educators only started to tap the infinite varieties of special education that could be used to improve instruction. During this decade of specialization they came to realize that the path to instructional improvement led to a diminution in scope of the duties of the individual teacher.

During this period teachers ceased trying to be psychologist–sociologist–group worker–counselor–therapist to their students. Specialists took over these jobs, and the teacher taught mathematics, or whatever his or her specialty was.

Throughout the twentieth century the urban school had played a role in both occupational and residential mobility—the more highly educated urbanites moved up the occupational ladder and out of the city. Despite all the nostalgic and romantic notions about the community voiced over the years by urban pedagogues, the urban school had in fact functioned as an escape hatch from the city. Finally, in the early sixties, Americans explicitly recognized this function.

CHAPTER 5

Economic Opportunity and the Schools

I

From the beginning Americans called their country the "land of opportunity." In America, Crèvecoeur reported in 1782, "one does not find, as in Europe, a crowded society, where every place is overstocked. There is room for everybody in America. Has he any particular talent or industry? He exerts it in order to procure a livelihood, and it succeeds."

Americans had little cause to doubt that America indeed was the land of opportunity until after the Civil War. In 1873, following a few years of jubilant postwar prosperity, the country entered a depression that lasted for six long years. There had been depressions before, but none like this. Depressions hit industrialized nations much harder than agricultural ones. Industrialization had mushroomed in America during and after the war so that the depression of the seventies took a deadly toll.

Three million workers faced unemployment, one fifth of the working class. Another two fifths worked but six to seven months a year. In New York City a quarter of the total labor force was out of work. According to Henry Pelling, "no other depression in American history, except that of the 1930s, was so severe." Only one fifth of the working class retained regular employment throughout the six-year period. In the fall of 1877, the low point of the depression, one New York worker rhetorically asked: "What are the carpenters doing? Nothing! What are the bricklayers doing? Nothing! What do they have to live on this coming winter? Nothing!"

Yet at the very moment the hopes of the many were fading, the fortunes of a few were soaring. Even before the depression, the progress of industrialization had been marked by the combination of businesses into bigger units. In 1870 the son of an itinerant medicine seller organized the Standard Oil Company of Ohio. Within eight years Standard Oil controlled 95 percent of the pipe lines and refineries in the United States. The 38-year-old John D. Rockefeller was well on his way to becoming "the most feared and hated man in America." Yet only later in the eighties did the public gain knowledge of the vast holdings of Rockefeller and the tactics of oppression, extortion, and price controls used by Standard Oil.

During the depression, the most widely known man of wealth was the rough-and-ready Commodore Vanderbilt. In 1855 Vanderbilt had been listed as merely one of nineteen New Yorkers whose wealth was estimated at more than a million dollars. By the end of the war he was the only American worth more than $20 million. Vanderbilt amassed his millions by keeping up with the technological revolution going on in transportation. Starting with a dilapidated ferry, the Commodore built a fleet of river steamboats. Then, moving from the waterways to the rails, he became the railroad king of the seventies. He died in January 1877, leaving an estate of $105 million. For a boy born in the one-room cabin of a ferryboat worker, Vanderbilt had done well, very well indeed! Here was proof that America was still the land of opportunity. Or was it?

Four months after the revelation of the Commodore's legacy, the railroad workmen read that their wages were being cut because the railroads were in trouble. The first announcement of a wage cut came from the New York Central, the line owned by the Vanderbilts. All the other lines followed. Opportunity, apparently, was limited to the few and denied to the many. On July 17, the day after the wage cut went into effect, the United States had its first major railroad strike. Starting on the Baltimore & Ohio line in West Virginia, it spread north to Canada and west to California. Frightened governors across the land called their militia. Railroad cars were burned; rifles and Gatling guns began going off. Violence flared in West Virginia, in Maryland, in New York, in Illinois, in Pennsylvania. A pitched battle between the strikers and militia reached the level of an insurrection in Pittsburgh. There, after killing twenty-six and wounding hundreds more, the militia retreated in the face of a wild, incendiary mob. For a day and a half law and order disappeared as the riotous mob proceeded to burn, loot, and destroy. When it had spent itself, the mob had destroyed over $5 million worth of railroad property. But the wage cut remained intact.

While the workers slunk back to work, a shocked nation wondered where it would all lead. One historian, James Rhodes, who had lived through the strike, later wrote, "We had hugged the delusion that such social uprisings belonged to Europe and had no reason of being in a republic where there was plenty of room and an equal chance for all." People wondered, Was America still the land of opportunity? More and more Americans began to feel that opportunity had all but disappeared from the land. And always someone appeared who would fan this discontent, like Henry George, a San Francisco newspaperman who wrote a book called *Progress and Poverty*. In it he argued that the progress of the few had been built on the poverty of the many. George's solution to eliminating the gap between the rich and the poor consisted of a plan for a single tax, a tax on land. Other reformers made different proposals, some more, some less radical than that proposed by George.

The ending of the depression in 1879 quelled much of the uneasiness, but the lesson of those hard times remained. If the workingmen of America were to lose their belief that theirs was the land of opportunity, this could open the door to radicalism and violence. At least this was how it looked from the top. The wealthy were getting frightened; to assuage their fears, the faith of working people in the ideology of individualism must be restored. And working people, ready and anxious to reaffirm their belief in America, avidly clutched at the words of those who told them there was room at the top.

II

Success literature was not unknown in America. One of the earliest—and most famous—"success manuals" had been compiled in 1757 by Benjamin Franklin under the title "The Way to Wealth." Others had written similar handbooks since the days of Franklin. But never had there appeared so many books "pointing out the high road to prosperity." Printing houses now turned them out by the thousands. Irwin Wylie has estimated that, of all the success manuals published before the year 1900, four out of five appeared after the Civil War. And more were published between 1880 and 1885 than in any other 5-year period.

In 1882, P. T. Barnum published *The Art of Money Getting*, followed by *How I Made Millions* (1884). The founder of the Mellon banking fortune published his autobiography in 1885, *Thomas Mellon and His Times*. In 1887 Henry Clews published his memoirs, *Twenty Years on Wall Street*. But most of the millionaires had neither the time nor the talent to write their own biographies. Journalists supplied the bulk of biographical data on the rich men of America. James Parton published a collection of biographies of millionaires in a two-volume work in 1884. He called it *Captains of Industry*. Other biographical accounts appeared in *Room at the Top*, edited by Adam Craig in 1883.

In addition to serving as the subjects for biographies most millionaires willingly gave interviews and responded to questionnaires. A large number of books based on such materials appeared in the eighties: William S. Speer, *The Law of Success* (1885); Wilbur F. Crofts, *Successful Men of Today and What They Say of Success* (1883); Francis E. Clark, *Our Business Boys* (1884). Clark, a clergyman, published a second book publicizing the secrets of success in 1885; he called it *Danger Signals, The Enemies of Youth from the Business Man's Standpoint*. Another clergyman, Lyman Abbott, wrote *How to Succeed* (1882). Nelson Sizer published *The Royal Road to Wealth* in 1882, followed by *The Road to Success* in 1884. Many books had similar titles. People sometimes confused Edwin T. Friendly's *The Secret of Success in Life* (1881) with William Farrar's *Success in Life* (1885). The prolific William Makepeace Thayer, who later edited a magazine simply called *Success*, gave one of his books the snappy title *Tact, Push, and Principle* (1881).

What were the secrets of success? Where could young people find the road to wealth? Did they have to be geniuses? Not at all. In fact, many of the authors noted that being a genius was frequently an obstacle to success since, as everyone knew, the genius was a lazy, vain, impatient, and undisciplined creature. In deprecating genius the authors of the success manuals made abundantly clear that almost everybody could be a success—since almost everybody was not a genius.

But, a youth might ask, what about the environment, did not that play an important role in success? The success handbook did not shrink from this topic, and most frankly admitted that certain environments contained more advantages than others. The most widely acclaimed was poverty. The best condition for success was to be born poor. The struggle against poverty, they argued, developed those personal qualities necessary for success. Climbing out of poverty gave testimony to one's worth of character. The greater the climb, the greater the testimony. So the children of the rich, deprived of the very conditions that developed those character traits necessary for success, had less opportunity for success than did the children of the poor. One of the staunchest defenders of poverty, Andrew Carnegie, pleaded: "Abolish luxury if you please, but leave us the soil upon which alone the virtues and all that is precious in human character grow; poverty—honest poverty."

In the race for success those born in rural areas also had a decided advantage, according to the handbooks. A childhood spent in rural life ensured a healthy body and a strong moral character. The fresh air, the good food, hardened one for the rigors of later life, while the daily round of chores allowed little time for developing mischievous habits. One clergyman in 1883 reminded readers that: "Our successful men did not feed themselves on boyhood cigarettes and late suppers, with loafing as their only labor and midnight parties for their regular evening dissipation. Such city trained bodies often give out when the strain comes in business, while the sound body and mind and morals of the man from the country hold on and hold out."

In stressing both poverty and rural beginnings, the literature of success reflected, for the most part, the early beginnings of most of the successful men of the times. But, at the same time, these writings were also indicating that success was possible for the majority of people, since the majority were poor and had been raised in rural areas. So to play up the advantages of poverty and country life was to play up the great opportunities that existed for most Americans.

Suppose, as was the case for most Americans in the 1880's, one had the dual advantages of poverty and rural beginnings. What then? Certainly a youth needed further guidance. The handbooks supplied this guidance, and the guidance differed little from that given by Benjamin Franklin over one hundred years earlier. (Significantly, a new, ten-volume edition of Franklin's writings appeared in 1887–1888.)

Neither management skills, nor production techniques, nor investment procedures were the qualities necessary for success; they were to be found within. Moral virtue—this was the key to success. America had not changed. The secrets of success still consisted of the familiar formulas of Franklin: industry, thrift, perseverance. Franklin, of course, had not invented these virtues. Indeed, through the history of Western civilization, men have praised these same virtues, especially Christians, and especially Protestant Christians. Through the practice of these virtues one accumulated material wealth and simultaneously identified oneself as one of God's elect.

In American success literature of the 1880s we find a forceful reaffirmation of this synthesis of business success and supernatural grace. William Makepeace Thayer, in 1881, noted that religion required every young man to "make the most of himself possible; that he should watch and improve his opportunities; that he should be industrious, up-right, faithful and prompt; that he should task his talents, whether one or ten, to the utmost; that he should waste neither time nor money; that *duty* and not pleasure or ease should be his watchword." Reliable shops and stores, of course, demanded the same things of young employees. Religion adds "those higher motives that immortality creates." Thayer clinches the union of Christianity and the cult of success with the comment: "Indeed, we might say that religion demands success."

Of all the qualities prescribed for success, none received more attention than the virtue of industry. Wilbur Crofts, in *Successful Men*, revealed that, in response to a questionnaire sent to some five hundred prominent men, three out of four attributed success to their own industriousness, to work habits they had cultivated in youth. Idleness, another author wrote, not only doomed men to obscurity and failure; it was a species of fraud upon the community, since idlers could not justify their existence. Who then could fail to understand why society condemned idleness?

Once again the moral came through clearly. Success came to the industrious, and who could not acquire this virtue? All Americans, then, had the opportunity to succeed. There were other virtues that helped. "Perseverance," said John D. Rockefeller, "is the great thing." The young person who sticks is one who succeeds. Ultimate victory, the handbooks pointed out, belonged to those who could plod on in the face of temporary setbacks.

Frugality won acclaim as an additional prerequisite for personal fortune. The spendthrift, all agreed, usually died poor. The thrifty, who saved and invested wisely, not only secured their own private fortune, but became public benefactors, by providing money for industrial enterprises.

In addition to the magic virtues of industry, thrift, and perseverance, young people needed to develop those qualities which most impressed employers. Those who came to work on time always won rewards. Punctuality counted, as did loyalty, and obedience. Loyal and obedient employees caught the attention of the employer when they placed the employer's interest above their own.

III

Most Americans had heard all this before. As children they had read these same notions in their school textbooks. The nineteenth-century readers saturated children with paeans to the land of opportunity while at the same time supplying sage advice about the secret of success.

The schools used a wide variety of different readers, raising the sales of some up into the millions. The most famous of all—"the unprecedented wonder of the publishing world"—*McGuffey's Readers,* sold 122 million copies between 1836 and 1920. The peak of popularity came during the 1870s and 1880s, when sales reached over 60 million copies.

The *McGuffey's Readers* from the first to the sixth grades contained stories and tales that admonished American children to be industrious, persevering, thrifty, and loyal. In these readers the idle boy almost invariably turns out poor and miserable; the industrious boy, happy and prosperous. Not just hard-working lads, but insects, like the industrious bee, were exhibited as models. The students of the second reader learned that

> In days that are sunny
> He's getting his honey;
> In days that are cloudy
> He's making his wax . . .
> From morning's first light
> Till the coming of night
> He's singing and toiling
> The summer day through.

The readers stressed perseverance over and over again. One story tells of a little boy who grows disgusted when he repeatedly fails to get his kite aloft. His aunt, however, insists that he try again and again until he finally succeeds. "Yes, my dear children, I wish to teach you the value of PERSEVERANCE. . . . Whenever you fail in your attempts to do a good thing, let your motto be TRY AGAIN." From an earlier reader the young scholar had already learned:

> If you find your task is hard
>   try, try again;
> Time will bring you your reward
>   try, try again;
> All that other folks can do,
> Why with patience, should not you?
> Only keep this rule in view:
>   try, try again.

McGuffey taught children the worth of obedience by recounting tales in which disobedience brought on disasters like overturned boats or cut hands. The fourth reader has a model of obedience in Casabianca, the boy who stood on the burning deck rather than disobey his father. He died, of course, but Casabianca "would rather die than disobey."

Central to most of the stories, poems, and tales is the theme of rags to riches. McGuffey pictures America as the land of opportunity, where virtue is always rewarded with material success. The second reader contains a typical story about one "Henry the bootblack," who fought against poverty, saving his widowed mother from starvation. The fourth reader featured fatherless

Henry Bond, who began to make his own way at the age of ten, when he shoveled snow to get money to buy his schoolbooks. Henry's efforts developed those qualities necessary for success, and from that time on "Henry was always the first in all his classes. He knew no such word as *fail*, but always succeeded in all he attempted. Having the 'will,' he always found the 'way.' "

After working through *McGuffey's Readers*, the American youth of the 1880s was ready to devour the success novels of Horatio Alger. A number of success novelists feverishly published their works during this period, but of all who played the rags to riches theme, none was better known than this one-time Unitarian minister. In the hands of Horatio Alger it received its classic treatment in novels like *Struggling Upward* and *Mark, the Matchboy*.

Alger's first, and wildly popular, *Ragged Dick* appeared in 1867. During the eighties he reached the peak of his popularity, becoming the most famous writer of children's books in the country. Using a sure-fire and unvarying formula, he wrote 106 books for boys, and using the same formula, publishers put out at least eleven other books under his name.

In story after story Alger tells of the poor boy who, through pluck and a little luck, capitalizes on the opportunities available to him and rises to the top. The typical Alger hero is never a genius. He is manly and self-reliant, embodying those traditional virtues of industry, perseverance, honesty, and thrift.

By the eighties, "the Horatio Alger boy" had become an American symbol, the theory of "work and win" synonymous with the name Horatio Alger. During this decade his books flooded the book stalls; copies stocked the shelves of every YMCA in the country. Often copies of these novels were bestowed on children as Sunday School prizes.

IV

Despite the flood of success literature during the eighties, or perhaps because of it, some Americans began to scoff. Although it purported to supply guidance to those aspiring to success, this literature actually did no more than supply reassurance that America had not changed. America—so went the message—was still the land of opportunity. But, of course, America had changed. The world described by these authors had disappeared. Nevertheless, schoolbooks, novels, biographies, and manuals all continued to preach the old formulas for success. The scoffers pointed out that these success formulas had become irrelevant in modern America.

The Horatio Alger hero, for example, always attained success by leaving the working class to become owner or a partner in a business of his own. But few of Alger's heroes have any connection with transportation, mining, manufacturing, or construction—the industries where the successful nineteenth-century men actually made their fortunes. Alger usually rewarded his hero with a partnership in a respectable mercantile house. As John Cawelti has noted, this is "a throwback to the economic life of an earlier period, when

American business was still dominated by merchants." The economic behavior of these earlier merchant types was unlike the devastating strategies of transcontinental railroad builders, iron and steel manufacturers, and other corporate giants of the 1880's.

Horatio Alger was not alone in recounting a version of success common to a bygone era. *McGuffey's Readers*, the manuals and handbooks, the biographies of wealthy men, all presented the same mythical version of success. The fact of the matter is that most who rose to the top during this period were not self-made men who started out as poor farm boys, but instead, men who had decided advantages in the race to the top. The typical successful man, as William Miller has shown, was "born and bred in an atmosphere in which business and a relatively high social standing were intimately associated with his family life."

By the mid-eighties the scoffers had convinced a number of people that the old success story was a myth. As a result the men of wealth began to lose some of their luster. In some quarters people now referred to them as the "robber barons." E. L. Godkin had called Cornelius Vanderbilt "a lineal successor of the medieval baron"—and the term stuck. Godkin was one of the first to write that the old mode of making a great fortune "by slowly working one's way up," by frugality, the practices of industry, and the display of punctuality and integrity, no longer applied. By the end of the eighties the old mode had indeed fallen into disrepute. Richard T. Ely wrote in 1889: "If you tell a single concrete working man on the Baltimore & Ohio Railroad that he may yet be the president of the company, it is not demonstrable that you have told him what is not true, although it is within bounds to say that he is far more likely to be killed by a stroke of lightning."

The literature of success had not pulled it off. More and more Americans came to admit that the old formulas were obsolete. True, the success manuals continued to be written. In 1894 Orison Marden published *Pushing to the Front*, which subsequently went through 250 editions. The Horatio Alger stories continued to appear, but at the same time the ranks of the scoffers increased.

Some did more than scoff. They rejected this new America, this new society that deprived them of opportunity. "Land of opportunity you say," a Chicago worker snarled in 1887, "You know damn well my children will be where I am—that is, if I can keep them out of the gutter." In radical protest against this new America, many in the late eighties turned away from the ideology of individualism to egalitarian ideologies, like socialism. Socialism had never been a great force in America, but in the aftermath of the great railroad strike of 1877, the socialist movement had begun a steady growth. In Chicago and St. Louis, socialist candidates had actually gained political office in municipal elections. Anarchism too found followers in America. In 1883 the red and black "internationals" issued the famous Pittsburgh Manifesto, expounding the revolutionary anarchist philosophy: "All attempts in the past to reform this monstrous [capitalism] by peaceable means, such as the ballot, have been futile, and all such efforts in the future must necessarily be so . . . there remains but one recourse—FORCE!"

V

More potent than the threat of socialism or anarchism to capitalism during the 1880s was the growing colossus, the Noble Order of the Knights of Labor. It was founded in Philadelphia in 1869 by Uriah Stephens together with some fellow members of a collapsing garment cutters benefit society. The order developed into a national labor organization during the depression. By 1879 it boasted 20,151 members.

The Knights of Labor symbolized a hankering for a simpler economic era, one antedating the wage system of industrialization. Under Stephens, the primary object of the Knights consisted of "educating the public" in order to create a healthy opinion toward labor. When Stephens stepped down as grandmaster of the order, he was succeeded by Terence C. Powderly, who preached a new brand of utopian egalitarianism: *cooperation*. Envisioning a new America, Powderly believed that, through establishing cooperatives, American workers could cross the chasm of inequality.

Powderly, however, could not control the large, sprawling Noble Order. The local assemblies, frequently consisting of the members of one trade, preferred strikes to cooperation. So during the early years of the eighties most of the activity of the Knights was spent directing strikes. The most important strike of this period took place in 1883, when the telegraphers struck against all commercial telegraph companies in the nation. Although it gained widespread public sympathy, this strike, like most others at that time, proved unsuccessful. Despite this lack of successful strikes the members of the Knights continued to increase, rising to over 51,000 by 1883. True, the Knights did have a rapid turnover in membership; many came in before and during a strike, then left when the strike proved futile. Over 25,000 left the order in 1883 alone. But the membership did keep rising, and the public now cast an uneasy glance at the dangerous, grumbling giant.

After the long series of unsuccessful strikes, some members were ready to make an attempt to establish cooperatives. They set up workers' cooperatives for mining, for foundries, for the manufacture of shoes, clothing, soap, and furniture. By 1887 the Knights had established 135 cooperatives. But, as would be expected, they soon failed, partly because of inexperience and inefficiency, but primarily because of the discrimination against them from the capitalists, who charged them exorbitant interest rates on loans, refused to transport their goods by rail, and refused to supply them with raw materials.

Before passing out of the scene, however, the Knights played a central role in what John R. Commons has called the great upheaval of 1886. The buildup began in the spring of 1885, when the Knights finally had a real success with strike action. Members of the order working on the lines of Jay Gould's railroad system launched an unpremeditated strike against wage reductions. Taken by surprise, Gould gave way. Later he attempted a lockout, which brought on a second strike; again Gould capitulated. The prestige of the Knights soared; membership mushroomed to 700,000. A reporter for the *New York Sun* concluded that, compared with the leaders of the Noble Order, the power of the President of the United States and of his cabinet "is a petty authority." The leaders of the Knights, the reporter warned, "can array labor against capital, putting labor on the offensive or the defensive, for quiet and stubborn self-protection, or for angry, organized assault, as they will."

Many recalled these ominous words when the next May the Knights of Labor, against the advice of Powderly, supported a general strike. The general strike for an eight-hour day had been called by a rival labor organization, the Federation of Organized Trades. Many workers belonged to both organizations, and most of the local assemblies of the order voted to strike. Four days after the strike began, the Haymarket bomb exploded, shattering the future of the Noble Order of the Knights of Labor.

On that May 4, a group of anarchists, speaking before a group of laborers in Haymarket Square in Chicago, were suddenly set upon by a cordon of policemen who advanced to break up the meeting. Suddenly a bomb was thrown at the police. In the melee that followed, one police officer was killed, a number wounded.

Panic and revulsion swept the country. Where will it all end, people asked. The Knights of Labor, the anarchists, the socialists, all wanted to do away with capitalism, wanted to replace it with some egalitarian utopian scheme. The country was full of groups of people formulating new utopian schemes. Between 1885 and 1890 forty different utopian novels appeared. Most of these pictured some sort of collectivized society. The most popular of all, Edward Bellamy's *Looking Backward* (1886), sold over a half a million copies in its first decade of publication. Nationalist clubs, inspired by the ideal collective society depicted in the novel, sprang up all over the country.

Were these reformers correct? Was it true that America was no longer the land of opportunity? Was individualism no longer a viable ideology? People were confused. Before the end of the decade, however, a new credo appeared that helped to dispel some of the confusion. According to the new creed America was the land of equal opportunity for all. If everyone did have an equal opportunity to succeed, then there was no need to turn to egalitarian remedies, like socialism. Once people stopped lamenting the diminished opportunities America now offered and adopted the new creed of equal opportunity, the function of American education had to undergo a profound change.

VI

As early as 1885, the year before the general strike, the Scots-bred Andrew Carnegie publicly admitted that America was no longer the land of opportunity it had been. Speaking to the students of the Curry Commercial College in Pittsburgh, he said: "There is no doubt that it is becoming harder and harder as business gravitates more and more to immense concerns for a young man without capital to get a start for himself, and in this city especially, when larger and larger capital is essential, it is unusually difficult."

The following year, the year of the general strike, Carnegie published his panegyric to American capitalism, which he called *Triumphant Democracy*. Once again he admitted that opportunities in America had diminished. "As the country fills," he explained, "these prizes naturally become more and more difficult to secure." Somewhat lamely he added that these diminished opportunities spur greater effort, "provide additional incentives to make hay while the sun shines."

Triumphant Democracy was essentially a long recital of the material achievements of America. Carnegie bragged how America surpassed the countries of the Old World in agriculture, in manufacturing, in commerce. With regard to education, religion, and art, Americans had more schools, more churchgoers, and more paintings than the countries of Europe. This remarkable material progress Carnegie attributed to the condition of political equality found in America. The removal of the taint of political inferiority—still existent in Europe—had freed the individual. Because of this freedom, some people had become millionaires: "The equality of the citizen is the fundamental law upon which is founded all that brings sweetness and light to human life." An emancipated people had wrought the "miracle of America." As he presented it, America was "Triumphant Democracy."

After tracing the material greatness of America to its condition of political equality, Carnegie pointed out that one of the bulwarks of American equality was American education. "The free common school system of the land is," he wrote, "probably after all, the greatest single power in the unifying powers which produce the American race." In these common schools, where all receive the same, good education, "the children of Irishmen, Germans, Italians, Spaniards, and Swedes, side by side with the native Americans . . . are transmuted into republican Americans and are made one in love for a country which provides equal rights and privileges for all her children."

In describing how the common schools brought about political equality, Carnegie was merely giving voice to the conception most Americans shared. Horace Mann, "the father of the common school," had declared in 1844 that, in America, education was "the great equalizer of the conditions of men . . . the balance wheel of the social machinery." Carnegie shared the unbounded faith of his adopted land in the power of education. "Just see," he intoned, "wherever we peer into the first tiny springs of the national life, how this true panacea for all the ills of the body politic bubbles forth—education, education, education."

In his paean to the material triumph of American democracy, Carnegie ignored the complaints from egalitarians that this great American wealth was largely in the hands of a very few Americans. Some of these complainers, the socialists, wanted the wealth distributed more evenly, more equally. Carnegie had paid no heed to the socialists in his book. But the general strike in 1886 and its aftermath revealed socialism to be a viable force in American society.

By 1889 Andrew Carnegie had an antidote for socialism. The antidote was a new creed, soon to be called the "gospel of wealth." Carnegie first expounded it in 1884 in the *North American Review*. The article, simply entitled "Wealth," was acclaimed by the editor as "the finest article I have ever published in the *Review*."

Carnegie began his article by dismissing socialism as something from out of the past, something that "belongs to another and long succeeding sociological stratum." The race has tried that, he admonished. We have displaced collectivism with individualism, so to return to socialism would necessitate "the changing of human nature itself—a work of eons." Better then, Carnegie concluded, to hold on to individualism, private property, the law of accumulation of wealth, and the law of competition; these are "the highest result of human experience, the sod in which society so far has produced the best fruit."

After disposing of socialism as an answer, Carnegie turned to the problem that troubled the socialists: the proper administration of wealth. Under capitalism, since great wealth accumulates in the hands of a few, the main problem is the disposal of surplus wealth. Carnegie admits to three possible modes of disposal. He dismisses two of them. He rejects passing it on to the family and bequeathing it for public purposes. He accepts only the third way: to have it administered by its possessors during their lives. This mode, he submits, is "the true antidote for the temporary unequal distribution of wealth." He pointedly remarks that this mode is founded upon "the present most intense Individualism." To carry it out requires "only the further evolution of existing conditions, not the total overthrow of our civilization," as advocated by the socialists and communists. With this mode of distribution of surplus wealth, Carnegie promises an ideal state, one where "the surplus wealth of the few will become, in the best sense, the property of many, because administered for all."

How can rich people administer their surplus wealth for the benefit of all? Carnegie supplies a list of projects. They can build and support hospitals, parks, meeting halls, even churches. These benefactions would indeed promote the common good, but they also smack of paternalism. Carnegie, however, did not envision the rich people of America as paternalistic philanthropists, especially not philanthropists who would mollify the masses, keeping them satisfied but poor. Carnegie's main hope was to cast the rich people of America into the role of saviors of American opportunity. Persons of wealth, he argued, have an obligation to increase and insure equal opportunity for all. For this reason he held that the best way to dispose of surplus wealth was to give it to educational institutions—to give it to universities or, his favorite, to free libraries.

During his lifetime Carnegie set up 2811 free libraries and gave $20 million to various American colleges and $22 million to the Carnegie Institute of Technology. His largest gift, $125 million, went to the Carnegie Foundation. Carnegie's heroes of philanthropy were men like Johns Hopkins (1795–1873), Ezra Cornell (1807–1874), Charles Pratt (1830–1891) and Leland Stanford (1824–1893)—all men of wealth who founded institutions of higher learning in the last half of the nineteenth century. A special tribute went to Peter Cooper (1791–1883), who had early seen the need and before the Civil War established a technical school in New York City, called Cooper Union. Carnegie cautioned all who advocated radical equalitarian change—the Communists, the socialists, the anarchists—to ponder the benefits to America that flowed from Cooper Union.

With his "Gospel of Wealth," Carnegie finally confronted the problem that had bedeviled Americans since the Civil War—the disappearance of opportunity. Before this, Carnegie had mouthed the same platitudes about opportunity voiced by the other millionaires. To the students of Curry Commercial College in Pittsburgh in 1884, for example, he had said: "Still, let me tell you for your encouragement that there is no country in the world, where able and energetic young men can so readily rise as this, nor any city where there is more room at the top." But the rising influence of the socialists had forced him to face the fact that opportunity had disappeared and to realize the possible consequences for his adopted land. The socialists called for an equal distribution of the wealth. But the canny Scot realized that most Americans were individualists and did not really aspire to the equality the socialists promised. Rather than seeking to be equal, most Americans aspired to rise higher than their neighbors, to achieve more success, more power, more wealth.

Since this is what Americans wanted, Carnegie merely pointed out that they could find it only in capitalism, not in socialism. And although capitalism does concentrate wealth in the hands of a few, the best interests of all are promoted, since these few can re-create opportunities for all by distributing the surplus wealth in benefactions that help people to help themselves. Through benefactions to educational institutions, especially to colleges, rich men provide, in Carnegie's happy phrase, "ladders upon which the aspiring can rise." Colleges already did exist in great numbers in America. But if people now regarded them as ladders to success, more would be needed. If he helped to fill this need, the rich would thereby prove themselves to be defenders of equality of opportunity.

The year after he published "Wealth," Carnegie wrote an article entitled, "How to Win a Fortune." Here he pointed out that most of the men at the top of the mercantile, commercial, financial, and industrial worlds had all started out at the bottom. Beginning by sweeping floors and filling inkwells, they had learned "on the job," and then moved up and out on their own. Carnegie supplied a long list of millionaires who had "started out as poor boys and were trained in that sternest of all schools—poverty." Then he made a significant admission to the young men starting out: "It is no doubt infinitely more difficult to start a new business of any kind today than it was."

Carnegie was right. Most everyone thought it was infinitely more difficult now to start a new business. The opportunities in America existed in the already established companies and corporations, and these corporations and companies, as Carnegie noted, looked to the colleges to supply them with the personnel they needed.

In 1903 a group of foreign observers took note of this new development in America. That year the Mosely Education Commission came from Great Britain to study the relationship between prosperity and education in the

United States. The investigators reported that, everywhere, businessmen had told them that as late as 1890 few employers hired college graduates, but that by 1900 many had developed a decided preference for the college man. The Pennsylvania Railroad, for example, had recently adopted regulations requiring all future executives to have some college training in engineering. In 1900 the famed corporation lawyer James B. Dill wrote that the "corporate tendency" in American business made college training necessary for success, "because the demand today for trained minds devoted to specific lines of work, has created a demand for college trained men."

By 1900 opportunity in America no longer existed "in the raw." The path to success was becoming much more structured. In the preindustrial days of abundant opportunity youths had tested themselves and proved their merit "on the job." Now the testing and proving was to take place before they ever entered the world of work. The schools were to take over this task. Youths who climbed the educational ladder would thereby prove their merit and be rewarded with the top echelon jobs.

In order to perform this new function of preparing people for the opportunities now provided in America, the American schools had to undertake a profound transformation, one that took place in the twenty years following publication of Carnegie's "Gospel of Wealth." Once Americans began to look at the schools as central to the economic life of the country, the number and the kinds of schools had to increase. Moreover, these schools had to be welded into a system of education, a ladder upon which the aspiring could rise.

VII

No system of American education existed in 1890. Nor could one find many educators committed to vocationalism. The colleges, especially, remained adamantly opposed to it, and so long as the colleges shunned the career-training function, the idea of an educational ladder to opportunity remained just that—an idea. In 1855 the president of the University of Alabama had written with assurance: "While time lasts, the farmer will be made in the field, the manufacturer in the shop, the merchant in the counting room, the civil engineer in the midst of the actual operation of his science." Since the days of the famous "Yale Report" of 1828 condemning vocationalism in higher education, the colleges had taken this stand, becoming, as a result, more and more irrelevant in American society. Nevertheless, the colleges continued to hold on to their traditional teaching function: transmitting liberal culture and imparting discipline and piety.

After the Civil War the ideal of research began to make some headway in American higher education, especially with the founding of Johns Hopkins University in 1867. Here, as Frederick Rudolph has written, "the university found its purpose in knowledge, in the world of the intellect." The first president of Johns Hopkins, David Coit Gilman, announced that the functions of the university were: "the acquisition, conservation, refinement and distribution of knowledge." Research, it seemed, had top priority. At the University of Chicago, founded in 1890, the president, William Rainey Harper, was more blunt: "It is proposed in this institution to make the work of investigation primary, the work of giving instruction secondary."

This research movement in higher education brought teaching closer to vocationalism. Ezra Cornell, the founder of the University bearing his name, declared: "I would found an institution where any person can find instruction in any study." With the help of Andrew D. White, its first president, Cornell University opened in 1869 with the expressed aim of uniting "practical and liberal learning." As Laurence Veysey has shown, however, vocationalism did not emerge as the dominant function of higher education until the end of the century. Throughout the nineties, the old and the new conceptions competed with one another. But by 1900 colleges began to welcome future merchants, journalists, manufacturers, chemists, teachers, inventors, artists, musicians, dieticians, pharmacists, scientific farmers, and engineers—training them in the skills of their profession, just as they had always trained the potential lawyers, ministers, and physicians. Departments, and sometimes whole schools, grew up where one could study business administration, forestry, journalism, veterinary medicine, or social work. By the beginning of the century most colleges and universities had been swept up into the movement toward vocationalism. In 1906, E. J. James, then president of the University of Illinois, declared that the state university must "stand simply, plainly, unequivocally and uncompromisingly for training, for vocation . . ." Scholarship was necessary, he added, only insofar "as scholarship is a necessary incident to all proper training of a higher sort of vocation . . ."

By 1900, vocationalism not only dominated all the new graduate programs, it invaded the undergraduate programs as well. Increasingly the undergraduate sought and got a specialist's education. Throughout the land, the traditional prescribed curriculum of the colleges gave way to the elective system, which permitted students to choose courses from a variety offered. Through this freedom of choice the student was supposed to become a trained expert in some special field.

The triumph of vocationalism was hastened by the lavish financial grants to colleges and universities made by the captains of industry. At Columbia University, for example, the philanthropic gifts received between 1890 and 1901 amounted to more than twice the total amount received from its beginnings. The list of donors read like a Who's Who of millionaires: Morgan, Vanderbilt, Havemeyer, Pulitzer, Schiff, Fish. New York University received gifts from Jay Gould. John D. Rockefeller founded the University of Chicago in 1900; he also gave large sums to Brown University. Mark Hanna gave to Kenyon, and George Eastman virtually created the University of Rochester. The money donated by these millionaires enabled the colleges to build the new schools, hire the new professors, and house the new departments.

More often than not these gifts were unsolicited by the institutions of higher learning. But gradually there emerged a new breed of college president, one who sometimes solicited these grants or at least sought to administer effectively and efficiently the newly gained wealth of his college. Veblen called these new administrators the "captains of erudition." They were a far cry from the old-time college president, who, usually a clergyman who taught moral philosophy to seniors, now found himself out of date in the new academia. Very few of the new administrators taught classes at all; they were too preoccupied with administering their rapidly expanding empires.

Before the first decade of the century ended, the university had become an American institution, holding out the promise of economic advancement to all who entered. The university now provided the key to opportunity in America. Moreover, there was increased opportunity for all to get this key, since by this time the university was widely accessible to all youths. During the same twenty-year period that vocationalism emerged as the primary function of higher education, Americans were creating an educational system. By 1910 the university had become the top rung of the American educational ladder to opportunity.

VIII

Back in 1890, Charles W. Eliot, the president of Harvard University, had complained to the delegates attending the NEA convention that no state in the union possessed "a system of secondary education." And so long as this gap between the elementary schools and the colleges persisted, no state had what could properly be called a system of education.

To create a system of education, the gap between the elementary school and the college had to be filled by a secondary school that prepared students for entrance into college. This the secondary schools failed to do. President Eliot informed the NEA delegates in 1890 that only nine high schools in all of Massachusetts sent pupils to Harvard College every year. He reported that, of 352 students admitted to Harvard in 1889, only 97 had been prepared at free public high schools. Since everyone considered the Massachusetts high schools far superior to those in other states, the conclusion was obvious: free public secondary education was in a sad condition throughout the nation. Plainly the public high schools were not preparing students for admission to Harvard College, or to any other college that had respectable admission requirements.

Eliot, perhaps, expected too much of the high school. Actually the free public high school had only recently come into existence in the United States. Boston had created the first public high school in 1821. But few cities or school districts had followed the lead of the Bostonians. By 1860, according to William T. Harris, onetime U.S. Commissioner of Education, there were but forty high schools in the entire United States. Others dispute this. I. L. Kandel, for example, claims that 321 existed in 1860. Not until 1890 do we have reliable records. In that year the U.S. Commissioner counted 2556 public high schools. By this time the number of public schools surpassed the total number of private secondary schools (1632) and enrolled more than twice as many students as the private schools.

The rapid increase in the number of high schools can be explained partly by the fact that the public high schools had become increasingly responsive to different expectations and demands of the people in the local school district. Since most of the financial support for the high school came from the local school district, the high schools had no choice but to become responsive to whatever demands were made. So during this period of rapid growth—from 1860 to 1895—one finds an amazing increase in the number and variety of public high school programs. A study of those in the north central area in 1860 revealed that 12 high schools offered only 1 course, the classical or Latin course; of the remaining 8 high schools, 6 had only 2 programs, while 2 offered 3 programs. By 1896 the number of high schools in the area had risen from 20 to 60. These 60 high schools offered a grand total of 35 different programs. Only 35 of the 60 high schools offered a single program. Thirty-two of them offered from 2 to 4 different programs, 2 offered 6, and one high school had 7 different programs.

What did these new programs consist of? Back in the 1860s the "general" and "normal" programs had appeared in the high schools, alongside the "classical" program. But now in the nineties one found, in addition to these, such newcomers as the "English and German" program, the "scientific," the "scientific engineering," the "technological" programs, as well as the "commercial English" program.

This tremendous expansion of subjects and programs made the high schools more popular with the masses. But although this expansion had brought about an increase in the number of high schools, at the same time it prevented the creation of an American school system. There could be no school system unless the high schools prepared students for admission to colleges, and the very proliferation of subjects and programs in the high schools had so lowered the quality of education that few self-respecting colleges could admit high school graduates.

In his 1890 address to the NEA delegates, Eliot had played up this theme. Because of the inferior quality of the high schools, he claimed, "one half of the most capable children in the United States, at a moderate estimate, have really no open road to colleges and universities." The conclusion was obvious: without a fully completed system of education the schools could never fulfill the function of career preparation.

Most public high school people agreed with critics like Eliot, but they argued that the fault lay with the colleges, not with them. First of all, the college entrance requirements were narrowly conceived in terms of a few traditional subjects: always Latin, Greek, and mathematics, usually English grammar, and sometimes history and geography. But even more disconcerting to the high schools was the fact that subject matter requirements varied so much from one institution to another. Some colleges not only expected applicants to pass a test in Latin, for example, but frequently tested their knowledge of a specific Latin author or even a specific text. Each college had its favorite authors and texts. High school principals across the land complained about the impossible task of preparing students for a number of different colleges, no two of which had the same requirements.

All were agreed on one point: the solution to the problem of articulation of high schools and colleges called for some kind of uniformity. But few Americans, including Eliot, had the temerity to suggest that all the high schools of the land should adopt the same program of instruction. He, however, did formulate one approach to the problem of uniformity in a talk delivered at the NEA convention in 1892 entitled "Undesirable and Desirable Uniformity in Schools." Eliot strongly rejected a prescribed, uniform curriculum, even within a single school, claiming that it "crushes and bruises those priceless individual endowments which systems of education should take infinite pains to bring out." The ideal school, he said, was one that had more different courses of study than any one student could possibly undertake. Eliot was, of course, advocating that high schools adopt the elective system he had so successfully introduced at Harvard.

After dismissing the "undesirable uniformity" of a prescribed course of study, Eliot turned to what he conceived as desirable uniformity. This, briefly stated, consisted of uniform standards of instruction for each course so that all who studied any elected subject would be taught the same topics, for the same amount of time, in the same way, and be given the same tests.

At this 1892 convention the NEA selected a committee, called the Committee of Ten, to investigate the problem of the articulation of the high school and college. As chairman of the committee they chose, naturally, Charles W. Eliot.

The final report of the Committee of Ten did reflect Eliot's ideas insofar as it prescribed no uniform program of studies for all high schools. And while not explicitly endorsing the elective system, it did sanction the basic principle of the elective system, the equivalence of studies. At Harvard College, Eliot had used this principle to shatter the traditional, narrow, prescribed curriculum. At Harvard the elective system had brought about the addition of a wide variety of new courses, all of which counted equally toward a degree. In the report of the Committee of Ten we find the principle of equivalence of studies being used to confine the high schools to a set of nine subject matter areas: Latin, Greek, English, other modern languages, mathematics, physical science, natural history, history, and geography. These nine subject areas were to be considered as equivalent for the purpose of admission to college.

The Committee of Ten proposed a truly ingenious solution to the problem of articulation. Confronted on the one hand with narrow but widely varied college entrance requirements, and on the other with a tremendous expansion of high school subjects and programs, the Committee of Ten proposed that the college entrance requirements become wider and more flexible—wide enough and sufficiently flexible to admit students who had followed a program of studies made up of some combination of the nine basic subject matter areas. Then it used this prize of college admission as a lever to get the high schools to restrict their programs to the nine basic subject matter areas.

The committee's report was no less than a blueprint for a type of secondary school that would fill the gap between the elementary school and the college. Once the gap was filled, Americans would have an American system of education—a solidly constructed ladder upon which the aspiring could rise. The committee report put it this way: "A College might say,—we will accept for admission any group of studies taken from the secondary school program, provided that the sum of the studies in each of the four years amounts to sixteen or eighteen, or twenty periods a week,—as may be thought best . . . On the theory that all the subjects are to be considered equivalent in educational rank for the purpose of admission to college, it would make no difference which subject [a student] had chosen from the programme . . ."

IX

The Committee of Ten had no legal power over the schools of America. Yet it did influence the programs and courses in American public high schools. In 1904 Commissioner Harris, who had been a member of the committee, declared that "the scheme of studies recommended by the Committee of Ten on Secondary School studies to the National Education Association in 1893 has become the model for all secondary, or high schools, public and private."

In 1909 the recommendations of the Committee of Ten got support from an unexpected quarter: Andrew Carnegie, or, more precisely, from the Carnegie Foundation for the Advancement of Teaching. The Carnegie Foundation had money to pay pensions to retired professors. This kind of philanthropy would "advance teaching" by encouraging the older and more recalcitrant professors to leave the colleges and create openings for new, young professors more attuned to the changes taking place in higher education.

The Board of Trustees had to decide how to disburse these funds. At that time the Board consisted of three bankers and twenty-two college presidents, including the president of Harvard University, Charles W. Eliot. The trustees decided to pay the pension money directly to the colleges, who would then disburse it to the retiring professors.

By deciding to give the money directly to the college, the Carnegie Foundation put itself into the position of exerting great pressures on the colleges throughout the land. The Foundation proceeded to draw up the standards that a college must meet in order to qualify for the pension funds. It decreed that a college must have at least six full-time professors, a four-year liberal arts course, and a high school course as a requirement for admission. What counted as a high school course? The Board decided that it should consist of 16 units of 120 classroom clock hours in one subject each. As to the subjects making up these sixteen units, the Trustees indicated their general agreement with the subjects identified by the College Entrance Examination Board (CEEB). The Board, which had been initiated by Nicholas Murray Butler, president of Columbia University, at the suggestion of Charles W. Eliot, had settled upon a list of high school subjects acceptable for admission to college and had established standard tests or examinations in these subjects. The CEEB's list of acceptable subjects differed little from that set out earlier by Eliot's Committee of Ten.

Since most colleges eagerly sought Carnegie pensions, they inevitably pressured the high schools to adopt the "Carnegie unit" as the basis for curriculum construction. Many high schools complied, so that, within a short time after 1909, practically all high schools measured their work in terms of the unit defined by the Carnegie Foundation.

Yet in spite of the president of Harvard, in spite of the U.S. Commissioner of Education, and in spite of the Carnegie Foundation—in spite of all that prestige and power—by 1920 only a minority of high school students followed the program of studies proposed by the Committee of Ten. The committee had hoped to provide a blueprint for the entire high school. Why had it failed?

Actually the Committee of Ten had not failed insofar as it did make a college education more widely accessible to all. By inaugurating a course of study in public high schools that colleges would accept, the committee had created greater opportunity for all to enter the ranks of the old and the new professions. But not all available jobs were at this professional level; in fact, most jobs did not require college training. So if the school system was to become a real ladder to job opportunities, then it must train people for these lower level jobs as well as the higher level ones. Obviously, then, the program of studies set forth by the Committee of Ten could not serve as a complete blueprint for the American high school. The committee's program of studies prepared youths for college, but those who did not go to college were disadvantaged by this program since they had to compete in the employment market with other job hunters who had vocational skills. In order to insure equal opportunity for all, the argument went, the school systems had to introduce new and different programs of vocational training.

X

Strident voices had called for new programs of vocational education in the high school back in the nineties. In 1892, Edmund J. James, then a professor at the Wharton School of Finance and Economy of the University of Pennsylvania, delivered a major address before the convention of the American Bankers Association at San Francisco. He called it "A Plea for the Establishment of Commercial High Schools." Four years later the National Education Association welcomed a new group to its fold: the department of business education. At the second meeting of this department, Charles H. Thurber, a professor from the University of Chicago, reported that a survey he had made showed that an overwhelming majority of Chicago businessmen supported the creation of commercial high schools. Within the next few years commercial high schools appeared in Philadelphia and Cleveland, as well as Chicago. By 1899 New York City had established commercial courses in three high schools and that year decided to set up a separate commercial high school.

Reviewing the progress of commercial education in 1899, W. C. Stevenson, of the department of bookkeeping and penmanship of the State Normal School of Emporia, Kansas, boasted to the NEA delegates of the recent "spontaneous sentiment in favor of the commercial high school from all parts of the country for the ninety and nine who go into business pursuits, as well as to the one who goes into the professions of law, medicine, teaching, or to the ministry." The professor from Emporia concluded with a final burst of rhetoric:

> The commercial high school is here. It is based on principles eternal, and is a product of the heart universal. Business is being recognized as more than secularity. Its mission is no less divine than teaching or preaching . . . So long as ambition lives in the hearts of men, or a government exists by the people and for the people, so long will the light of education for use, falling upon the fields of human toil and the pathway of human sorrow, help to transform earth into a suburb of the New Jerusalem.

The delegate from Kansas had given a rousing victory speech; by the end of the century most of the major cities had set up commercial courses and commercial high schools. Here they trained the future clerks, bookkeepers, stenographers, and typists. But not all youths were destined for office jobs. What about the blue collar workers? Could the schools train them? Here the school system moved more slowly.

Back in 1879 Calvin Woodward had established the first manual training school in the country. This school, located in St. Louis, had spawned a host of imitators so that by the nineties public manual training schools could be found in Philadelphia, St. Paul, Chicago, Denver, Boston, and Brooklyn.

Calvin Woodward had established the first school to "fit [young men] for the actual duties of life in a more direct and practical manner than is done in the ordinary American School." But in the eighties so many educators attacked the manual training movement for its crass vocationalism that its proponents shifted their grounds. Now they pointed up the disciplinary powers of their subject. Through manual training, they argued, the school could educate the whole child, disciplining not only his or her mind, but his or her hands as well.

Throughout the nineties, the manual training movement continued to grow. In 1894 Massachusetts, for example, passed a law that required cities of 20,000 inhabitants to include manual training in the high school courses. The manual training educators, meanwhile, took great pains to distinguish their work from technical, trade, or industrial education. Manual training, as they saw it, was a part of general education, not to be counted as vocational preparation. But while these experts in manual training spent time justifying their work to their fellow educators, laymen became increasingly impatient with the impracticality of this kind of schooling.

At the 1899 meeting of the NEA, Charles F. Warren of the Mechanic Arts High School of Springfield, Massachusetts, pointed out to the members of the manual and industrial department that "manufacturers are looking forward to the time when manual training schools can turn out graduates who are really proficient in some line of work, and able and willing to join forces with their employers as producers." Then, after expressing the hope that he would not be stigmatized as "a deserter from the ranks of true educational manual training," Warren offered the timid suggestion that manual training in the schools be somehow connected with trade education.

Whether in response to Warren or not, the members at that 1899 meeting decided to change the name of the department from manual and industrial department to department of manual training. But Warren's plea apparently did have some influence, since the following year the department of manual training set up a committee to study the relations of manual training to trade education.

The work of the committee led to a symposium on trade education held at the 1903 convention of the NEA. Here Arthur Henry Chamberlain delivered the most significant speech. He started off by telling the manual training educators that they flattered themselves if they thought manual training had been introduced into the American schools as a result of the "powerful" educational arguments. "Manual training schools have come to stay," he declared, "because there is a demand for that form of education which shall connect itself with productive industries and with the employments which the youths of our land are by force of circumstances bound to follow. . . . It is our duty to appreciate their full mission and see that they fulfill it."

At this symposium of 1903 few self-respecting educators accepted any longer the theory of mental, or manual, discipline. Schoolmen now justified school subjects by their practical, not their disciplinary, value. Speaker after speaker at the symposium pleaded for practical, vocational education. And when the stalwart, old-line defenders of manual training had their chance to respond, many acceded to the pleas for vocationalism. They asked only that the public schools not become "trade schools." They could accept vocationalism so long as the youths were taught, in the words of Woodward, "the processes that underlie a group of trades," not just the processes of a single trade. They argued against trade schools on the grounds that this narrow education, or training, would not prepare youths for a variety of different job opportunities.

But manual training had had its day. In 1906 the Massachusetts Commission on Industrial and Technical Education, called the Douglas Commission, announced that it found widespread indifference to manual training as a school subject. The commission found that many cities disregarded the 1894 law that required them to include manual training in the high schools. It traced this indifference to the narrow views of manual training prevailing among its chief advocates, the educators, who looked upon it as a cultural subject—"a sort of mustard relish, an appetizer—to be conducted without reference to any industrial end." The final verdict was that manual training "has been severed from real life as completely as have other school activities."

The Douglas Commission recommended that all towns and cities provide elective industrial courses in high schools. In addition to day courses for full-time students, they asked cities and towns to provide evening courses for persons already employed in trades, as well as part-time day classes for employed youths between the ages of fourteen and eighteen.

In the fall of 1906, the year that the Douglas Commission gave its report, the National Society for the Promotion of Industrial Education (NSPIE) held its first meeting. The delegates to this meeting selected Henry S. Pritchett as their president. He had been president of Massachusetts Institute of Technology and was currently president of the Carnegie Foundation for the Advancement of Teaching.

According to Pritchett, the underlying purpose of the national society was "the thought that we are no longer fitting our youths for their opportunities in the way in which they must be fitted." Industrial education was needed to prepare young people for the opportunities that America offered. To promote industrial education, the NSPIE brought together industrial workers, manufacturers, schoolteachers, and interested members of the public at large.

The vocational education movement now took on the proportions of a Klondike gold rush. Demands that school systems establish programs of vocational education came from both schoolpeople and other public leaders. The movement took hold in great part because the promises held out by its proponents appealed to individualists and hierarchs alike. The individualist saw vocational education providing increased job opportunities so that people could become autonomous, no longer victimized by industrialization. The hierarchs also saw vocational education as the means of providing increased job opportunities, which they found desirable since this would restore stability to American society. They saw unemployed and unoccupied youths as the most serious threat to that stability. If these youths could be kept busy in school, learning something practical that would guarantee employment once they got out, then by all means vocational education was needed.

The NSPIE achieved remarkable success. By 1910 it enlisted the support of *both* the National Association of Manufacturers (NAM) and the American Federation of Labor (AFL) for public vocational schools. Although the high point of the vocational education movement had been passed some five or six years earlier, in 1917 the lumbering machinery of the United States Congress finally passed the first Vocational Education Act. Called the Smith-Hughes Act, it provided federal funds to establish high school vocational programs in agriculture, home economics, and trade and industrial subjects. Although commercial education received no help, the members of Congress had been persuaded to provide support for the vocational training of both boys and girls, for both urban and rural vocations.

So in the twenty years following the publication of Andrew Carnegie's "Gospel of Wealth," the Americans had created a national system of education. What kind of system was it? Did it solve the problem posed in 1884? Did it ensure that all would have equal opportunity for success in America? Did it provide a ladder upon which an aspirant could climb?

XI

When they stepped back to look at the system they had created, Americans saw that they had done more than expand and articulate the different schools. They had wrought a change in the function of the American school. Until the nineties, as Carnegie had correctly observed, the American school had functioned as a unifying force, providing a common education for all children. But the school system that now emerged at the end of the nineteenth century abandoned the ideal of commonality. The school system still carried out the function the hierarchy wanted—serving as the "balance wheel of society," as Horace Mann had put it—but now it maintained a stable society by becoming "the great selector." The new, articulated system of education permitted only the most talented to climb to the top of the educational ladder, the ladder that led to the professional jobs. Moreover, the new, differentiated school system not only selected the most talented for the higher level jobs, it selected from the rest those destined for office jobs and those destined for factory jobs. The educational ladder to opportunity really was several ladders. Upon the schools now fell the somewhat awesome responsibility of selecting which one a child should climb.

Charles W. Eliot had made this quite clear in a talk he gave at the 1908 meeting of the NSPIE in which he pointed out that, once industrial schools are established, someone will have to decide who will attend them. "Here we come upon a new function for the teachers in our elementary schools," he said, "and in my judgment they have no function more important. The teachers of the elementary schools ought to sort the pupils and sort them by their evident or probable destinies."

This sorting out of people according to their probable destinies was a totally new function for the American school. In the past the American school had not decided the probable destiny of the children who attended it. In America, most people, being individualists, had insisted that a person can take up any job, any occupation: America was the land of opportunity. The idea that any person could take up any job did not mean that any person could do a job as well as any other. Americans did not believe that all people were, in fact, equal. What they did insist upon was that each person should have the opportunity to try his or her hand at any job he or she sought. Here they contrasted their land with the countries of Europe, where laws, institutions, and customs denied these opportunities to most men. The Americans had tried to eliminate all such discriminatory laws, customs, and institutions. Moreover, they had relied on the schools to provide all children with a common, unifying experience. Once freed from the artificial restrictions imposed in other countries, once equipped with a common school education, young Americans were prepared for the unexpected. They could take up almost any job. But in an industrialized society this just could not be done. Eliot had emphasized this very point in his 1908 talk to the NSPIE. "We must get rid of the notion," he declared, "that some of us were brought up on, that a Yankee can turn his hand to anything. He cannot in this modern world; he positively cannot."

Eliot had made clear what was happening. All now realized that America was no longer the land of opportunity, in the sense that anyone could try his or her hand at any job. But not everyone realized that this meant that the school must sort out the young for their "probable destinies." In spite of the convictions of the president of Harvard University, many Americans, especially American educators, felt uneasy about this change in the function of the

American school. For the next fifty years most educators refused to accept "career selection" as the primary function of the schools. By various stratagems they were able to deny that the schools selected students for their "probable destinies."

XII

By 1918 some cities had taken a few hesitant steps toward institutionalizing the selection process. Beginning in 1910, first in Berkeley, a number of cities created special intermediate schools called junior high schools where the selection took place. The junior high school, consisting of grades seven through nine, sorted students into one of three courses of study: the general, the commercial, or the industrial. This institutionalized differentiation received official endorsement at the NEA convention in 1915 when the department of superintendence passed a resolution approving "the increasing tendency to establish, beginning with the seventh grade, differentiated courses of study aimed more effectively to prepare the child for his probable future activities."

In addition to attempts to institutionalize the selection process in the junior high school, a number of cities now created a "professional selector"—a guidance counselor. By 1910 there were enough guidance counselors to hold a national conference in Boston. Three years later a National Guidance Association came into existence.

In spite of these attempts to institutionalize and professionalize the career selection function, by 1918 a reaction had set in. That year the NEA's Commission on the Reorganization of Secondary Education (CRSE) issued its final report. Called "The Cardinal Principles of Education," it muted the vocational function of the schools, burying it exactly in the middle of the seven aims of education: (1) Health, (2) Command of fundamental processes, (3) Worthy home membership, (4) Vocation, (5) Citizenship, (6) Worthy use of leisure time, and (7) Ethical character.

The report of the CRSE did more than mute the vocational function of the schools. It reasserted the notion proposed by the hierarchs in the nineteenth century that the task of the school was to provide a common education for all. But now that notion had become quite abstract. The educational objectives set forth in the seven cardinal principles were to be aims for all students. So, if all teachers committed themselves to these seven aims, then all students would receive essentially the same common education, the argument went—even though they took different courses of study and prepared for different careers.

The CRSE report recognized the existence of separate courses of study "based on future vocations," but it urged the schools to incorporate various stratagems to "unify" the students in these different courses. The report suggested that all students take certain common studies together, like social studies and English. They also suggested that all students should participate in common activities—athletic games, social activities, and the government of the school. Finally, they recommended that all students attend a comprehensive high school—a school containing a variety of different courses of study— rather than separate specialized secondary schools. In the comprehensive school, the report claimed, pupils became "friendly with pupils pursuing other curriculums and having educational goals widely different from their aim." As a result, "the pupils realize that the interests which they hold in common are, after all, far more important than the differences that would tend to make them antagonistic to others."

American educators tried to have it both ways. They would work in a system that selected students for different careers, but the teachers would focus their efforts on the task of unifying the students. The compromise, of course, was largely a verbal one. It marks the beginning of the substitution of educational slogans for concrete educational policies in America. No one could argue against the seven cardinal principles of education, for example, but at the same time no one could take these aims seriously as policy to guide practice. They were a slogan, one that educators invoked to convince themselves and others that the schools could, and did, unify all students.

Other proclamations of common aims appeared in the next twenty-five years, most of them more vacuous hence even less helpful as policy guides than the original seven cardinal principles. In 1938, for example, the Educational Policies Commission of the NEA recommended the following as goals for American education: self-realization, human relationship, economic efficiency, and civic responsibility.

Until the late fifties American teachers refused to accept career training as the primary function of the schools. In their quest to equalize all students they continued to give allegiance to sets of aims for *all* American youth. Moreover, they retained their faith in the prescriptions issued by the CRSE in 1918: common courses for all in general education, common extracurricular activities, and the comprehensive high school. But neither the commitment to common aims nor the emphasis on common experiences succeeded in unifying the students. The structure of the educational system—a selective system—defeated all rhetoric and all stratagems.

Study after study of the American schools revealed that they failed to unify; they merely sorted and selected students for different careers, different ways of life. In their study of a typical midwestern town first in the twenties and then again in the thirties, Robert and Helen Lynd reported that the school system of Middletown sorted out students for different careers. In the twenties they quoted the president of the board of education as saying: "For a long time all boys were trained to be President. Then for a while we trained them all to be professional men. Now we are training boys to get jobs." In the twenties they reported that the cleavage among groups had "become more rigid in the last generation." Nor did the schools of Middletown succeed in unifying the people during the thirties. When the Lynds returned during that decade, they noted that more children were in school and that they were staying there longer. But rather than unifying them, the schools were still sorting them out and preparing them for jobs. The Lynds noted that the high school had expanded its course offerings and had inaugurated a complete program of vocational guidance. They credited these changes, not to the teachers, but to the parents, those "hard-working folk," who wanted "something tangible—a better job, the ability to earn more money—as at least one dependable outcome of 'an education.' "

In the forties, W. L. Warner and his associates studied a number of typical American communities. He reported that, even though the schools brought all children together and gave them a common experience and common literacy, one could still see that "as early as ten or twelve, these children all were travelling different paths in life."

In the fifties, Patricia Sexton found that the schools still failed to equalize children. Focusing on "Big City," a large midwestern city, she charted the "inequalities of opportunity in the public schools." She discovered that in the high schools the children from low-income families were almost completely separated from children from high-income families. Children from each group tended to take different subjects and to enroll in different programs. When they took the same courses, the upper-income students were sorted into the higher ability sections of these courses. Moreover, she confirmed other studies, like *Elmstown's Youth*, that reported that the upper-class students dominate the school's extracurricular activities.

Despite the plethora of studies documenting the fact that the schools failed to fulfill the unifying function, most teachers continued to believe that they could carry it off, if they only tried harder. Even some of the investigators who reported the failures of the schools to equalize students continued to urge teachers to try harder. Some, like Warner and his associates, repeated the familiar prescription of "common educational experiences."

At the same time as the schools failed to provide a common education for their students, some people complained, they failed to do a good job of career preparation. The schools got complaints from factories, from offices, from colleges. The schools, so said the complaints, either improperly selected students or poorly trained them, or both. Nevertheless, the schools, in most instances, did an adequate job of sorting and preparing youths for the factory, for the office, or for a professional career. The selection was not perfect, the training not of the highest quality possible, but, on the whole, the schools did a fairly good job of selecting and training youths for their future careers. However, by the fifties many realized that fairly good was not good enough.

XIII

By the fifties the United States had become what Burton R. Clarke called "the expert society." Industrialization had reached the advanced stage where the service industries increasingly overshadowed the others. From 1900 to 1950 the proportion of agricultural workers in the American labor force had declined from 37 percent to 12 percent; during the same period unskilled laborers declined from 12 percent to 7 percent. On the other hand, skilled and semiskilled workers increased from 23 to 35 percent, clerks and sales workers from 7 to 19 percent. In the fifties these trends accelerated. From 1950 to 1958 alone, professional-technical workers increased from 9 to 11 percent of the labor force.

The rapidly changing occupational patterns spawned a new genre of educational research—manpower studies. During the fifties these researchers confirmed the suspicions of many people when they announced that the United States had too few skilled technicians and professional workers and too many unskilled workers. The need for technicians reached crisis proportions in 1957 when the Soviet Union launched its first sputnik. The Americans transformed this technological defeat into an educational problem. America, too, could launch satellites if it had an adequate supply of trained manpower. In less than a year, the normally sluggish Congress had whipped together legislation to provide federal aid to the schools, appropriately called the National Defense Education Act. This Act provided funds to improve the quality of instruction in the vital areas of science, mathematics, and foreign languages. It also provided funds to expand and improve the guidance and counseling services of all schools. And it supplied funds to enlarge the existing programs of vocational education.

Once the United States Congress had made clear that the primary function of the school was career selection and preparation and proceeded to back up its position with substantial federal funds, many educators came into line. One now heard less about the function of providing a common education for all children. Educators now busied themselves "tooling up" the system in order to supply the country with the needed manpower. They now spent lots of time setting up quality programs in the vital subject matter areas, inaugurating special programs for the gifted, and initiating comprehensive programs of guidance and counseling. At the same time they began playing down, even eliminating, some of the old, general education courses—now labeled "the frill courses"—that had supposedly operated to unify the students.

During this period of rapid transformation some wondered aloud about the comprehensive school. Could it perform this function of career selection and training? Admiral Hyman Rickover declared it could not perform this task satisfactorily and therefore should be abolished. But at this point an old combination appeared on the scene to confer its powerful endorsement on the comprehensive high school.

In 1957 the Carnegie Foundation contracted with James Bryant Conant, former president of Harvard University, to conduct a study of the American school system. Conant issued his first report, *The American High School Today*, in 1959. Here he argued that the comprehensive high school, provided it made some necessary changes, could adequately prepare some students for college, give others a vocational education, and at the same time provide a general education for all. Addressing himself to the members of the local school boards throughout the nation, Conant announced that almost all schools could raise the academic quality of instruction. But more pointedly he called for a sharpening of the selection devices used in the comprehensive high school.

As his first recommendation he insisted that all schools had to improve and expand their counseling and guidance services. He not only recommended that students be grouped according to ability in all subjects but went on to call for complete special programs for the academically talented *plus* an additional special program for the *highly gifted* (estimated as the top 3 percent of the population). Perhaps the most blatant recommendation was the fifth one: the supplement to a high school diploma. "In addition to the diploma," Conant wrote, "each student should be given a durable record of the courses studied and the grades obtained. The existence of such records shall be well publicized so that employers ask for it rather than merely relying on a diploma when questioning an applicant for a job about his education." Here was career selection with a vengeance! "The record might be a card that could be carried in a wallet," Conant added.

As noted earlier, the manpower studies of the fifties pointed up a surplus of unskilled workers as well as a shortage of skilled, technical, and professional workers. The uneasiness this "surplus" problem created found expression in the new concern for the "dropout." Children had been dropping out of schools ever since schools first opened. In fact, over the half century the "dropout rate" had declined. But now the dropout was a problem; he or she could not get a job. Therefore, the dropout had to be lured back to school. But once he or she had been lured back, what could the teachers do for or to him or her? Most students had dropped out because they could not get along in school. They found the work too difficult or too irrelevant. More of the same could only succeed in driving the returned dropout out of school again, permanently.

James Conant used part of his Carnegie Foundation grant to study this problem. He published his findings and recommendations in 1962 in *Slums and Suburbs*. In the suburban schools he found that, since most students go on to college, the main problem these schools faced was to select the appropriate college for each student and to convince the parents of the wisdom of the choice. This problem seemed trivial in comparison with the problem the schools faced in the slums. There, the unemployed, out-of-school youths had become, in Conant's famous phrase, nothing less than "social dynamite." To preserve the society itself, these youths had to be lured back to the schools, where together with other "potential dropouts," they should be taught vocational skills—equipped with what Conant was fond of calling "marketable skills." He recommended that the high schools in the slum areas take on all the functions of an employment bureau, keeping in close touch with the employers and the labor unions, as well as keeping job records for all graduates until the age of twenty-one.

By the sixties public pressures (and financial inducements) from Washington and quasi-public pressures from the Carnegie Foundation helped convince many American educators to accept career selection as the primary function of the schools. In some instances, particularly among the younger teachers, one found that they gravitated toward the career selection function in revulsion against the old slogans, the rhetoric, associated with the unifying function. These younger teachers, in rejecting the slogans that had justified it, discarded the function as well. A new, hard-headed realism now made its way among members of the teaching profession, including many of the older teachers who had spent much of their professional lives trying to give their students a common education. After years of failure they succumbed to disenchantment with the unifying function, especially as their younger colleagues declared that *they* would not try to do the impossible.

Finally, as one aspect of this hard-headed realism, one sensed that some teachers now actively sought out the role of philosopher-king. Consciously, or perhaps unconsciously, they wanted to have the job of sorting and selecting the next generation.

XIV

Americans had created their educational system at the end of the nineteenth century at a time of widespread lamentation for the disappearance of opportunity in America. The robber barons, the entrepreneurs who "got there first," had accumulated vast wealth, power, and prestige so as to leave no room for the little man to get ahead. To restore opportunity, the Americans built a school system, a system to provide, in Carnegie's words, "a ladder on which the aspiring could rise." They expected their schools to guarantee all Americans an equal opportunity for success.

In order for the schools to serve this function, the school system had to be the only ladder to success. Entrance to the top jobs through the back doors of family connections or private wealth had to be sealed off. During the twentieth century this is exactly what took place. The duress of modern technology caused what some have called the corporate revolution—the accumulation of productive property into larger and larger aggregates, the corporations. The corporate revolution undermined the old class of property holders by putting the control over the corporation property into the hands of nonowners—the executives and the managers. These organization men constitute what David Bazelon has labeled "the new class." One gains entry into this new class through education. People, in Bazelon's words, "translate achieved educational status into organization advantage." Studies in the sixties revealed that the old "pull" of wealth and family no longer opened the gates of the prestige universities. One study in 1963 of the New York Social Register revealed that, "while nearly two-thirds of the men listed went to Harvard, Yale, or Princeton, fewer than half of their sons had done so."

Yet at the very moment the Americans congratulated themselves on creating an educational ladder to the (corporate) land of opportunity, they had to face up to the fact that this same educational system reinforced the gross inequalities already existing in American society. Once they accepted the career selection function built into their school system, they could see that these sorting procedures discriminated against those who had low achievement levels, those who hated school, those with low I.Q.'s. These, the schools selected for the lower level jobs, selected them by allowing them to

drop out of the system, by dumping them into some pseudo "vocational training" program.

Since most educators and educated laymen during the sixties had con-
ceded that the children's environment largely determined their school-mind-
edness, their achievement levels, and even their I.Q., this meant that in the
very act of accepting "career selection" as the primary function of the schools,
Americans had to face the fact that their school system discriminated against
what was now called the "culturally deprived" child. So long as they had
refused to accept career selection as the primary function of the school, so long
as they had believed that the primary function was to provide a common education for all, Americans could have faith that their schools were doing something positive for the lower classes. Once, however, they accepted career selection as the primary function of the schools, that faith could not be sustained.
The schools did not provide a common education for all, nor did they help the
lower classes to rise. For the lower class the school system now became, to use
Paul Goodman's phrase "the universal trap"—a compulsory, selective school
system that sorted them out from the competition for the opportunities in
America. In 1961 the distinguished psychologist Kenneth B. Clarke bluntly
stated that the schools of America had become "an instrument of social and
economic class distinctions in American society."

What were the Americans to do? Could they persist in developing and
improving these instruments of selection that discriminated against the "culturally deprived" children? Could they continue to busy themselves with ability grouping, tests and measurements, vocational guidance and counseling?
As a way out of their dilemma many turned to a stratagem called "compensatory education." This consisted of special supplementary aid, counsel,
instruction, and attention for the "culturally deprived" child. Compensatory
education was nothing less than an attempt to use the schools to equalize children, not by giving them all the same "general education," but by making up
for their "lacks."

If incorporated fully into the educational system, compensatory education
would undermine career selection. But the Americans did not want to destroy
the career selection function; they wanted to make it less discriminatory
against the "culturally deprived." Thus, the most widely implemented form of
compensatory education was that provided for preschool children. This kind
of compensatory education would not interfere with the career selection carried on by the school system proper. Preschool compensatory education
proved so popular that the United States government provided funds to support it throughout the nation, labeling it, appropriately, "Operation Head
Start." Educators hoped that, if "culturally deprived" children got a "head
start," then the selection and sorting process carried out by the regular school
would no longer discriminate against them.

No one expected Operation Head Start programs to eliminate "cultural
deprivation." But at the same time none, save a few utopian thinkers like Paul
Goodman, wanted the schools to abandon the function of career selection. The
system was doing a good job in providing opportunities for success to the rest

of American youths. For all but the culturally deprived, the school system was still a ladder upon which the aspiring could rise. Those who climbed to the highest rungs could get the top jobs. The system itself, of course, determined who could climb to the top. But this, most people felt, was as it should be. And so in the 1960s, the mass media shouted slogans like, "Stay in School and Get a Good Job!" "Education Is for the Birds—the Birds Who Get Ahead!"

CHAPTER 6

The Government and the Schools

I

Before the Civil War some Americans sought political positions as a means of personal gain. After the war, the floodgates were open, and many, many more sought and secured political offices in order to make money. Graft and corruption became so commonplace that, by the 1870s, the average citizen used politics as a dirty word and called politicians "spoilsmen."

Many have attributed this upsurge of corruption to the abundant temptations provided by the greatly expanded operations of the government. First the war, then the rapid expansion of business after the war, created a multitude of new government jobs. To finance the war, the federal government had to hire hordes of new tax collectors, and securing arms and supplies for the troops required an additional army of purchasing agents and government inspectors. After the war the government had to employ many new custom house workers to enforce the high tariffs designed to protect American industry. All of these jobs were filled by the recommendation of a political boss—ward leader, senator, or chairman of the political party. The control wielded by these bosses over such a vast and rapidly expanding empire of patronage opened opportunities for graft, payoffs, and bribes. Moreover, those politically appointed to these public offices frequently exercised their powers in ways that further promoted corruption and chicanery.

The state and local governments also offered many new political jobs. Rising birth rates and increased migration swelled the populations of many cities and states, thereby increasing government responsibilities. The rapidly growing cities added thousands of employees to their payrolls to fight fires, keep the peace, build sewers, install lighting systems, pave streets, administer laws and ordinances. Here, too, all jobs were filled on the recommendation of a political boss. So during this period politicians could become rich by selling jobs, contracts, franchises—whatever they had in their power. As Thomas Cochran and William Miller put it, "politics . . . became one of the great businesses of the nation," and those in politics sought profits "like any other enterprise in a competitive society."

Some of the profits went to support the political machines. In some states, for example, the excise on whiskey filled the coffers of the party treasury. Often the profits went directly to politicians themselves, for in addition to selling patronage, officeholders were open to private financial inducements that determined whether or not they would regulate business, tax it, or protect it from regulation or taxation. Since the federal politicians dealt in federal lands, they could sell their favors to those entrepreneurs anxious to build railroads, mine coal and other minerals, drill oil, or sell and settle the empty spaces remaining in America. To secure the necessary land grants, protection, and freedom from regulatory legislation, capitalists donated campaign funds to the politicians, supplied them with investment opportunities, paid them fees, and bribed them outright.

The capitalists spent fabulous sums. In an age of raw competition entrepreneurs vied with one another in bribing the opportunistic politicians in order to gain any advantage over their rivals. According to Hofstadter, the Union Pacific Railroad spent $400,000 on bribes between 1866 and 1872. Few officeholders remained untainted; the graft and corruption seeped deeply into both parties. A Republican senator, Grimes of Iowa, declared in 1870 that he believed his party to be "the most corrupt and debauched political party that ever existed." Few politicians listened, however, since most eagerly sought the rewards of office that only the capitalist could supply. And capitalists paid no heed, since they needed the favors only the politicians could confer. In time, the unlimited greed of the politicians was their undoing. They continued to up the prices for their services and in some instances double-crossed their benefactors. In New York state a classic case occurred when one of Boss Tweed's senators accepted bribes from both Vanderbilt and a competitor in return for his vote on a matter affecting control of the Eric Railroad. Tweed's man voted for the highest donor. By the 1870s many Americans began to call for political reform. The businessman, rebelling against the excesses of bossdom, were especially eager for some kind of reform.

In 1871, the New York Citizen's Committee, led by corporation lawyer Samuel Tilden, began the campaign that ultimately put Boss Tweed in the penitentiary. In other cities leaders similar to Tilden were organizing crusades against their own bosses. Even earlier in Missouri a coalition of Democrats, dissident Republicans, and Independents had elected a reformer to the U.S. Senate—the highly cultivated Carl Schurz.

In the weekly *Nation* the editor, E. L. Godkin, kept up a continual demand for reform. The root of the evil, he argued, lay, not in corruption, but in the system. The alliance between industrialists and politicians bred corruption in the form of benefits for business: high tariffs, grants of public land, and federal subsidies. In 1870 Godkin had called for a party "having for its object Tariff Reform, Civil Service Reform, and Minority Representation."

Some of the most avid readers of the *Nation* were what Eric Goldman has labeled "the best people." These came from "families a cut above the middle

classes, in which, even if great wealth was lacking, money was no daily problem, a good education was assumed, and the next generation did not have to
suffer from the nationality, religion, or reputation of a previous one." In keeping with the hierarchical ideology, these patricians of America considered
themselves the national elite, the natural leaders born to rule. But in the new,
postbellum America they had been usurped. They saw the country being run
by a gang of "spoilsmen" in cahoots with the "new rich," people who lacked
the "restraints of culture, experience, the pride, or even the inherited caution
of class or rank." The hierarchy looked about and found themselves in agreement with Godkin's description of America as a "gaudy stream of bespangled,
belaced, and beruffled barbarians." Viewing the mad scene, "the great barbe-
cue," these hierarchy decided to save America. Morality must be restored to
political life. To do this, the unholy alliance between business and government
had to be severed. This meant a return to the policies of limited government
and laissez-faire—policies at that time identified as political liberalism.

They decided to begin at the top. The man occupying the White House
symbolized all the evils of the age. Under the administration of Ulysses S.
Grant corruption and graft had invaded all branches of all levels of government. "Grantism" had to be eradicated from American life. As the 1872 Presidential election approached, the hierarchy set out to create a new political
party, a liberal reform party, a party that would purify government.

II

The Liberal Republican party held its 1872 convention in Cincinnati. The
keynote address by Carl Schurz set the proper tone. The new reform party represented the conscience of the nation. "We saw jobbery and corruption, stimulated to unusual audacity by the opportunities of a protracted Civil War. . . .
We saw those in authority with tyrannical insolence thrust the hand of power
through the vast machinery of the public service into local and private affairs.
. . . We observed this, and . . . the question might well have been asked, 'Have
the American people become so utterly indifferent . . . that they should permit themselves to be driven like a flock of sheep by those who now assume
to lord it over them?' " This convention, Schurz cried, was the answer.

But the reformers, much to their dismay, soon learned that an age of
reform called for more than determination and moral righteousness. It
required organization. And the hierarch reformers were poorly organized.
Their convention had served as a magnet for dissidents of all stripes from the
Republican party and a strong contingent from the Democratic party as well.
The genuine liberal reformers proved so few in number and so ineffective in
the political arena that they failed to keep control of their own convention. The
hierarchs had expected to supply a slate of candidates who had a sense of
responsibility to the entire nation, educated men who wished nothing from
office save the opportunity to serve the public good. We want men of "superior intelligence, coupled with superior virtues," Carl Schurz declared. In

Charles Francis Adams, a patrician's patrician, they found the logical choice for the Presidential nomination. Unfortunately, the convention nominated Horace Greeley, a man opposed to reducing the tariff, scornful of civil service reform, and a vegetarian and prohibitionist to boot.

The landslide election of Grant came as an anticlimax. The American people had answered the hierarch reformers. The people wanted none of it. Throughout the nation, Henry Adams wrote, the men of talent, the men of virtue, the natural elite, folded their tents and stole silently away.

Not all men of talent gave up so easily, however. Those who persisted in saving America realized that a third political party just would not do; in fact, they now scorned all political parties, seeking to be Independents. Known to the party stalwarts as "mugwumps," the independent reformers did frequently exert enough influence to determine the outcome of elections. At the national level, the two major parties were so equally balanced that, from 1874 to 1894, neither could dominate the federal government for any length of time. The five Presidential elections held during this period were all closely contested, with the Democrats losing one, in 1880, by a mere 7000 votes. Moreover, throughout these twenty years a largely Democratic House of Representatives confronted a largely Republican Senate. Only twice did a single party control both the Presidency and Congress. Under these conditions the reforming mugwumps could exert considerable influence. Through exercising discriminating judgment between the major parties, they helped defeat James G. Blaine's nomination in 1880 and his election in 1884. They also helped defeat Cleveland's first bid for a second term in 1888 and did the same thing to Harrison in 1892.

The mugwump strategy did no more than create a political stalemate, producing no sustained working majority for twenty years. At the same time this strategy destroyed the possibilities for any political leadership. Grover Cleveland, in Hofstadter's words, was "the only reasonable facsimile of a major President between Lincoln and Theodore Roosevelt." In addition to obstructing all bids at strong leadership, the mugwump strategy did not produce the kind of legislation the reformers sought. Although some reform legislation was passed, it did not destroy the unholy alliance between politics and business.

The principal bond between these two spheres was the high tariff, and when a bill finally emerged from the mysterious recesses of the Senate as the Wilson-Gorman Tariff, it did not reduce the tariff; in fact, it incorporated increases from 10 to 300 percent on some items. The politicians continued to protect American businessmen. A second bond connecting politics and business consisted of the favors, immunities, and privileges the politicians extended to the giant corporations, the "trusts," which included the railroads. Between 1874 and 1885 more than thirty measures for the regulation of interstate railroads were introduced in Congress; all died in the Senate. Finally, during the first Cleveland Administration, the Interstate Commerce Act set up a federal commission to regulate the railroads. But as Cleveland's Attorney General, Richard Olney, assured the president of the Chicago, Burlington, and Quincy, the act satisfied "the popular clamor for government supervision of the railroads at the same time that that supervision is almost entirely nominal." As Olney predicted, the act became "a sort of barrier between the railroads and the people and a sort of protection against hasty and crude legislation hostile to railroad interest." Finally, during the election year of 1890 Congress passed a bill to regulate the trusts, the Sherman Anti-Trust Act. But this act too was a sop to the reformers, being easily circumvented by the capitalists; in fact, they used it as an effective instrument to combat labor organizations.

Although the mugwump strategy failed to produce legislation adequate to the task of destroying the links between politics and business, there was another tactic that did much to purify politics—civil service reform. At all levels of government, civil service jobs were regarded as the spoils of office that the victorious party expected to distribute as patronage to party stalwarts. The liberal reformers wanted to distribute these jobs on the basis of competitive examinations. Expectedly, they met with furious opposition. But when President Garfield was assassinated by a disgruntled office seeker, a shocked Congress in 1883 passed a Federal Civil Service Law, the Pendleton Act, and a number of states and municipalities followed the lead of the federal government.

This merit system struck at the very root of party power. At the same time it provided entry into public service for those men of "superior intelligence, coupled with superior virtue." Finally, civil service examinations circumvented popular deliberation. The reformers now could secure public office without depending upon the voters. After the fiasco of 1872 the liberal reformers had lost all faith in the intelligence, virtue, or even good will of the masses. They realized, too late, that they had placed too much faith in democracy, had relied too much on popular deliberation. Popular deliberation had cost them control of their political convention; it had returned Ulysses Grant to the White House. The liberal reformers now agreed that the people could never be trusted to elect men of superior intelligence and virtue to public office. This fear of popular deliberation, which amounted to a fear of expanded democracy, is clearly revealed in the way the liberal reformers approached education. After the debacle of their Liberal Republican party, the reformers turned to education—to the schools—not with the hope of raising the level of popular deliberation, but with the intention of curtailing it.

III

Probably the most direct expression of the liberal reformers' educational creed came from Carl Schurz in his Phi Beta Kappa oration at Harvard in 1882. A republic like the United States, he explained, needed two levels of formal education: "the elementary popular education which does not impart a high degree of knowledge, itself, but makes . . . men open, accessible, susceptible to the influence of superior knowledge and culture when they come in contact with it; and that higher education which enables and incites . . . those to whom it imparts superior knowledge and culture, to make their influence felt." No one did more to implement this educational creed of the liberal reformers than America's foremost educationist, William T. Harris.

Born in New England, Harris moved to St. Louis in 1857, after attending Phillips Andover Academy and Yale College. In St. Louis he taught school, rapidly rising to become superintendent of schools in 1868. Harris was more than an educational administrator. A member of the famous St. Louis movement in philosophy, founder and editor of the *Journal of Speculative Philosophy*, he was one of the leading philosophers of his age. Like his philosophic-minded friends in St. Louis, Harris considered himself a disciple of Georg Hegel, a philosopher that nineteenth-century Americans regarded as a political liberal, a spokesman for the republican movement in Europe. According to one commentator, one reason for the popularity of Hegel's philosophy in the United States was that many Americans, including the members of the St. Louis movement, saw it as a philosophy that both explained and healed "the tragic dialectic of the civil war." In accordance with the dialectical progress of civilization, the Hegelians had philosophical certainty that the North and South would now reunite.

When Harris applied Hegel's philosophy to American education, he did no less than articulate the American liberals' conception of the political function of the school. The school, Harris taught, had four cardinal duties to young children: to train them in the habits of regularity, punctuality, silence, and industry. Unless he had these habits, the child could not adjust to the social order. For Harris the school was the "nursery of civilization," "the center of discipline" that helped to preserve and guarantee the continuation of the social order. As superintendent of schools in one of the nation's largest cities, he saw at firsthand that the urban newcomers lacked these necessary social virtues. In his schools he insisted that the children must learn to accept authority. Through direct moral training of the will the pupil got used to "the established order" and obeyed it "as a habit." Moreover, the child would try to maintain that social order after leaving school, "whether he has ever learned the theory of it or not."

Harris, however, insisted that this direct disciplining of the will had limited efficacy, and he advocated it only for very young children. Ultimately he wanted the child brought to the point of freely and voluntarily accepting discipline and authority. For this to happen, the child had to appreciate the underlying rationality of social existence. As a Hegelian, Harris held that whatever was rational was necessary. So, as he said in one of his St. Louis school reports, education emancipated by giving insight into the origins and function of the " 'conventionalities of society'—*thus into their necessity.*"

The school's job was to supply children with the tools that enabled them to appreciate the common stock of ideas and cultural values of the civilization of which they were a part. Harris called these tool subjects "the windows of the soul." He listed them as: grammar, the mastery of the word; arithmetic, the mastery of numbers; geography, the mastery over place; history, the mastery over time. Once they had mastered these subjects, the students could approach the world of intelligence, studying the literature and art of their civilization. Once they perceived its underlying rationality and accepted their culture, once it had become "a living reality," children could participate in that culture—no longer isolated, no longer alienated.

To be prepared for the exigencies of modern life, the child had to gain insight into the reasonableness of moral commands. Harris was quick to point out that this was a political necessity in America. If the schools aimed for unreasoning obedience from their pupils, they were preparing future adults who would give unreasoning obedience to a demagogue or to a leader in crime. So without the proper education, the masses, especially the immigrant masses, would remain alienated, corrupting the body politic. In a speech delivered to the NEA in 1874 Harris explained that "all the evils which we suffer politically may be traced to the existence of an immense mass of ignorant, illiterate, or semi-educated people who assist in governing the country while they possess no insight into the true nature of the issues which they attempt to decide."

Combining the skills of the practical schoolman with an intensely idealistic philosophy, Harris was, in Lawrence Cremin's words, "the commanding figure of his pedagogical era." In 1889 he became U.S. Commissioner of Education, serving in this position until 1906. Few people have ever had such widespread influence over the American schools. At the time of his death in 1909 a contemporary observed that Harris was "the most quoted," "the best loved," "the most widely known," and the most influential "educator in this or any other country." In him the hierarchical reformers had found a vital force, one that made reasonable Charles Francis Adams's boast to a political club in New York City that: "we do not care which [party] is in office and which is in opposition . . . we who manage the schools, the press, the shops, the railroads, and the exchanges . . . are moving this country, you run the political machine."

In the last decades of the nineteenth century the hierarchs had control of American education from the bottom to the top. Under the forceful guidance of William T. Harris, the American schools now prepared citizens who accepted rational authority, citizens who accepted the leadership of men of superior intelligence and virtue. To complement the influence of Harris on the schools, the hierarchs had in their camp the most important man in higher education, the president of Harvard University, Charles W. Eliot.

IV

Charles W. Eliot was a patrician to the core. He was born in Boston in 1834 to a family that traced its roots in New England back to the late seventeenth century. For generations the family name had been familiar to Harvard students. Charles's grandfather, a prosperous merchant, had founded the Eliot Professorship in Greek. His father had served as treasurer of the university. One cousin, Charles Eliot Norton, was an established Harvard professor; another cousin served as a member of the Board of Overseers. With these family ties, no one thought it strange that young Charles became an instructor in mathematics at Harvard, after receiving his B.A. from that institution in 1853. Then, after President Hill resigned in 1868, no one was too surprised to hear that the Board of Overseers had selected the thirty-five-year-old Charles Eliot for the job of president.

At the time of his appointment to the presidency, Eliot held a position at Massachusetts Institute of Technology as a professor of chemistry. This M.I.T. background made some of the Harvard faculty uneasy—the arts people feared having a scientist as president, the scientists worried about having as president a man from a school of technology. Reluctantly, they finally approved the appointment. Within three years their new president had reformed the law school, purged the medical school, and established a graduate school.

Before appointing the new president, the Board of Overseers had expressed the desire to transform Harvard into a "noble University," a "seat of learning which shall attract the best teachers and most ardent students, a university which shall retain all the good of the past and go forward to welcome the advancing light of the future." When they elected Charles W. Eliot, they picked the right man. In his inaugural address he presented a declaration of beliefs that guided him for his forty years as president. Not that Eliot had any master plan for Harvard University in 1869. He merely expressed his firm commitment to the task of transforming Harvard into a great, national institution. Doctrinaire, firm, supremely self-assured, the young president proceeded to turn Harvard University over "like a flapjack." At a meeting of the medical faculty where new reforms were proposed, one of the senior professors asked: "How is it that this faculty has gone for 80 years managing its own affairs and doing it well—and now within three or four months it is proposed to change all our modes of carrying on the school?" Eliot, who was present, immediately spoke up: "I can answer [the doctor's] question very easily. There is a new president."

There was a new president, and he was strong and determined. By 1871, three years after taking office, he had reorganized the medical school. Instead of getting their salaries directly from their students' lecture fees, as had been customary, all medical professors now received regular salaries from the university, and students paid regular tuition fees to the university. Eliot initiated stiff entrance examinations where none had existed before. Prior to his reforms, a future physician had only sixteen weeks of required attendance at lectures. The only examination he took was a final oral, where he had to receive a passing grade from five of the nine professors who quizzed him for ten minutes each. Eliot asked for, and got, a required three-year course of study for all candidates together with a series of written examinations to be taken at the end of each year.

Other universities soon copied the reforms Eliot inaugurated at Harvard. Medical schools were soon set up on this model at the University of Michigan and the University of Pennsylvania. And in similar fashion, other institutions followed the lead of Harvard in reforming their law schools. In 1870, Eliot brought Christopher Langdell into the school that three practicing lawyers had been conducting as the Harvard Law School. With Eliot's encouragement and support, Langdell drew up a three-year course of study, replete with written examinations. Most important, he introduced the revolutionary "case method" of studying law. By 1893 Christopher Langdell had become the first dean of the Harvard Law School, making it the first graduate school of law in the nation.

After revolutionizing both medical and law education, Eliot created in 1872 a third professional school, the Graduate School of Arts and Science. Now the serious student, instead of going abroad for advanced training, could study and prepare for a Master of Art degree or a Doctor of Philosophy degree at Harvard University. Harvard could not claim a first here, however. Yale University had established, twenty years earlier, a graduate school of arts and science, which remained definitely subordinate to the undergraduate program. Would this be the case at Harvard? Wasn't there a real danger that a graduate school would weaken the college? Eliot, as always, had a ready answer. The graduate school, he said, "will strengthen the college. As long as our teachers regard their work as simply giving so many courses for undergraduates, we shall never have first-class teaching here. If they have to teach undergraduate students as well as graduates, they will regard their subjects as infinite and keep up that constant investigation which is necessary for first-class teaching."

Under Eliot's guiding hand, Harvard did become a great national university. True, reforms in the medical and law schools resulted in an initial decline in enrollments. This brought a typical nostrum from the unflappable Eliot: "the only way to drive people out of a school permanently is to let it be a poor school." He was, of course, correct, and before the end of the seventies enrollments in both schools had risen above the pre-reform days. Most important, the number of students from outside the New England area had doubled. By the end of Eliot's forty-year tenure as president, Harvard had become the largest and wealthiest university in the country. In 1869 he had inherited a faculty of 60; he bequeathed one of 600. When Eliot took office, Harvard had an endowment of $2 million; when he left, that endowment equaled $20 million.

Of all his reforms none did more to transform Harvard University than the undergraduate elective system. This, Eliot said in 1894, "has proved to be the most generally useful piece of work which the university has ever executed." Electives existed at Harvard University before Eliot came on the scene, but as peripheral subjects, inferior to the prescribed studies. Eliot proceeded slowly but surely to abolish all prescribed subjects, finishing the job in the nineties. This extension of the principle of election to the exclusion of all prescribed subjects rendered all subjects of equal worth—the notion of equivalence of studies. Under the "radical electivism" of Eliot, students were free to choose their own course of studies.

While many commentators, including Eliot's immediate successor, President Lowell, have complained about the quality of the education Harvard students received, or elected, under this system, few have noted the impact of this elective system on the quality of education that Harvard professors provided for students. Radical electivism was a lever that Eliot used to widen the scope and increase the depth of studies pursued at Harvard. In this laissez-faire atmosphere, each course, each professor, each department was in competition for students. To secure students, one had to be a top-flight teacher, and have something meaningful and significant to teach. In addition to improving the caliber of instruction, free, or radical, election brought about an enormous increase in the number of subjects, courses, and faculty. This meant that the Harvard undergraduate could receive a broader and a deeper education than ever before. Nevertheless, to many professors the elective system was a form of blackmail. They opposed a system that had such built-in pressures—on their subjects, their courses, their teaching, their very personalities. Their most effective argument was that American college students were too immature to choose wisely; they chose courses flippantly, or in accord with the laxity or popularity of the professor. These opponents assumed an ideal of the educated person, which, they said, was not being attained by students freely electing their courses of study. Eliot, of course, had his own ideal of the educated person: the expert. Indeed all of his reforms—the professional schools, the graduate school, and the elective system for undergraduates—were of a piece. All contributed to the creation of experts.

In establishing an institution of higher education that functioned to train experts, Charles Eliot differed from most of the hierarch reformers of his day. They, for the most part, looked to the college to turn out an elite steeped in the genteel tradition—persons of culture, persons of virtue. These educated people, they felt, had claim to authority, not because of any technical competence, but because they possessed a liberal education, which gave them general competence and the right to lead. Eliot, who was more aware than most of the changing times, maintained that the college graduate's claim to leadership must be based upon technical competency. He constantly argued that the American failures of government—at all levels—could be traced to the refusal to employ experts. "The democracy must learn," he argued, "in governmental affairs, whether municipal, state, or national, to employ experts and to abide by their decisions." Like other hierarchs, Eliot sought to restrict popular deliberation. But he not only distrusted the masses to run the government, he also distrusted the "educated man" who had no expertise. "Such complicated subjects as taxation, finance, and public works, cannot be wisely managed by popular assemblies or their committees," he cautioned, "nor by executive officers who have no special acquaintance with these most difficult subjects."

As Eliot saw it, unless the universities trained experts, there would be no check on the masses. The hierarchs had placed their faith in the power of elementary education, which would make the masses, in Carl Schurz's words, "open, accessible, susceptible to the influence of superior knowledge and culture when they came in contact with it." But Schurz had not explained just how this was to be done. William Harris, on the other hand, had relied upon a Hegelian faith that the authority of the elite would be a rational authority that the masses, trained to "reasonable obedience," would accept. Lacking Harris's Hegelian faith, Charles Eliot wanted elementary (and secondary) schools to make the masses aware of their limitations. Then, he concluded, they would be willing to trust most of the tasks of government to the experts. The masses could be made aware of their limitations if the schools would concentrate on training them how to think. Once people learned the importance of accurate observation, exact description, and correct inference, then they would "naturally acquire a respect for these powers when exhibited by others in fields unknown to them." People who have been trained to think will recognize that their own competence is limited to a few subjects and "will come to respect and confide in the experts in every field of human activity."

Perhaps because he never held political office, Eliot clearly saw that one need not hold political office in order to exert political influence. He realized that legislators and administrators increasingly came to depend upon "the researches of scholars, men of science, and historians and follow in the footsteps of inventors, economists, and political philosophers." These experts, he felt, were the ones who exerted the real power in America. But Eliot was not so naïve as to discount the importance of institutions as well as people. He realized the political power of a great institution like Harvard University. By fulfilling his commitment to make Harvard University into a great national institution, Charles Eliot provided the surest guarantee that people would listen when one of its experts spoke—be he or she an alumnus, a professor, or the president.

V

In 1906, William T. Harris retired from his post as U.S. Commissioner of Education. Three years later he died. In the same year Charles W. Eliot stepped down from the presidency of Harvard University. An educational era had ended. The influence on education these "hierarchical reformers" had shared now passed to a new band of reformers, called progressives. Like their predecessors, these new educational reformers took their cues from the political scene, turning to the schools to help solve political problems.

The political problems in America had changed in the years since 1870, when the hierarchs zeroed in on political corruption. They had divined the root of this corruption in the unholy alliance between the businessmen and the politicians. But as early as the 1890s things began to change. By then many of the infamous spoilsmen had passed to their just rewards. At the same time, many businessmen, fed up with paying ever-increasing amounts of money to the politicians, decided to enter politics themselves. In 1888, for example, a New York banker, Levi Morton, entered the White House as Benjamin Harrison's vice-president. Moreover, the cabinet of this administration included the merchant John Wanamaker, and Redfield Proctor, the so-called marble king of Vermont. People called it the "Businessman's Cabinet." The entrance of businessmen into politics was even more pronounced in the Senate. This body came to be called the "millionaire's club." There one found lumbermen, bankers, industrialists, publishers, and railroad magnates. These businessmen senators rapidly became a ruling clique that, according to Thomas Cochran and William Miller, "controlled every bill that tried to run the gauntlet of the Senate." The highpoint of this period came in 1896, when Mark Hanna, a capitalist turned political boss, maneuvered William McKinley into the White House.

This emergence of business politics in the eighties and nineties was not precipitated solely by the businessmen's reluctance to continue paying the politicians. The businessmen's decision to enter the political arena was also due to their fears of the increasing agrarian discontent. During the eighties and nineties, the farmers became louder and louder in their denunciation of the existing economic order. They had begun to complain right after the Civil War, when farm prices began to decline. Some analysts explained the low prices in terms of the law of supply and demand: the farmers had increased production, so the selling price, naturally, went down. But the farmers would have none of this. They blamed their plight on the middlemen—the railroads, the grain elevators. The cost of storage and transportation ate up all their profits. Frequently the complaint was heard that it cost a bushel of corn to send a bushel of corn to market. There were other villains. The manufacturers of farm equipment—protected from foreign competitors by the high tariff—charged exorbitant prices for their wares, the farmers argued. Another group that took advantage of them was the bankers and moneylenders. They had steered the economy into a strict hard-money policy, which worked adversely on debtors.

It was the vociferous complaints of the farmers that had induced Congress to pass the legislation purported to eliminate these evils: the Interstate Commerce Act (1887), and the Wilson-Gorman Tariff Act (1894). As noted earlier, none of these laws did what they were supposed to do. This, naturally, fanned the flame of agrarian discontent, and in the nineties the farmers turned to politics themselves, forming a People's party. This Populist party called for truly revolutionary changes, including public ownership of the railroads, a drastic lowering of the tariff, and an inflationary monetary policy based upon free silver.

The radical thrust of the Populists, which in the South included a black–white coalition, frightened many Americans into voting against them. The 1896 election sealed their fate when the American people rejected the Populist candidate, William Jennings Bryan, and chose instead the businessman's president, William McKinley. After this abortive escapade, the Populist party disappeared from the scene. But the evils that the Populists had decried continued to haunt the American public. The accusations the Populists had made could not be ignored: Political power had fallen into the hands of the rich. The United States was ruled by a plutocracy.

In the last years of the nineteenth century, these charges gained more credence as the people witnessed the proliferation of gigantic, monopolistic corporations. In 1898 there were 82 trusts in America. Within the next six years 234 additional trusts appeared, with a capitalization of over $6 million. These trusts included such giants as Consolidated Tobacco, Amalgamated Copper, American Smelting and Refining, and largest of all, United States Steel.

Could this plutocracy be destroyed? For that matter, should it be destroyed, or would its destruction serve to destroy America itself? The Populists had wanted to destroy the plutocracy. They had aimed for a revolution. But the voters had rejected them because of the fear that such a revolution would undermine the very progress and prosperity Americans had enjoyed since the Civil War. Was reform compatible with progress? It was their affirmative answer to this last question that hurled the progressives into political prominence.

VI

Theodore Roosevelt, perhaps the leading progressive politician of the era, sincerely believed in the compatibility—the necessary connection—between progress and reform. He distinguished, for example, between "good trusts" and "bad trusts." In 1902 he said, "Our aim is not to do away with corporations; on the contrary, these big aggregations are an inevitable development of modern industrialism, and the effort to destroy them would be futile unless accomplished in ways that would work the utmost mischief to the entire body politic . . . We draw the line against misconduct, not against wealth." Roosevelt argued that regulation rather than dissolution was the answer. "The government," he wrote "must now interfere to protect labor, to subordinate the big corporation to the public welfare, and to shackle cunning and fraud exactly as centuries before it had interfered to shackle the physical force which does wrong by violence . . ." In pursuing his policy of regulating "bad trusts," he carried out forty-three proceedings for violations of the Sherman Anti-Trust Act.

The progressives stood for increased governmental powers of regulation and control. Roosevelt called for effective regulation of railroads, for federal child-labor legislation, direct income and inheritance taxes, curbs on labor injunctions, federal inspection and regulation of foods and drugs, and protection of the nation's natural resources. He got some of his demands, but some had to await the progressive administrations of his successors, Taft and Wilson. Their administrations expanded and strengthened the power of the government to control the trusts; they also lowered the tariff and reformed the banking credit and currency system.

The federal government was not alone in its attempt to protect the American economy from domination by the plutocracy. The state governments, caught up in the progressive movement, passed legislation to protect workers and employees from exploitation. With Wisconsin and Oregon usually leading the way, state legislatures passed laws to curtail or regulate the child and female labor laws, to establish health and safety standards in industry, laws setting up minimum wages and maximum hours, laws providing workmen's compensation.

During this period progressivism also dominated local or municipal government. Here too, the reformers expanded the powers of government to

restrict and curtail the plutocracy. Led by reformers like Tom Johnson, mayor
of Cleveland from 1901 to 1909, the progressives called for, and frequently got,
public ownership of the streetcar system and other utilities that served the
cities. They passed new municipal tax laws to replace those that granted privileges or immunities to the plutocracy.

In a special sense, as Richard Hofstadter has shown, the progressives were
the spiritual heirs of the liberal reformers. Both the progressives and the liberal reformers worried about the power and influence of the plutocracy. The
liberals, who subscribed to the ideology of hierarchy, thought that the political problem was a moral one and believed that the solution lay in having men
of superior virtue and intellect exert influence over the polity. The progressives, however, subscribed to the ideology of individualism and saw the political problem as one of restoring equality of opportunity. The liberals had
wanted to restrict governmental power. Only in this way, they thought, could
the unholy alliance between politics and business be destroyed. The progressives, on the other hand, wanted to expand government power. They wanted
the government to regulate, control, and restrict the powerful business interests. The progressives were the first to denounce the doctrine of limited government and laissez-faire. In practice few government administrations had
successfully adhered to this doctrine, but none had ever rejected the doctrine
itself. From the beginning, Americans of all political persuasions had opposed
the idea of strong government. They had traditionally equated strong government with tyranny. But now at the end of the nineteenth century the progressives pointed out that the plutocrats, in fact, had become the tyrants in America. Moreover they insisted that the government was the only institution able
to resist or eliminate the powerful plutocracy and restore equality of opportunity.

Americans, however, would not give up their commitment to weak government without some guarantee that a strong government would not itself
become tyrannical. Here we come to the heart of the progressive movement,
the essence of its political philosophy. If the American democracy became truly
a democracy, the progressives argued—if the people participated more fully
in governmental decisions; if they, in short, became the government itself—
then the perennial fears of strong government would disappear. The people
could not fear government if they were themselves that government. The
genius of progressivism lay in its adoption of a wide variety of strategies to
increase public participation in political and governmental decisions. The progressives did not invent all of these devices. Some they copied from abroad,
like the Australian secret ballot; some they stole from the Populists, like
the direct primary and the initiative and referendum. These devices, used at
all levels of government, would permit the people to participate in direct
democracy.

Across the nation, progressive reformers in the cities fought for and got
municipal home rule. This right to form their own charters permitted many
cities to inaugurate direct democratic practices—the initiative, the referendum,
and recall of public officials. At the state level, some states not only adopted

the direct primary, the initiative, and referendum, but went on to set up commissions, committees, and leagues of interested and knowledgeable citizens as part of the government machinery. Under the progressive governor Robert La Follette, for example, the state of Wisconsin established a railroad commission as well as an industrial commission to regulate health and safety conditions in the future. At the national level, the progressives secured two amendments to the constitution that served the cause of direct democracy; one, the seventeenth amendment, provided for the direct election of senators; the other, the nineteenth, gave nationwide suffrage to women.

The progressives' theory of direct democracy assigned a central role to the schools. Americans had long insisted that a democracy required an educated citizenry. Now the progressives' hope of creating a direct participant democracy meant an even greater demand for an educated citizenry. The very success of this direct democracy depended on the schools. To fulfill this political function, the schools now required a new, progressive theory of education.

VII

So long as they had insisted upon weak government, Americans had to contend with the danger of anarchy, and they had depended upon the schools for protection. The common schools—free and open to all—had the task of taming, civilizing, Americanizing all who attended. In the common schools the schoolmaster molded, shaped, and formed the character of the young, training them so that later as adults they would abhor anarchy. This education would produce citizens who would live in an orderly, law-abiding way in a society that was free from the coercion of a strong government. Foreign observers had noticed this strange American commitment to "anarchy plus a schoolmaster." De Tocqueville, for example, had noted in the 1840s that "in the United States politics are the end and aim of education." He also pointed out that "in the United States instruction of the people powerfully contributes to the support of the democratic republic; and such must always be the case, I believe, when the institution which enlightens the understanding is not separated from the moral education which amends the heart."

When in the twentieth century the progressives abandoned limited government, this link between the schools and democracy became even more crucial. Once the government was free to grow and become strong, the danger of anarchy disappeared. But in its place arose the danger of governmental tyranny. And, as we have seen, the progressives hoped to ward off this danger by creating a participant democracy, so that the people themselves became the government. Many progressives realized that, if people were ever fully to anticipate and contribute to the processes of government, then a new kind of education was called for. A participant democracy needed schools that would release and unblock people, schools that could uncover and help develop the capabilities and talents of every citizen.

The old education, that traditionally given in the common public schools, tried to tame children and mold them into respectable people who controlled their passions. Frequently their school experience repressed the children and stifled their talents. The progressives urged the schools to forget their traditional role as "the great stabilizer" of American society, in favor of a new role as "the great liberator." The progressives believed that, once the schools helped children realize their own particular talents and abilities, once the school "liberated" them, then they could make a more worthy contribution to the political life of the society, enriching the quality of direct democracy.

In this new quest to liberate the child, American educators began to advocate what has been labeled a "child-centered" theory of education. This child-centered theory had first been voiced by Jean Jacques Rousseau in the eighteenth century, when he advised teachers to begin "by making a more careful study of your scholars, for it is clear that you know nothing about them." In *Emile,* Rousseau had charted the normal, or natural, development of children, which, he insisted, should guide educational practices. But his conception of human development had been purely speculative, based upon his own limited experience. After the time of Rousseau a science of human development came into being, a science greatly influenced by the theories of Charles Darwin. These scientists of human development saw the child as an evolving organism, and they hoped to determine scientifically just how the child evolved. Once educators knew how children developed, they would be better prepared to foster and aid that development by clearing away obstacles that might block or retard it.

One of the most influential of these scientists of human nature was G. Stanley Hall, a psychologist, once referred to by a contemporary as "the Darwin of the mind." Human development, according to Hall, followed the general psychonomic law which stated "ontogeny recapitulates phylogeny." This meant that, as the individual organism, the child, matures, it recapitulates the evolution of the human race, going through the same or similar stages that the race itself had gone through. By means of numerous questionnaires, Hall accumulated a mass of data to support this theory of human development.

In 1901, in the early days of the progressive movement, Hall gave what Charles Strickland and Charles Burgess have called his single most important pronouncement on education. Speaking at the NEA convention, Hall presented a paper entitled "The Ideal School as Based on Child Study." He described his school as "pediocentric" (child-centered). Instead of fitting the child to the school, Hall wanted teachers to fit the school to the child. In the ideal school, the child would develop naturally, while the teacher kept "out of nature's way," defending "the happiness and rights of children." Hall's conception of children as plants, with the teacher as a kind of gardener who protects them from harm while allowing them to grow and develop according to their nature, is not unlike that of Friedrich Froebel, the German educator who originated the kindergarten—"the children garden." Hall recognized Froebel as one of the "deepest of all modern educational thinkers."

Although Hall found himself in agreement with Froebel, he found others who disagreed with him. For many Americans, including Hall's former teacher, William James, the recapitulation conception of human development smacked too much of determinism. James, a staunch opponent of determinism, propounded an entirely different conception of human development, yet one still within the framework of evolution. He saw people as free agents interacting with their environment. Out of this interaction between the self and the environment, one develops habits, which James called "the flywheel of human behavior." By the time we reach adult life, according to James, "ninety-nine hundredths, or, possibly, nine hundred and ninety-nine thousandths of our activity is purely automatic and habitual." A person is nothing more than a "walking bundle of habits."

As early as 1892 James had urged teachers to use the findings of the psychologists, "which may enable you to labor more easily and effectively in the several schoolrooms over which you preside." In his *Talks to Teachers* he insisted that "the teacher's supreme concern should be to ingrain into the pupil that assortment of habits that should be most useful to him throughout life." In James's theory of instruction then, we find that the teacher does not, as Hall proposed, stand aside and allow matters to take their course. Instead, the teacher must select those habits he or she wants the child to acquire, and then proceed to "ingrain them into the pupil." James's theory of human development was not based upon any empirical procedures; thus, he never determined just how habits came into being. This empirical task was carried on by another of his famous pupils, Edward Lee Thorndike.

Taking James's view of habits as the result of the interaction between the self and the environment, Thorndike tried to search out the scientific laws that accounted for this phenomenon. Using a "problem-box" and a supply of chickens, cats, and other small animals, Thorndike discovered that, after a series of trials, a boxed animal more quickly pressed the lever that released it from the problem-box. He called this "learning." At this point Thorndike used the terms "situation" and "response" to describe the interaction of the self with its environment. The environment or situation (e.g., trapped in a "problem-box") calls forth a response from the organism (e.g., stepping on the lever that opens the door). When a specific response becomes "wedded" to a specific situation, when, that is, the same situation always calls forth the same response from the organism, then we can say that learning has taken place. We might use James's term and say that a habit has been formed; or, in Thorndike's terminology, we might say that the organism has become conditioned. After looking at interaction in terms of situation–response, Thorndike was able to discover the laws that explained how a specific response became wedded or connected to a specific situation. One of the most famous of these laws of learning is "the law of effect" according to which responses that are *rewarded* are "stamped in."

Thorndike, like James, had the teacher deciding what habits or connections to ingrain into the students. He had developed a fairly sophisticated theory of instruction, but it was not the theory the progressives were looking for. In spite of the fact that Thorndike and James looked at the child as an evolving organism, and the teacher as an agent to maximize that evolution or development, the role they gave the teacher was too authoritative for the progressives. The progressives did not want the teacher to supply a set of fixed goals for the students. They wanted the teacher to bring out the potential talents of each student, no matter what these might be. The work of James and Thorndike merely provided a psychological theory of instruction that gave support to the old ways of training, molding, and forming children according to some set of fixed aims.

On the other hand, Hall's theory of instruction was no more acceptable to the progressives because of its implicit determinism. According to Hall the child will—if left alone and protected by the teacher—naturally realize his or her fullest development. But one could never be sure that this would, in fact, occur. The progressives wanted a theory of instruction that had the teacher guide and direct the development of the child, without, at the same time, imposing his or her goals on that child's growth. John Dewey provided just such a theory.

VIII

Like both James and Thorndike, John Dewey saw human development, or growth, in terms of the interaction between the self and the environment. This interaction he called "experience." He cautioned, however, that not all experience contributes to growth, or, put another way, not all experience is educative. Educative, or growth-producing, experiences are those that alter our traditional patterns of behavior in such a way that we are better able to function in the world in which we live.

Dewey viewed people as goal-seeking organisms. People act purposefully. So long as they are behaving rationally, their behavior is directed toward some "end-in-view." The environment sustains this behavior, or this activity. Thus, one is able to walk to the store to buy a six-pack because there is a sidewalk to walk on, traffic lights to permit crossing streets, a store supplied with beverages, and so forth. However, the environment not only sustains activity, it sometimes frustrates or hinders pursuit of the end-in-view. The store, for example, might be out of what I want. When the environment presents us with obstacles, hindrances, or frustrations, we have the initial and necessary conditions for growth or development. People, Dewey insisted, grow or develop only when they are confronted with problems, or have what he called "felt difficulties." In trying to overcome a difficulty, hindrance, or problem, people must alter their traditional behavior. Sometimes they must develop new ways of behaving. If the new behavior overcomes the difficulty and solves the problem, then we can say that the organism has developed, has grown.

There are, Dewey said, definite steps the organism takes in creating new ways of behavior. These steps are no less than the scientific method. People grow through making experiments. Like a scientist, they encounter problems, formulate hypotheses, and test them. When the hypothesis works out in practice, when it is confirmed, then the problem is solved, the difficulties overcome. Thus, when I discover that the store is out of my regular brand I might look for another store, or try a new brand. Each of these suggestions can serve as a hypothesis that I could test. In this case the test would be: does this way of behaving satisfy the need I feel for my usual beverage? If none of these hypotheses meets the test, I keep searching for one that does. When I discover a hypothesis that works out, then I have developed a way of behaving that will be appropriate whenever I again encounter the same problem. Or I might even switch brands, or become a steady customer of another store, or make some other new radical change in my traditional behavior. Whatever course of action I take, if I solve my problem, then I have furthered my ability to cope with, or function in, the world in which I live.

This theory of human development provided Dewey with the basis for a theory of instruction in which the teachers could guide and direct the growth of a child without imposing their own goals on the child's growth. The teacher's primary task is to supply the child with problems, the initial and necessary conditions for growth. The teacher must exercise care in selecting the problems, since they must be the *child's* problems, not the teachers. So the problems must consist of obstacles to the pupil's own ends-in-view. Moreover, care must be taken to ensure that the child is ready to confront the problem—ready psychologically, physiologically, and intellectually. When possible the problems should not be totally novel but should have some connection to, or continuity with, the child's past experiences. Finally, if an experience is to be truly educative the teacher must pay attention to the quality of the experience. That is, the experience must not be a disagreeable one that might repel the student, and at the same time it must be an effective experience, one that "will live fruitfully and creatively in subsequent experience."

For Dewey there were no "ends" or "goals" in education, nothing fixed and determinate. Education was growth, and growth was a process with no end, or goal, save further growth. The teacher had the job of maximizing the possibilities for growth, both present and future, by supplying children with *real* problems, helping them to formulate hypotheses and guiding them in testing them. In this way children learned how to learn—they learned the scientific method of discovery.

Dewey's theory of instruction became the instructional theory of the progressives. By taking the growth of the child as his central concern and by analyzing the process of growth itself in terms of the scientific method, Dewey provided a theory of instruction that liberated the child, and still provided a crucial, guiding role for the teacher.

John Dewey went further. He gave the progressives a theory of education as well as a theory of instruction, a theory of education that cast the school into the role of model for a truly participant democracy. In the schools, Dewey admitted, the child may acquire technical, specialized ability in algebra, Latin, or botany. But if this is mere "isolated intellectual learning," then the school contradicts its own aim. Its aim is to educate the child, but unless the child understands "the meaning which things have in life of which he is a part," he or she is not educated, merely trained. Students, Dewey said, had to acquire the "social sense" or the "social direction" of the "disposition acquired." One way to do this, he suggested, was to engage in joint activities that call these technical abilities into play. Therefore, the problems teachers confront their students with should be *shared problems* that will generate this joint activity. These shared problems must be "real" problems; that is, problems that "reflect the life of the larger society." This makes the school an embryonic community, in which the child is saturated "with the spirit of service," and provided "with the instruments of effective self-direction." In this way, Dewey concludes, "we shall have the deepest and best guarantee of a larger society which is worthy, lovely, and harmonious."

For Dewey then the school was to be the model for the larger society precisely because democracy, participant democracy, is nothing more than people engaging in joint activity to solve their common or shared problems. With Dewey progressive political theory became one with progressive educational theory. Democracy for him was more than a form of government; it was a way of life, and children would learn that way of life in the American schools.

IX

John Dewey's educational theory clearly exposes the epistemological differences between the earlier liberal reformers and the progressives. The liberal reformers were pessimists. They had lost faith in the ability of the masses to know the truth, much less to use it as a guide to action. So they designed an educational program to produce both an elite who would lead and a disciplined mass that would willingly accept the rational, virtuous leadership of that elite.

The progressives, in contrast, were epistemological optimists. They believed that all men could perceive the truth once it was made manifest. Moreover, they believed that all men would use this truth as a guide to action. The progressives' educational program, Dewey's version of it, envisions a society wherein all citizens are nothing less than scientists, working together and jointly solving their common problems.

The same optimism is reflected in higher education during the progressive era. The liberal reformers had looked to colleges and universities to supply a cadre of leaders. Through civil service examinations these college graduates were to gain access to positions of political power. The progressive, in contrast, stressed the power of ideas, rather than the power of people. They showed less enthusiasm for civil service reform, concentrating instead on developing ways of releasing and promulgating information, facts, knowledge, and ideas to the masses. The best example of a progressive university during this period was the University of Wisconsin. Here, Charles Van Hise, who served as president from 1903 to 1918, declared that he expected the university to "carry out knowledge to the people."

At Wisconsin a vast network of agencies came into being to perform this task of carrying knowledge to the people. Correspondence courses were established in all fields of study. And to supplement this the university conducted college extension classes throughout the state. In addition, it set up institutes, held conferences, promoted lectures, and designed exhibits to educate all people in all places "for the daily occupations of life." Perhaps the creation of the Department of General Information and Welfare expresses best the service function the university had now adopted. This was a clearinghouse of almost any kind of service or information, serving individuals, clubs, cities, counties, or commercial organizations. Frederick Howe described it as the "questions and answers department of the state."

While the liberal reformers had looked to the colleges and universities to supply leaders, or even experts, the progressives now looked to them for consultants. Unlike leaders and experts, consultants make no policy decisions; they only advise. During this period the University of Wisconsin provided a host of advisers and consultants. By 1908, for example, forty-one members of the faculty were serving as members of one or more state commissions. In fact, Van Hise and one of his deans each sat on five state commissions. Many have referred to the University of Wisconsin of this period as "the fourth branch of government." What this quip distorts is the important though obvious fact that the university had no intention of becoming an official branch of the state government, nor did its faculty want to get into political offices. The job of the university was to reveal the truth—to the politicians as well as the people. And so long as those in office were open and ready to receive the truth, it did not make too much difference who they were or what political party they represented.

X

The First World War broke the back of political progressivism. Robert La Follette had argued against American entry into the war, predicting that this would "set progress back a generation." Even Woodrow Wilson, when he finally decided that America must enter the conflict, did so with forebodings of gloom. The night before he asked Congress to declare war, he confided to newspaperman Frank Cobb: "To fight you must be brutal and ruthless, and the spirit of ruthless brutality will enter into the very fiber of our national life, infecting Congress, the courts, the policeman on the beat, the man in the street."

Knowing that the progressive impulse was rooted in a humanitarian concern for others, Wilson tried to preserve these humanitarian feelings by couching the entry into the war, and the later peace negotiations, in the language and rhetoric of the progressive movement itself. He explained intervention in lofty phrases, using moral terms to justify America's role—tying it to altruism and to self-sacrifice. America was opening a crusade to make the world safe for democracy. But, as Hofstadter has observed, by linking the war to progressive rhetoric and progressive values, Wilson unintentionally ensured that the American people would repudiate progressivism, when they ultimately, but inevitably, repudiated the war.

During the twenties, Americans euphemistically referred to their repudiation of the war as "the return to normalcy." At this point hedonism replaced the spirit of self-sacrifice, the sense of responsibility gave way to neglect, and civic participation disappeared in the face of widespread apathy. Progressivism was dead. The participant democracy the progressives had hoped to create never materialized. During the twenties the initiative, the referendum, and recall were invoked sparingly. Moreover, when the practices introduced by the progressives were actually used, they produced little change in the political or economic situation. Female suffrage made no appreciable difference, nor did the direct election of senators. And the direct primary left nominations where they had always been, in the hands of party managers. Summarizing the impact of progressivism on the twenties, Eric Goldman has concluded that "the most conspicuous result was the lack of any result."

In the twenties American intellectuals bade farewell to reform, losing all hopes of creating a participant democratic society. To many, reform and democracy seemed incompatible. After all it was a democratic society that now tolerated the Ku Klux Klan, jailed Sacco and Vanzetti, staged the Scopes Trial, and imposed a nationwide prohibition on alcoholic beverages. Henry L. Mencken, one of the heroes of the age, declared that democracy in the end came to nothing but the mob, which was "sodden, brutal, and ignorant." Mencken made interest in social questions ludicrous and unfashionable. Democracy became a farce. "All the known facts lie flatly against it." It was he who wrote, "I enjoy democracy enormously. It is incomparably idiotic, and hence incomparably amusing." Mencken stirred up violent opposition, but not against his political satire. Few cared. "It was characteristic of the Jazz Age," said F. Scott Fitzgerald, "that it had no interest in politics at all."

During this apolitical period, a group of educators in 1919 founded an organization they named the Progressive Education Association (PEA). Ignoring the union between political and educational progressivism that John Dewey had forged a few years earlier in *Democracy and Education,* the leaders of this new association set out to impose the dogma of child-centered pedagogy on American educational reform. The Progressive Education Association ignored the political function of the schools, disregarding thereby the fact that American educational reform had come into being as an integral part of American political reforms. Nothing better illustrates how oblivious these educators were to this than their choice of Charles W. Eliot as the first honorary president of the PEA. Significantly, John Dewey refused to join. After the death of Eliot in 1926, he finally did accept the honorary presidency.

According to Stanwood Cobb, the first executive secretary, the early members of the PEA "aimed at nothing short of reforming the entire school system of America." But as Lawrence Cremin has noted, "one looks in vain for the reformism that had been the leitmotif of the movement before 1919." Severed from its connection with political progressivism, progressive education lost its momentum as a reform movement, becoming merely a pedagogical attitude. The editor of *Progressive Education,* writing about the 1926 conference of the PEA, reported that "each speaker had his own intimate message and no two would agree on the ramifications of technique. Yet all were invested and animated with an inquisitive attitude, a searching for the best way to enrich and to cultivate the essence of children. . . . Progressive education can never formulate more than an inquisitive attitude. Each child is a law unto himself."

During the twenties the main work of the PEA was in the area of "creative expression." *Progressive Education* devoted a number of special issues to this theme in the fields of art, literature, music, and dramatics. "Creative expression" was the central theme of the decade's most representative educational book, *The Child-Centered School*, written by Harold Rugg and Ann Shumaker. In the child-centered school, they exclaimed, "the lid of restraint is being lifted from the child in order that he may come to his own best self fulfillment." "The new school," they wrote,

> assumes that every child is endowed with the capacity to express himself, and that this innate capacity is immensely worth cultivating. The pupil is placed in an atmosphere conducive to self-expression in every aspect. Some will create with words, others with light. Some will express themselves through the body in the dance; others will model, carve, shape their idea in plastic materials. Still others will find expression through oral languages, and some through an integrated physical, emotional dramatic gesture. But whatever the route, the medium, the materials—each one has some capacity for expression.

The authors of *The Child-Centered School* related this child-centered education to John Dewey's concept of growth. They thought that this concept "cut through the crust of the disciplinary conception of education," uncovering what they took to be the most crucial question of all: "How shall the activities and materials of instruction be organized to guarantee maximum child growth?" Rugg and Shumaker were not alone in finding a rationale for child-centered education in John Dewey's theory of instruction. And like the others who bolstered "creative expression" by references to Dewey's conception of growth, they ignored his *theory of education,* which made the growth of the individual the means to create a community, a participant democracy. These "progressive" educators of the apolitical twenties showed little concern for this side of John Dewey. As Rugg himself later confessed, they were "radical in educational method . . . but not in social philosophy." Then, after 1929, things began to change. After 1929 those who called themselves "progressive" educators could no longer ignore the social realities in America.

XI

"I have no fears for the future of our country," Herbert Hoover intoned in his inaugural address in March 1929. "It is bright with hope." Seven months later the stock market crashed, following which America entered the worst depression of its history. As wage cuts and unemployment increased, the people sank into an abyss of despair.

The Depression dispelled the apolitical outlook of the twenties. Something had to be done to revive the nation, and the government seemed to be the only agency powerful enough to do this. As the elections of 1932 approached, people looked for a candidate who could solve the economic crisis. The Democrats found a leader in Franklin D. Roosevelt. In his acceptance speech he told the people just what they longed to hear. The American people, he said, wanted two things, "work, with all the moral and spiritual values that go with it; and with work, a reasonable measure of security—security for themselves and for their wives and children." Then, before a roaring convention throng he declared, "I pledge you—I pledge myself to a new deal for the American people."

To give the people work and security, "a New Deal," the powers and functions of the government had to be expanded. Roosevelt proceeded to expand and strengthen federal control over banks and railroads, security issues and security exchanges, public utility holding companies, motor carriers, and industrial and agricultural production. Under Roosevelt the federal government for the first time forbade employers to interfere with their employees' right to organize and engage in collective bargaining. It established minimum wages, maximum hours, and child-labor regulations.

In addition to expanding its regulatory functions, the federal government now began to provide extensive services for citizens: jobs for the needy and unemployed, housing for lower income families, cheap electric power, and loans to farmers and homeowners, as well as to banks and railroads.

As a reform movement the New Deal stood squarely in the tradition of political progressivism; indeed, it made the work of the progressives seem timid by comparison. Nevertheless, the New Deal represented a departure from the progressive tradition. Ideologically, the progressives were individualists, fighting against privileged monopolies in an attempt to give the little man a better chance. In carrying out this fight the progressives had expanded the powers of government. In granting the government an expanded, positive role, however, the progressives had viewed that role as a preventive one, or a regulatory one.

With the New Deal this preventive role of the government gave way to the role of protector of all the people. Ideologically, the New Dealers were egalitarians. Under them the government had the task of providing security for all, to protect all people from any and all hazards—unemployment, accident, illness, and old age. Equally important was the thrust of the New Deal—it came from the top. Unlike the progressives, the New Dealers had no concern with bringing about a participant democracy, they did not crusade to "restore government to the people." The New Deal, in Richard Hofstadter's words, was a "managerial reorganization of society." Most Americans accepted this thrust from the top, this governmental organization of society. Their traditional fear of government tyranny had given way to the greater fear for their own welfare and security—freedom from government seemed much less important than freedom from want.

Franklin Roosevelt had no master plan. The New Deal did not represent economic planning so much as "a chaos of experimentation." Roosevelt had in 1932 prescribed "bold persistent experimentation," explaining that he thought it was "common sense to take a method and try it. If it fails, admit it frankly and try another." He defended this drive to do something with the warning that the people would not "stand by silently forever while the things to satisfy their needs are within easy reach."

His role, the role of the government, was to do something about those needs of the people—farmers who needed markets, unemployed who needed jobs, the hungry who needed food, the banks that needed money, and so on. Roosevelt was not a philosopher, nor did the New Deal and its program of social welfare emerge from a political theory. The New Deal rested on a point of view, the ideology of egalitarianism: the government's job was to meet the needs of all the people. It was an opportunistic point of view, one that suited practical politicians, administrators, technicians—men who wanted to get things done.

The needs of one group of people attracted the particular attention of the New Deal: American youth. Those between the ages of sixteen and twenty-four made up the largest number of all unemployed in the nation. Between 1929 and 1935 the number of all unemployed youth increased by about 30 percent. Most American youths needed jobs but could find none; some needed further education, but could not afford it. What were they to do? Or rather what could be done for them? Could their needs be met?

One attempt to meet the needs of youth was the Civilian Conservation Corps (CCC), which Roosevelt established within three months after taking office. This program employed youths to perform useful public work—planting trees, restoring streams, protecting wildlife, fighting dust storms. Housed in camps built and managed by the war department, they were able to send home to their families a good part of their dollar-a-day wages.

To further reduce unemployment the New Deal set up the National Youth Administration (NYA) in 1935. This program kept youth out of the competition for regular jobs by creating new part-time public service jobs that permitted them to continue their schooling. Through this program thousands were able to pay their way through college and over a million able to stay in high school.

XII

And what about the schools? If America in the thirties had a "youth problem," were the schools able to cope with it? Could the schools help to meet the needs of youth? Many thought not. The American Council on Education, for example, organized an American Youth Commission in 1935 with the declaration: "Recent social and economic changes in the United States have given rise to difficulties in the care and education of young people with which existing institutions are quite unprepared to deal adequately."

Earlier, at the 1932 convention of the PEA, George S. Counts had challenged the child-centered doctrine that continued to dominate American educational practice. At that meeting, in an address entitled "Dare Progressive Education Be Progressive?" Counts urged the members to focus more on the society, less on the child. He dared them to "face squarely and courageously every social issue, come to grips with life in all its stark reality, establish an organic relation with the community, develop a realistic and comprehensive theory of welfare, fashion a compelling and challenging vision of human destiny. . . ." He wanted them not only to become society-centered, but actually to reconstruct American society. Dismissing as "bogeys" the fears of *imposition* and *indoctrination,* Counts proclaimed that competition must give way to cooperation, the urge for profits to careful planning, and private capitalism to some form of socialized economy.

In his speech Counts was expressing an ideological position that had been developing among his colleagues at Teachers College, Columbia University: egalitarianism. In 1933, one of them, William Heard Kilpatrick, edited a book of position papers under the title *The Educational Frontier.* This volume contained articles that expressed deep concern about socioeconomic conditions in America and a plea for educators to confront them. As if to explain what Counts had meant in his earlier address when he dismissed the fears of indoctrination, Kilpatrick now wrote: "If to prepare individuals to take part intelligently in the management of conditions under which they will live, to bring them to an understanding of the forces which are moving, to equip them with the intellectual and practical tools by which they can themselves enter into direction of these forces, is indoctrination, then the philosophy of education which we have in mind may be adjudged to be an instrument of indoctrination."

The notions of these social reformers found expression in two further ventures: *The Social Frontier,* a journal first published at Teachers College in 1934, and the John Dewey Society for the Study of Education and Culture, organized in 1935. The John Dewey Society published its first yearbook, *The Teacher and Society,* in 1937. Kilpatrick, who edited it, explained that it was devoted to the study of the teacher in relation to society because "under existing conditions the teacher is the crucial factor in any conscious effort to bring school and society effectively together." The book contained a number of different articles dealing, in Kilpatrick's words, with the "various phases of the problem in such a way as to help both teacher and teaching serve more vitally the cause of a better society."

The movement to use teachers and the schools as the lever to reconstruct the society never gained much headway among American schoolpeople. But whether it was the pressing reality of the youth problem or the work of men like Counts and Kilpatrick, most educators during the thirties did shift the focus of concern away from the child to the youth. Most educational discussions now attended to the secondary level of education. Moreover, these discussions went beyond the psychological concerns of the child-centered twenties to include appraisals of the social context.

The best illustration of this shift of pedagogical concern is the work of the Commission on Secondary School Curriculum. This commission, created by the PEA, published its most important report in 1934, *Reorganizing Secondary Education*. In it, the commission adopted an approach to schooling that soon dominated all educational literature. It reorganized the curriculum around "the needs of youth."

Rather than reconstruct the society, these investigators wanted teachers to recognize and to meet both the personal, or psychological, needs of their students and their social needs. The members of the commission took the psychological needs to be those demands society makes on the individual. They insisted that "a working concept of an educational need must always be both personal and social in reference; it must always incorporate both the present desires of the individual and what they should desirably become." The commission was not the first to suggest basing the curriculum on the needs of youth. Keaton and Koopman had published *A College Curriculum Based on Functional Needs of Students* in 1936. And the year before Goodwin Watson had delivered an address at the NEA convention entitled "Problems of Youth— What Does Youth Most Need?" But in *Reorganizing Secondary Education*, the Commission on Secondary School Curriculum did provide the most comprehensive and far-reaching program for curriculum reform.

The commission organized the resources of six fields (science, social studies, mathematics, language, literature, and art) into four basic areas: immediate personal-social relationships, social-civic relationships, economic relationships, and personal living. Each of these "basic areas" was further analyzed in terms of "needs," to guide the reorganization of the secondary schools. For example, the needs identified under economic relationships were: (1) the need for emotional assurance of progress toward adult status, (2) the need for guidance in choosing an occupation and for vocational preparation, (3) the need for wise selection and use of goods and services, and (4) the need for effective action in solving basic economic problems.

Of course, the American secondary schools never adopted the entire reorganization plan of the commission, but the concept of meeting the needs of youth soon became the basis for all educational planning. By 1942 Donald C. Doane could write in his published doctoral dissertation: "If there is one point upon which most educators today appear to be in agreement it is that educational programs, particularly those of the secondary school, should be founded upon the needs of the children concerned." This work, *The Needs of Youth: An Evaluation for Curriculum Proposals,* was an attempt to analyze and classify the many different opinions "as to just what these needs are and what they imply for the curriculum."

Despite the efforts of Doane, no agreement was reached by American educators as to what the needs of youth were. As a result the concept of need lent support to a rapidly expanding curriculum. In 1934 there were almost double the 68 subjects offered a mere 12 years earlier. By 1944, according to John F. Latimer, one could find 141 different subjects in the high school curriculum. But more significant than the numerical increase was the shift in the quality of the curriculum. As late as 1934 the leading fields of study in the high schools were foreign languages, mathematics, and science. By 1949 more students were studying health, music, and art than any other fields. By this time more than half the subjects in the curriculum were in the fields of social studies, vocational education, home economics, and agriculture, and student concentration in these fields was almost as great as the concentration in the fields of foreign language, mathematics, science, and English.

In the fifties, as we shall see, the scope and the quality of the high school curriculum came under violent attack. Most of these attacks came from outside the profession, but within the profession itself the concept of need came under searching analytic scrutiny. In " 'Need' and the Needs-Curriculum," B. Paul Komisar showed the triviality, the vagueness, and the indeterminacy of the concept of need and its total inadequacy as a basis for making educational policy.

Still, the concept of need and the needs curriculum had brought to the fore the welfare function of the American school, a function very much in keeping with the ideology of egalitarianism. Ideological egalitarianism not only generated many new functions for the public school, it also wedded the school to the government. The school was now one of the agents of welfare—an agent of the state.

XIII

One hundred and fifty years earlier Thomas Jefferson had written: "If a nation expects to be ignorant and free, in a state of civilization, it expects what never was, and never will be." When Lyndon B. Johnson delivered his State of the Union address in January 1965, he revealed the profound change that had taken place in America when he announced: "Thomas Jefferson said no nation can be both ignorant and free. Today no nation can be both ignorant and great."

In the 1960s Americans seemed less concerned with freedom than with greatness. They would have, in President Johnson's words, a "Great Society." Yet, it would not be accurate to say that they were less concerned with freedom than heretofore; it was just that Americans no longer regarded their own government as a threat to their freedom. The New Deal, the Second World War, and the Cold War had all fostered the growth of government and governmental power. By the sixties, the traditional Jeffersonian distinction between the society and the state was disappearing as governmental control over society increased. By this time, as Daniel Bell has written, the United States had become a *national society*. Now "all crucial political and economic decisions" were made by the government, creating a national economy and a national polity. The state, in short, directed social change.

This expanded governmental power had not produced government tyranny. Indeed, the expanded powers of the government had raised the general welfare of the society, giving the people social security against those who threatened "the American way of life."

By the sixties most Americans not only no longer feared governmental tyranny, they felt that only the government could guarantee the blessings they enjoyed. Above all, only the government could secure the nation against those foreign powers that threatened to "enslave" America.

The only way to be secure was to be powerful, to be great, greater than any other nation. In the late fifties, John F. Kennedy could base his successful campaign for the Presidency largely on the warning that the United States was in danger of losing its hegemony. Lamenting the missile gap, the declining rate of economic growth, and the loss of prestige abroad, he promised to "get the country moving again." Kennedy's New Frontier led, naturally, to Johnson's Great Society.

To create this Great Society President Johnson turned to the schools. In July 1964 he said: "If we are learning anything from our experiences, we are learning that it is time for us to go to work, and the first work of these times and the first work of our society is education." Johnson, a former school-teacher, confessed that he would like to be remembered as the "education President." Yet he was not the first Cold War executive to give such high priority to education. Back in 1949 President Harry S Truman had said, "Education is our first line of defense." He went on to add, "In the conflict of principle which divides the world today, America's hope, our hope, the hope of the world is in education. . . . Education is the most important task before us."

Truman, like most, saw the conflict with the Communist nations as an ideological one. The educational task then consisted of instructing all in the knowledge of good and evil; that is, all people—both at home and abroad—must learn to recognize the virtues of democratic capitalism and the evils of communism. This ideological conception of the Cold War continued into the fifties. It was how the Educational Policies Commission saw things in its 1951 report, *Education and National Security*. After describing the world that Americans then faced, the report announced that there was a moral task to be performed. Regretting the "profound misunderstanding of the meaning of America in most parts of the world—and among some Americans," it declared that "we must come to know ourselves" and to others "we must make clear our devotion to moral purposes." Turning to the role of the school, the members of the commission found little to disturb them in the emphases and programs of the schools. Above all, they insisted, "the schools must educate for moral and spiritual values," since "the problems which now most urgently require solution are not physical or technical, but moral and social."

What worried the commission most, as it did most concerned observers, was the matter of staffing and financing the schools of the nation. During the Second World War many teachers had left the classroom, and now with the war babies beginning to enter the schools, the nation faced a severe teacher shortage. Moreover, the increased school population necessitated increased expenditures for new buildings and new equipment. The need for money was dire indeed, and the Educational Policies Commission merely reflected a widely held opinion when it declared: "If we dedicate to our schools sufficient funds to operate them well, we shall have taken important steps to safeguard our future."

Inevitably, the requests for money for school equipment, school buildings, and schoolteachers brought forth angry opposition from many taxpayers. The American principle of local control of the schools gave homeowners the opportunity to express their dissatisfaction with the rapid inflation of the postwar years. And express it they did as time and time again proposed school bonds went down in defeat at the polls. In their fight to prevent new expenditures, these tax-conscious citizens turned a critical eye toward the current ones. Here they discovered, predictably, that much of their tax money was being spent on "fads and frills" and "costly palaces." They also uncovered teachers who defended the fads and frills but who couldn't teach Johnny to read. The criticisms frequently extended to the teacher-training institutions, the schools of education that foisted such ill-prepared teachers on an innocent public. Viewing them as part of the establishment that conspired to control teacher certification, the public affected shock and dismay at revelations that Einstein could not be hired to teach science in the schools of many states, nor Beethoven to teach music. They, you see, had not taken enough credits in "methods courses" in a school of education.

This searching reappraisal of American education led, in 1956, to a White House Conference on Education. The delegates to this conference identified the most urgent problems facing the American schools. The first problem was one of objectives. But the remaining ones all centered about the issues of staffing, equipping, and building. Of greatest importance, according to the conference report, was the problem of public interest and support.

During the very year of the White House Conference on Education some Americans began to see the role of the schools in a new light. In April, William Benton, one-time United States senator, reported the following in *The New York Times Magazine:* "A recent trip to the USSR has convinced me that education has become a main feature of the cold war; that Russia's classrooms and libraries, her laboratories and teaching methods may threaten us more than her hydrogen bombs."

The senator seemed to be right, for when in October of the following year Americans witnessed the first Russian sputnik, they attributed this feat to the superior schooling provided in the USSR. The chancellor of the University of Kansas, for example, in an address before the American Council on Education six months after the Russian triumph, declared: "The message which this little ball carries to Americans, if they would but stop and listen, is that in the last half of the twentieth century . . . nothing is as important as the trained and educated mind. This sphere tells us not of the desirability, but of the utmost necessity of the highest quality and expanded dimensions of the educational effort."

The message was clear. While the schools in the United States had concentrated on ideology, the Soviets had stressed quality instruction in basic subjects. Technological supremacy was the payoff. And the Russians had won the first round.

So now Americans must have quality education. Admiral Hyman Rickover, the "father" of the atomic submarine, in his best-selling book on American education, announced: "Now that we have been aroused to the danger-ous effect which poor education has on our strength and influence as a world power, let not men of little vision with their soothing words hold back our righteous anger. We must sweep clean the temple of learning and bring back quality."

Some educators tried to defend the American school system on the grounds that it served the needs of *all* people and did not cater to an elite of gifted students, as was the case in Europe and in the USSR. But the American public was in no mood for this kind of argument. John Gardner, who wrote "Pursuit of Excellence," the Rockefeller Report on Education, answered in the form of an ultimatum: "From time to time one still hears arguments over *quantity* versus *quality* education. Behind such arguments is the assumption that a society can choose to educate a few people exceedingly well, *or* to educate a great number of people somewhat less well, but that it cannot do both. But a modern society such as ours cannot choose to do one *or* the other. It has no choice but to do both."

The infusion of quality into American education now came to be one of the primary concerns of the federal government. The first move was the pas-sage of the 1958 National Defense Education Act. This set up institutes to upgrade teachers of foreign languages, mathematics, and science, and pro-vided improved guidance programs to urge more students to become lin-guists, scientists, and mathematicians. During the next seven years the federal government expanded this initial narrow outlook to a concern for the *total quality* of American education. Since 1958 it has passed the Higher Education Facil-ities Act, the Library Services Act, the Vocational and Technical Education Act, the Nurses Training Act, the Economic Opportunity Act, the Civil Rights Act, the Higher Education Act, the Federal Arts and Humanities Foundation Act, and the International Education Act. And when Congress renewed the National Defense Education Act it broadened the number of different fields of study included in its benefits. The culmination of this landslide of educational legislation was the Elementary and Secondary Education Act of 1965—"An Act to strengthen and improve educational quality and educational opportunities in the Nation's elementary and secondary schools."

XIV

When Congress passed the Elementary and Secondary Education Act of 1965, President Johnson declared that it was "the greatest breakthrough in the advance of education since the Constitution was written." Whether or not it advanced education, this act did culminate *the* greatest federal breakthrough into American education.

By supplying all American schools with money—a total commitment of over $4 billion for 1965 alone—the government had guaranteed that they would be agencies of the state—agencies of national defense, or national secu-rity, or national welfare.

The federal breakthrough penetrated most deeply into higher education, where it had begun long before sputnik. During the Second World War the government had turned to scientists in the laboratories of universities throughout the country for technical assistance. This cooperation continued into the period of the Cold War, leading, during the Eisenhower Administration, to the creation of the National Science Foundation to support university research and to pay for the training of researchers. This twenty-year or so period of common-law marriage between the states and institutions of higher learning produced what Clark Kerr termed a transformation of the university. In his remarkable Godkin lectures of 1963 he described the results of this transformation: the "multiversity"—a federal grant university that served as "a prime instrument of national purpose." By 1960, Kerr reported, the federal government had given about $1.5 billion to higher education. Of this, $1 billion was for research, and this accounted for 75 percent of all university expenditures on research. "Clearly," he concluded, "the shape and nature of university research are profoundly affected by federal monies."

This *statification* of the universities did more than affect the shape and nature of university research. As Kerr himself noted, the university's control over its own destiny had been substantially reduced. Moreover, the individual scholar, by engaging in the negotiations for federal funds, reduced the authority of the department chairmen, deans, and the president. Understandably the schools had already been used to help meet the successive challenges of Depression, hot war, and Cold War. But now more than ever before, they were mobilized, or ready to be mobilized, *by the government* to meet *national* needs. Many faculty members now shifted their loyalties from their university to Washington, D.C. This transformation also included a great shift in emphasis within the universities—toward the physical sciences, the biomedical sciences, and engineering, and away from the humanities and social sciences. Not only the balance among the fields, but the balance among institutions also changed, since federal grants concentrated research at certain universities.

Finally, this transformation greatly reduced the quality of undergraduate instruction as professors spent more and more time on their research projects with graduate students. Most observers point to this as the underlying cause for the 1964 undergraduate revolution at the University of California—Clark Kerr's own university. Kerr, earlier in his Godkin lectures, had neither approved nor defended the transformed university; he merely analyzed and described "the wave of the future." The implication, however, was that all realistic people must bow and accept it, like it or not. The students at Berkeley, however, refused to concur. Their revolt set off a torrent of commentaries and analyses from academics, some filled with admonitions for the student protesters, but many more filled with self-incriminating praise for them.

By 1965 Americans had abandoned their traditional fear of their own government. The consensus among most Americans was that in acting on behalf of what was called the national interest, their government was acting on behalf of them and society. Many now expected the schools to engineer and to perpetuate this consensus.

* * *

After the Civil War the public school became the panacea for all social problems. I have tried to show that the school failed to solve the multiple problems generated by urbanization, industrialization, emancipation, and nationalization. Moreover, in some cases this faith in the power of the schools actually aggravated these problems. Rather than bring about a racially integrated society, the schools reinforced segregation; rather than educate people to cope with life in the city, they accelerated the flight from the city and aided in the spread of urban blight. By 1965 the schools had polarized American society into self-satisfied whites and victimized blacks, into despondent city dwellers and indifferent suburbanites.

In their attempts to cope with industrialization by providing equality of opportunity in the success race, the schools once again polarized the society by identifying, indeed creating, the winners and the losers. And with regard to their political function the schools by 1965 had completely reversed themselves, moving from the original role of preventing governmental tyranny to become a primary agency of the state in its pursuit of the national purpose. Once again the result was polarization, this time a polarization of students into conformers or radicals. The conformers—those who did not object to the fact that their schools and their school careers were being shaped to serve the national purpose—the schools rewarded. The radicals—those who rebelled— were not rewarded, and usually ended up ignored, or expelled by the system.

Yet, Americans still had faith in education, still believed that the public school was the panacea for all of society's ills. Since 1965, however, many Americans have undergone a crisis of faith, a loss of belief in the ability of the public schools to solve society's problems.

PART THREE

The Imperfect Panacea

CHAPTER 7

The Decline of the
Public School

I

The long-standing faith Americans have in education has its roots in a particular conception of education, a conception of education as a process of socialization. Construed in this way, education becomes an authoritarian transaction—a matter of changing, shaping, molding, processing people to some
predetermined end or goal. If schools could do this, then any, or all, of society's problems could be solved through education. In other words, the notion
that the school is a panacea for all of society's problems carries with it the
assumption that people are the root of every social problem: *they* have to be
changed; *never* the existing arrangements, *never* the system.

When looked at from this angle of vision, the authoritarianism of General
Armstrong, Booker T. Washington and W. E. B. DuBois stand out clearly: each
of them prescribed an education that would change black people and thereby
solve America's racial problem. This authoritarianism is also manifest in the
efforts to use the schools to solve the social, economic, and political problems
caused by industrialization, urbanization, and immigration since the time of
the Civil War: think of the proposals of Charles Eliot, Andrew Carnegie, John
Dewey, James Conant—all of whom urged the schools to change people in
some predetermined way so that they would then readily accept and fit into
the existing social, political, and economic arrangements.

Yet those who proposed what the schools should do *to* people did not
see education as an authoritarian enterprise. Rather, they saw it as something that helped people, benefited them; schools enhanced people's life
chances—socially, politically, economically. And this is how those who
attended the schools viewed them, too—as a panacea: going to school was the
way out of poverty, or the way to secure prestige, or the route to success and
power.

Television changed all this. With the coming of television, more and more
people became aware of the authoritarianism of the American schools.

II

Much has been written about the effects of television, most of it variations on the same theme of technological determinism. According to this theme, television molds and shapes the thought and conduct of those who watch it. We become what we perceive on the TV screen. If we watch violent shows, we become violent. If the shows are sexist or racist, the viewers become sexists and racists. The problem I have with all such explanations of the influence of television is that they deny agency to viewers. Technological determinism casts all viewers as more or less passive receptors of messages that shape and mold them, somewhat in the way a current of water shapes and molds the rocks in its path. A rock has no agency; it becomes what it is simply as a result of external forces that impinge upon it. But human beings are not rocks; they *do* have agency. They *can* make choices, judgments, decisions, and criticisms about what life—or television—presents to them.

What television presents to us is something markedly different from what is presented to us by newspapers, magazines, and books. The messages we get through print are discursive—they are descriptions, explanations, arguments presented in a more or less logical, rational manner. The messages we get from television, however, are nondiscursive. They are visual images, usually of people, of people interacting with other people. The focus of television, the bias of this medium, if you will, is on interpersonal relationships. Whether we are watching a drama, or a situation comedy, or the news, our attention is drawn primarily to the relationships among the people we see presented on the screen. We pay less attention to the content of the programs we watch than to the patterns of relationships revealed to us as people interact with one another. What we remember is not what they said or even what they did, but rather, the kinds of relationships that exist between Archie and Edith, Crockett and Tubbs, Dr. Craig and Ehrlich, Cagney and Lacey, Hugh Downs and Barbara Walters.

Because television is a different kind of medium from print, we respond to it differently. We respond to print cognitively, but to television we respond affectively. When we watch television, questions of truth and validity give way to questions of liking or not liking what we view. Television provokes feelings more than thought. Our criticisms, therefore, take the form of "this is good" or "this is bad" rather than "this is true" or "this is false." Television educes moral criticism from us, criticism focused on the relationships we see encoded on the screen. Note that I do not claim that television makes people more moral but only that it evokes moral criticism.

As I understand it, what television did in the sixties—which was about the time when most American families owned a TV set and watched it on a regular basis—was to encode and present to the public the existing, stereotypical relations common among people at that time. This was not by design but simply an outcome of the bias of the medium: it focuses on relationships. There on television, Americans could see in a way never before possible the relationships common in society between men and women, between blacks and whites, between young and old, between cops and criminals, between rich and poor, between political leaders and citizens, between the clergy and their congregations, between teachers and students. When they viewed these relationships—encoded in dramas, comedy shows, newscasts, documentaries—people could begin to see the moral inadequacies, the social injustices inherent in those relationships that society accepted or found acceptable. These commonplace, heretofore accepted, relationships were now uncovered as being unfair and unjust: racist, sexist, elitist.

Television created a national awareness, first, that the problems of the society were national problems, not local; and second, that the problems were the problems of groups—blacks, women, the aged, the young—not the problems of individuals. Finally, and perhaps most important, television helped people to recognize that the traditional American way of dealing with social problems—through education, that is, by changing people so that they would fit into the existing arrangements—was the heart of the problem itself. Through television, many people became critical of the existing social, political, economic arrangements. They now perceived them as unfair and unjust.

One way to put this is to say that television brought about a rise in the ideology of egalitarianism. Through television people saw that some groups—blacks, women, the non-English-speaking, the disabled—were not being treated the same as others. Much of the resentment, envy, and outrage about such unfair treatment focused on the schools, since the schools functioned to socialize people to accept these unfair arrangements. The schools were perpetuating an immoral society. Unable to shake the concept that education is a process of socialization, these critics of the 1960s insisted that the schools always served the existing system, always socialized people. So the only way to secure social justice, many concluded, was to radically change the system by gaining control of the schools. Then they could use the schools to socialize the young to the beliefs, the understandings, the attitudes, the conduct that *they* wanted the young to have. This, they hoped, would help undermine the existing unfair and immoral social, political, and economic arrangements and lead to the creation of new and better ones. The schools, they believed, could create a more egalitarian society, a society where everyone was treated equally. Thus began one of the most turbulent decades in the history of American education, a time of turmoil set afoot by television.

III

In 1964 Congress passed the Civil Rights Act, followed the next year by the Voting Rights Act. Now, for the first time in 300 years, black people gained a sense of power and dignity, a sense of true citizenship. Things had gotten better. The federal government had acted to protect their rights: the courts had declared segregation to be unconstitutional, Congress had passed laws to guarantee their rights, and the executive branch had given vigorous support in the form of federal marshals and federal voting registrars dispatched from the attorney general's office.

Yet although things had gotten better, in some ways the situation for blacks had worsened. Television had helped to make it worse, and television had also made more people aware of how much worse it was. The sympathetic network coverage of the nonviolent black protest demonstrations had actually heightened white resistance in the South and intensified physical attacks on blacks—all of which television dutifully reported. This dialectic with television brought the logic of nonviolent protest to the saturation point. How many beatings could one take? How many times could one go to jail? And were the beatings and the jailings worth the prize? Did the suffering win freedom now, as the protesters demanded? Increasing numbers of protesters grew weary of nonviolence. "I'm not going to let somebody hit up the side of my head for the rest of my life and die," one young protester complained. "You got to fight back. We don't demonstrate to get beat up. We demonstrate to show people what has to be done."

By escalating the violence against blacks, television had now lowered the commitment of many blacks to the philosophy of nonviolence. Television also clearly revealed that nonviolence was a tactic of the powerless. It did work— most of the time. But it left blacks still beholden to white people: *they* determined what rights, what freedom, blacks could enjoy. Blacks still lacked autonomy, lacked control over their own lives. Because television faithfully encoded the relationship between the races, blacks could now more clearly see how dependent upon, thus inferior to, white people they really were in this society. These encoded relationships also revealed in a way never possible before that being black in this society was a curse. Being black was a condition to lament; it was never a source of pride. In this racist society, whatever self-esteem a black person had came only from being like a white person or being the kind of black that white people esteemed.

Perhaps most important of all, television made the battle against racism a moral crusade, and moral crusades are rarely content with gradual, slow, piecemeal change. The black protesters, especially the young ones, had less and less patience with the snail-like pace of political action, which always required compromise, negotiation, bargaining. The antipolitical attitude had surfaced on national television at the 1964 Democratic National Convention, when the Mississippi Freedom Democratic Party refused a compromise to accept two seats as convention delegates. To these blacks, combatting racism was not a political matter where compromise is appropriate; it was a moral matter.

This moral crusade gathered force and took on a new focus in the summer of 1966, when the police of Greenwood, Mississippi, arrested Stokley Carmichael, the leader of the Student Non-violent Coordinating Committee (SNCC). Released in time to address a protest rally that evening, an infuriated Carmichael told the audience of 600, and the television cameras covering the rally: "This is the twenty-sixth time I have been arrested. I ain't going to jail no more." He pointed out that blacks had been demanding freedom for six years and had gotten nothing. "What we gonna start saying now is 'black power.' " He shouted the slogan repeatedly. Each time, the audience shouted back, "Black power." Another member of SNCC leaped to the platform and asked, "What do you want?" Again and again the audience shouted in unison the phrase that had suddenly galvinized them—and the television audience— into a new consciousness.

In a number of ways, television had prepared blacks for this new consciousness, this new awareness of the need for black power. From television, they had learned how their brothers elsewhere in society lived—how they lived in the urban ghettoes of the North, how they lived in the rural South. More than this, from television blacks had also learned how whites lived in American society. Through the medium of television—*the* reference source for black–white relations—they had become increasingly aware how their people were deprived in relation to white people. And many had come to the conclusion that black people would always remain deprived unless they gained power.

Television also engendered receptivity to the need for black power by exposing blacks to the increasing precariousness of their lives in this society. So long as blacks had accommodated to the existing social arrangements, they had been relatively safe. And so long as they had accepted those existing arrangements, they had believed—especially in the South—that they could count on "decent white folks" to protect them against arbitrary and wanton attacks from cruel whites. But now, blacks no longer accepted the social arrangements whites had imposed on them, and so, now they *were* more vulnerable to victimization than ever before. At any moment, they might be attacked, or even killed—television continually fed them information about bombings, beatings, and killings of their people. There was no one to protect them. They had to protect themselves. To do this, they needed power.

Television had also made blacks ready for the demand for black power by raising false expectations. Many black people had watched President Eisenhower send federal troops to desegregate the schools of Little Rock. And many had seen Presidents Kennedy and Johnson declare their support for the black movement. Had not President Johnson himself used the words "we shall overcome" on television? And hadn't he denounced all forms of racial discrimination on television when he signed the Civil Rights Act in 1964: "It cannot continue. It must not continue. Our constitution, the foundation of our republic forbids it. The principles of our freedom forbid it. Morality forbids it. And the law I will sign tonight forbids it." But the continued bombings, the beatings, and killings of blacks in the South revealed that the United States government *could* not, or *would* not, protect black people. Nor could the franchise really change matters. After all, Northern blacks had the franchise, and they still remained victims—deprived and discriminated against socially, politically, and economically.

So when someone like Malcolm X appeared on their TV screens as the embodiment of black pride, black independence, and black militancy, many were ready. Perhaps, as Malcolm had been saying for a long time, and as Stokley Carmichael and Floyd McKissick and others were saying now, perhaps black power *was* the answer. Blacks *had* to become proud of being black, *had* to stop seeing their blackness as a curse, as a badge of infirmity. Blacks *had* to identify and accept what was quintessentially their culture—they had to take pride in "soul." They *had* to find solidarity with their black brothers and sisters. "The most important thing the black people have to do is to begin to come together, and to be able to do that, we must stop being ashamed of being black," Stokley Carmichael said in many of his speeches. "We are black and beautiful." Through racial pride and racial stability, many black people now believed they could move on to self-determination as a group. No longer dependent upon or beholden to whites, black people would finally be in control of their own destiny.

At this point, many blacks became increasingly critical of the schools, calling them racist institutions. Earlier, black leaders had recognized that the decentralized structure of American education prevented their children from ever securing equal educational opportunities at the local level. So their strategy had been to seek help at the federal level. The Supreme Court had declared segregated schools were unconstitutional, but now, many blacks realized that the *Brown* decision did not go far enough: it did not outlaw racism. And while Congress had passed the Elementary and Secondary Education Act with specially ear-marked funds for educationally handicapped children, many blacks now realized that this so-called compensatory education was itself racist.

Compensatory education rested on the assumption that children were educationally handicapped because they were "culturally deprived." Compensatory education thus involved the schools in socializing "culturally deprived" black children, trying to make them more like white children. Such an authoritarian approach perpetuated racism by undermining black children's self-confidence and self-esteem. Not all black people viewed compensatory education as inherently racist, but the federally sponsored programs for promoting it did much to make blacks aware of how racist the American schools were. The federal programs required the "maximum feasible participation" of local residents, which brought black parents into contact with the schools. Here they witnessed firsthand the racism of school personnel and of school arrangements.

These parents soon saw that many teachers had low or minimal expectations of their black students simply because they did not believe they could learn. This certainly did not inspire confidence in the children. Parents also discovered that school personnel treated black children unfairly, suspending them or failing them more readily than white children. Moreover, the reading materials provided in schools all reflected a white outlook and focused on problems and situations not relevant to black children. The readers, as well as the textbooks used in literature and social studies, contained little or nothing about black people. Gradually, black parents realized that their children were failing in schools, not because they were "culturally deprived," but because the schools were incompetent to teach black children. Indeed, black children were not culturally deprived; they had a culture, a different culture. And many now argued that the schools should teach that culture to their children, and instill pride in it.

This line of thought led to demands for new textbooks that would portray the black experience and reinforce black children's positive self-image. It led to demands for arithmetic problems relevant to blacks. It led to literature courses where students read Claude Brown, Langston Hughes, and Malcolm X instead of Shakespeare, Longfellow, and Hemingway. And it led to demands that schools accept and respect Black English. It also led to demands for changes in discipline and grading, as well as demands for more black teachers who would have higher expectations of black students and who would serve as role models for them.

None of these changes came about easily or readily. Most took place only after black parents staged protest rallies, or sit-ins—actions that usually appeared on the local evening news and, when exceptionally dramatic, on the network news.

The most dramatic, and therefore widely televised, attempt to control the education of their children occurred when blacks tried to take over the governance of the schools—the so-called community control movement. This began in Harlem in 1967, where, after months of picketing, boycotting, and demonstrating, black leaders got three "demonstration districts" in New York City that were to be run by local governing boards. But within a year, this project ran into opposition from the teachers' union, which stridently opposed attempts to replace white teachers with black ones in the demonstration districts. After three bitter citywide strikes—accompanied by turbulent counterdemonstrations by the supporters of community control—the state legislature adopted a decentralization plan for the city that eliminated the demonstration districts and undermined the local community control movement. Television cameras extensively and avidly captured the animosity and violence that erupted during this period, sowing fright and bitterness throughout the entire metropolitan area.

The most prolonged struggle of blacks to control the education of their children was that directed at having their children attend racially balanced schools. In 1966 the federally sponsored report, the so-called Coleman Report, entitled *Equality of Educational Opportunity,* found that the academic achievement of children from minority groups was one to two years behind that of whites in the first grade and three to five years behind by the twelfth grade, even though the resources provided were almost equal. What seemed to be a factor, the report indicated, was the racial isolation of black students. The notion that racial integration of the schools provided the key to improving black achievement received further endorsement seven months later with the publication of the U.S. Commission on Civil Rights report *Racial Isolation in the Public Schools.* According to this report, black students in majority-white schools generally achieved more than did black students in majority-black schools, even when the latter had better teachers.

Armed with the findings of these two reports, the U.S. Office of Education began to apply pressure on local school districts to create racially balanced schools by threatening to cut off the federal funds provided by the Education Act of 1965. This course of action, the Secretary of Education pointed out, was required by Title VI of the Civil Rights Act, which authorized a cutoff of federal funds for any program in which there was illegal discrimination.

The main struggle to secure racially balanced schools took place in the courts. There were two phases here. In the first phase, black lawyers sought to overthrow the traditional interpretation of the Supreme Court decision in the *Brown* case, which held that the court had merely prohibited segregated schools. So long as this interpretation prevailed, the Southern states could use obstructive tactics, like tokenism and so-called "free choice" plans, to perpetuate the isolation of black children in racially segregated schools. The first victory came in 1968, when the Supreme Court in *Green v. County School Board of New Kent County* struck down a free-choice plan in Virginia. Here and in subsequent cases, the court affirmed that the *Brown* decision required racially balanced schools. Then in 1971 *(Swann v. Charlotte-Mecklenburg Board of Education)* the Court directed the school authorities to use "every available device," including racial quotas and busing, to achieve racially balanced schools.

In the second phase of the struggle against racial isolation, black lawyers sought to apply the *Brown* decision to schools outside the South. In the South, schools had been racially segregated by law *(de jure)*, whereas in the rest of the nation it was residential segregation that resulted in *de facto* segregated schools. Until now, the courts had taken the *Brown* decision to apply only to *de jure* segregated schools. But in 1973 in *Keyes v. School District No. 1*, the Court held that the Denver School Board had pursued an *intentional* policy that resulted in *de facto* segregated schools. Since the segregated schools came about as the result of public policy, the Court found such segregation to be a violation of the *Brown* decision. It ordered the Denver School District to create racially balanced schools, even by busing if necessary. Following the Denver racial-balancing order, lower Federal Courts ordered Boston and San Francisco to create racially balanced schools. At the same time, other northern city school districts, either voluntarily or under threat of a court order, adopted school desegregation plans. But at this point, the movement toward racially balanced schools ran aground, largely because of the influence of television.

Years of watching racial turmoil on their television screens had generated considerable "white blacklash" to the efforts of blacks to control the education of their children. The attempts to replace white teachers with black ones, to change the curriculum, to "force" racial balance through quotas and busing had turned many white people against black demands for social justice. So, although racist conduct had diminished in American society in the 1970s, racial resentment had increased. And at the very point blacks began to experience increased white backlash, they discovered that their protest movement was leaderless and unfocused. The assassination of Martin Luther King in 1968 had deprived the movement of its most charismatic and respected leader. Moreover, television had eaten up the other national black leaders. Relentless exposure of the leaders and their doings had made all of them predictable, thus not

newsworthy. Indeed, there seemed no longer to be a need for leaders: the consciousness of blacks had been raised—by television—and they now took their
cues from television. New and different spokesmen appeared on television—
often leaders of local groups never heard of before, nor heard from again—all
of whom broadened and increased the number and kinds of issues and
demands: community control of schools, reparation, group identity, black consciousness, and hiring quotas were only some of the causes they promoted.
What the television screen now primarily conveyed was the frustration, anger,
and hatred many blacks felt toward whites.

In the face of these diffused, unfocused, yet often violent and hate-filled
protests, many white people now became critical of the entire black protest
movement. All the more so since the world they saw displayed on television
revealed that blacks had attained tremendous progress in the culture: black
people now appeared regularly in many commercials, black actors now starred
in prime time shows ("Sanford and Son," "Julia," "Shaft," "Good Times," "The
Jeffersons") and appeared in bit parts as lawyers, judges, physicians, teachers,
professors, business executives, policemen, clergymen, and political leaders;
and there were critically acclaimed "specials" that celebrated the character and
intelligence of black people ("Roots," "The Autobiography of Miss Jane
Pittman," "A Woman Called Moses"). In television commercials, blacks were
found playing and working together with whites. Moreover, the news shows
and network special reports frequently contained accounts of blacks in the arts,
in the professions, and in politics.

Television had moved from stereotype to myth. Blacks *had* made progress
in American society, their life chance had improved, but not nearly so much
as now appeared on the television screen. But since television had become the
reference source for what was happening in the culture, many whites believed
that the black protesters were wrong, wrong about their facts, wrong in their
methods.

In urban America in the 1970s, white backlash turned into "white flight."
Whites had been leaving the cities since the end of World War II, but now the
threat of mandated busing accelerated this exodus. Early in the decade, white
students became a minority in the schools of Chicago, Philadelphia, New York,
Detroit, Cleveland, and Washington, D.C. These demographic changes meant
that it was no longer possible to construct racially balanced schools within
these city school districts. The only solution, local black leaders concluded, was
to combine the city and suburban school districts into metropolitan school districts. Within such a metropolitan district, white students from the suburbs
could be bused back to the schools in the city and black students from the cities
could be bused out to the schools in the suburbs. But when a federal district
judge ordered the integration of the Detroit School District with fifty-three pre-
dominantly white suburban districts, the Supreme Court reversed the decision
(*Miliken v. Bradley, 1974*). Five years later, in 1982, the court reaffirmed its position when it supported California's state constitutional amendment forbidding
court-ordered busing.

During the 1970s not only the court but also the other branches of the fed-

eral government drew back their support for the efforts of black people to control the education of their children. Richard Nixon, as president (1968–1973),
repeatedly tried to get Congress to pass legislation prohibiting the busing of
students. Congress passed no such legislation, but neither did it pass any legislation designed to help black people secure social justice in the schools. Moreover, President Nixon repeatedly withheld monies already appropriated to
finance educational programs. According to one investigator, the Nixon
administration "forestalled or forebade the spending of approximately $1 bil-
lion in educational funds."

As support from the federal government waned, advocates of racially balanced schools turned to market strategies that were supposed to secure voluntarily racial integration in the urban schools. The most widely adopted
incentive was the so-called magnet school. Each magnet school has a particular focus, such as computer applications, creative or performing arts, math and
science, honors classes, or "fundamentals" like the 3Rs. As part of a consciously designed desegregation plan, magnet schools control enrollment to
ensure a specific racial balance. In such systems, parents are free to choose any
school in the district—so long as there is no adverse effect on racial balance—
with the option of staying in the neighborhood school if they wish. During the
seventies, magnet schools were established in San Diego, Los Angeles, Dade
County, Cincinnati, Savannah, Buffalo, and New York City's District 4 in East
Harlem. Milwaukee extended the voluntary magnet school to a metropolitan
school district that joins twenty-three suburban districts with the city school
system.

The turn away from federally mandated racially balanced schools did slow
down the pace of desegregation. Magnet schools generate what can only be
called incremental desegregation. Moreover, they do diminish the power of
black parents to control the education of their children. Yet in light of the
repeated public polls that reveal that the public rejects mandatory busing,
many argue that magnet schools provide a more democratic approach to racial
desegregation. In 1993 New York City announced that it would open thirty-
seven theme high schools, each one with a specialized course of study. These
include: The School for Computer Science, The High School for Economics and
Finance, The Science Skills Center for Science, Technology, and the Creative
Arts, The Foreign Language Academy of Global Studies, The Brooklyn School
for Global Citizenship, The Coalition School for Social Change, The Urban
Peace Academy, and the El Puente Academy for Peace and Justice.

* * *

The history of the education of black children during this period points up
what happens in a democratic, pluralistic society that subscribes to the notion
that education is socialization.

Television made most Americans aware of the victimization of black people, thereby bringing about a rise in egalitarian sentiments throughout the society. To create a more equal society, black Americans, not surprisingly, turned

to the schools. But the newly racially conscious blacks now recognized that the schools were part of the problem, not the solution. The schools were racist; they functioned as agencies of socialization, as institutions that tried to socialize black children into white people by imposing white culture on them.

When black people tried to combat these racist practices and policies in the schools, they did not reject socialization, they simply tried to use the schools to socialize their children as *they* wished. But their attempts to control the education of their children met with only limited success. Racial segregation continues. The emergence of magnet schools in the late seventies simply signaled that the white majority was reasserting *its* control over the nation's public schools—to use them to satisfy *their* wants.

Is this what schools are for?

IV

Television also brought forth demands for social justice from women. Although some had long complained about it, through the medium of television, most everyone could now see that, in the American society, men regarded women simply as sex objects: in commercials, in situation comedies, in westerns, in dramas; and if they appeared there at all, the television "news shows" of the early sixties presented women as "weather girls," subject to chauvinistic put-downs from the male announcers. Older women saw themselves limited to the television role of housewife and mother, alternatively silly, scatterbrained, or melodramatic. Commercials depicted women as stupid and incompetent, unable to select a laundry soap or dog food without a man (or a male voice-over) telling her what to do.

The relationships women had with men, when encoded on television, exposed to all the fact that women were in the world but not of it. They were not involved in politics, art, or science; they didn't even understand those fields. Their only interest in life was in attracting men. Although some television analysts have argued that television stereotypes perpetuate the existing social arrangements, I think they do the opposite: they help to destroy the existing social arrangements. Thus, by encoding the stereotypical relationships of women in this society, television revealed women to themselves. Television became *the* reference source for women. Through the medium of television, women came to recognize their own lack of autonomy and freedom of choice. They now saw that women for the most part lived in residential ghettos, shut off from the life of the world. And they came to realize that those women who were engaged in any activity outside the home were not taken seriously. Through television, they found out what they had been allowed to do and what not allowed to do; they saw what doors were shut and how sanctions were applied against the violators of assigned roles. And through the critical analysis of the relationships encoded on television, women began to trace the consequences of subscribing to the notion that the traditional role of women is to live for others and to find their identities in personal relationships—as mother and wife. They began to see that to live in response to others is to live a life that is necessarily fragmented and ephemeral.

In serving as the reference source, television did more than reveal women to themselves; it also revealed comparative information about men: the rewards, advantages, and privileges they enjoyed. Men initiate, lead, advise, and dominate; women follow. Television exposed men at work—as doctors, lawyers, detectives, firemen, and so on. And as situation after situation unfolded, the message was: women had no place in the man's world. More-over, "You don't belong here" clearly meant "We don't want you here." So television also became the reference source for what men thought of women, what behaviors men deemed were proper for women. They learned that males thought women were innately inferior and regarded females who thought oth-erwise as sick, bad, crazy, stupid, ugly, or incompetent. They learned that males believe that they know and understand everything because they, unlike females, are logical, rational, and objective. This is why, they say, women are not capable of knowing what's good for them, why women are a bundle of contradictions, and why they are not worth arguing with. This is also, of course, why women are not good at arithmetic or science. The message women received from male-dominated television is that she is weak and cannot cope with the world by herself. But she can be dependent on *him; he* will do it for her. *He* is indispensible.

Women responded to all these exposures with moral outrage. The limita-tions these male–female relationships placed on them were unfair, unjust. The designated roles imposed by the culture curtailed their growth and weakened their sense of identity. In this culture, women were childlike cripples.

Now, many women had long known and resented all this: they did not need television to tell them how unsatisfactory their condition was. But prior to television, most women were inclined to view this as a "personal failure"; their own personal inadequacies, they thought, prevented them from accept-ing and adapting to the existing male–female relationships present in the cul-ture. Television diminished this self-blame by providing normative references that enabled women to see that other women, *all* women, were victims of male discrimination. Instead of blaming themselves, women now began to blame the system, the culture. Their feelings of deprivation were not due to personal inadequacies but to the inadequacies of the system.

One of the bulwarks of the system, of course, was the school. From the earliest grades in elementary school through college and graduate school, American educational institutions followed sexist policies, practices, and pro-cedures that socialized girls to accept their inferior status. Thus, elementary schools invariably typed children according to their sex: boys sat on this side of the classroom, girls on that side; boys lined up here, girls there; boys wore trousers, girls wore dresses and skirts. Having typed them, the schools then socialized girls to accept the existing sex roles in the society. In the lower grades, girls played quieter games, listened to fairy stories, and engaged in activities like sewing and housekeeping. Boys played with trucks and trains and engaged in generally more active, noisier, more physical games. Schools conditioned girls to be silent, neat, docile, passive. The textbooks perpetuated the traditional sex roles by portraying females stereotypically as mothers, nurses, or teachers—never as problem solvers, like scientists, or mathematicians. Women were rarely mentioned in history and social studies textbooks. Even the math textbooks posed problems for girls in areas of dressmaking and cooking, whereas boys' math problems focused on activities like building things, climbing mountains, sailing a boat.

The schools not only typed girls and trained them for stereotypical sex roles, it also actively discriminated against them. The stories in the school readers, for example, were mostly about males, whether they were stories about children, adults, or animals. Moreover, the males in these stories—but never the females—displayed traits like courage, perseverance, and autonomy. Children's fiction repeated the same themes. A male character in the 1967 Newberry Award-winning children's book, *Up a Road Slowly,* says to the heroine: "Accept the fact that this is a man's world and learn to play the game gracefully." By telling girls in many and varied ways that they were not only different from but inferior to boys, the schools undermined female pride and self-esteem.

High school reading materials were not different. History texts omitted mentioning women; literature and language textbooks portrayed them as insipid, passive, ineffectual. Sex typing in high schools led to the segregation of boys and girls in many classrooms; home economics for girls, industrial arts for boys; girls rarely took advanced science or advanced math, and physical education classes were rigidly separated, as were most of the extracurricular activities—clubs, societies, teams. In some urban areas, entire schools were segregated on the basis of gender. In New York City, two academic high schools (Stuyvesant and Brooklyn Technical) that prepared students for higher education leading to careers in math, science, and technology, did not admit women. Vocational-technical schools also segregated students along the lines of gender. New York City had seventeen segregated vocational schools for boys or girls only—twelve for boys, five for girls. In the coed vocational schools, courses were segregated by gender.

The guidance counselors in the high schools cemented the sex role socialization process by guiding girls into those occupations and courses "appropriate" for women: legal secretaries, not lawyers; nurses, not doctors; and, of course, teaching. For the most part, high schools encouraged girls to excel socially rather than academically. Indeed, one of the most important lessons girls learned in high school was to make themselves as appealing as possible to boys. This usually meant that adolescent girls began to accent their own physical attractiveness and play down their intellectual ability. At all costs, they avoided being considered "too brainy."

Institutions of higher education continued the pattern of discrimination against females: admission policies and practices favored males, males received more financial aid; the health services were inadequate for female needs, and the counseling services irrelevant and unsympathetic to their problems.

Many colleges subjected women to much more restrictive parietal rules than men, rules that regulated where they could live, whom they could admit to their rooms, how late they could stay out at night. The same sexual biases appeared in textbooks and course materials and the same separation in classes and extracurricular activities. In addition to suffering discrimination from policies and procedures, college women sometimes found themselves the object of sexist comments and even sexual harassment from their professors.

Behind the sexist practices, procedures, and policies in American schools stood a male-dominated power structure. Until 1970 about 80 percent of the principals of elementary schools were men, even though over 85 percent of the teachers were women. There were even fewer female principals of secondary schools. This discrimination against women followed from the patterns of socialization males and females had undergone as students in the American schools. Men make better principals than women because men are (and should be) assertive, bold, inventive, energetic, and strong; women are (and should be) passive, gentle, sweet, shy, and kind. Women, therefore, held very few administrative posts in the educational establishment. In 1971 there were only two women among the 13,000 district superintendents in the United States.

In the nation's colleges and universities women made up only 25 percent of the faculty nationwide, but less than 10 percent in the more prestigious universities. Few deans and presidents were women.

The most glaring inequalities appeared in salaries. Systematically, at all levels of the system, women received less pay than men for the same work.

The schools were sexist. Not usually by design or intent. Sexism was simply part of the society, a normal, heretofore accepted condition found in all the activities people participated in. But the television they had watched during the sixties had raised the consciousness of many, and increasing numbers of women would no longer accept sexism—neither in their own lives nor in the lives of their children. A resolve to make this a more egalitarian society now took hold of many women . . . and men. Understandably, then, the late sixties and early seventies witnessed a nationwide attack on sexism in the schools. The National Organization of Women (NOW), at its first national convention in 1967, adopted a Bill of Rights that included the following: "WE DEMAND that the right of women to be educated to their full potential equally with men be secured by Federal and State legislation eliminating all discrimination and segregation by sex, written and unwritten, at all levels of education."

In 1972 pressure from lobby groups like NOW and other feminist groups helped push through three acts of legislation: (1) the Higher Education Act of 1972 included the provision that no person in the United States shall, on the basis of sex, be excluded from participation in, be denied the benefits of, or be subjected to, discrimination under any education program or activity receiving Federal assistance; (2) the Civil Rights Act of 1964 was amended to include education institutions under the ban on discrimination in employment; (3) the Equal Pay Act of 1963 was amended to remove the exemption of professional and executive employees. This federal legislation became the basis for numerous court cases and threatened court cases that compelled educational institutions to revise their hiring practices, award female faculty members back pay, adjust their salaries, and promote them to tenured positions. At the same time, the Office of Civil Rights (OCR) issued guidelines to educational institutions telling them: (1) they could not spend disproportionate amounts of money on male athletic programs, (2) they could not maintain different parietal rules for girls, (3) they could not favor male students in giving financial aid, (4) vocational programs could not steer men and women into different occupational activities, and (5) all school districts had to report how many classrooms had more than 80 percent of its students of one sex. The OCR also monitored textbooks in order to weed out books that contained sex stereotypes.

The Women's Educational Equity Act passed in 1974 provided additional federal support in the battle against sexism. This act created a National Advisory Council on Women's Educational Programs that granted funds to individuals, institutions, and school districts to produce nonsexist handbooks, curricula, and instructional materials, as well as money for training and research activities related to women.

At the state and local levels, commissions, committees, and task forces emerged that helped formulate legislation and policies intended to stamp out sexism in the schools. Students and their parents brought legal suits against sex-segregated schools and programs, petitioned to abolish dress and clothing regulations, demanded that sexism be purged from textbooks, including sexist language ("Ms." instead of "Miss" or "Mrs."; "salesperson" instead of "salesman"; "the history of human beings" instead of "the history of man"), insisted that schools provide information on contraception, requested that schools teach women's studies courses, and initiated questionnaires, as well as discussion and consciousness-raising groups for teachers to help them uncover the sexual biases in their attitudes and conduct. ("Do you stop one sex from making demeaning comments about the other, such as: 'I don't want to read any dumb girls' book?' ")

By the end of the 1970s these criticisms of American education had totally changed many of the policies and practices in American schools. The schools had not stopped socializing girls, they just socialized them differently. Now schools taught them they were not inferior to boys; they were equal to them. Schools taught girls to be active and assertive rather than passive and docile, fostering in girls the same attitudes, the same values, the same beliefs, the same understandings, the same conduct as they did in boys. Now, teachers and guidance counselors encouraged them to enter nontraditional fields to compete with men as equals. Some indication of how successful schools have been come out in the movement of women into traditionally male-intensive fields: from 1970 to 1979, the percentage of women earning degrees in law grew from 5.4 to 28.5 and in medicine from 8.4 to 23. From 1974 to 1979 the percentage of women earning bachelor's degrees in business and management grew from 12.8 to 30.5.

One of the unanticipated consequences of this moral crusade against sexism was the decline in the number of talented women entering the teaching profession. Other unanticipated consequences were the dramatic social changes that came in the wake of this new kind of female socialization. Since 1970 the marriage rate has declined, first, because many more women have delayed their first marriage, and second, because there has been a declining propensity to marry. The number of separated and divorced women grew from 3 million in 1960 to 9.6 million in 1983, at which time 10.3 percent of the female population over age fifteen was divorced, compared to 4.6 percent in 1960. Female-headed households have grown more rapidly in recent years than any other type, an 81 percent increase between 1970 and 1979. Most people, however, applauded the new egalitarian tack the schools had taken in the socialization of women. This, they believe, is what schools are for.

<h1 style="text-align:center">V</h1>

Television raised the consciousness of other groups in America. Not only blacks and women, but those who belonged to ethnic groups, now became aware of the discrimination they suffered in this society. By presenting the then current stereotypes of Italians, Mexicans, Poles, and Asians on the screen, television helped members of these ethnic groups to see the actual relationship of their group to the rest of society. What they saw was not flattering. In most cases, they found these portrayals demeaning. In the late sixties Italian ethnics created the Italian American Civil Rights League to denounce those television programs that implied all gangsters were Italian. Mexican-Americans complained about the Frito Bandito commercials. In response, the potato chip company replaced the Frito Bandito, who stole potato chips, with the Frito Amigo, who gave them away to children. Polish-Americans fought against the television picture of Poles by publishing newspaper advertisements that informed the public about Copernicus, Chopin, and other Polish notables. Seeing themselves so deprecatingly portrayed on television brought back to many memories of how the schools had tried to "Americanize" them by eradicating all ethnic pride and consciousness. Here is how Michael Novak recalled his experience growing up in a largely Slovak community in Johnstown, Pennsylvania, in the 1930s: "The strategy was clearly to make an American of me. English literature, American literature, and even history books, as I recall them, were peopled mainly by Anglo-Saxons from Boston (where most historians seemed to live.)"

Yet in the late sixties neither the Slavs nor the Poles, nor any other European ethnic group, felt so victimized by this cultural imperialism as did the Hispanics and the Asians. Ever since the Immigration Act of 1965 had abolished national origin quotas, the tide of immigration had shifted. The number of European immigrants had declined steadily until, by 1976, more than half of all immigrants came from Asia and Latin-American countries. These were the newcomers who complained most bitterly about discrimination. Television heightened the situation through its coverage of the Vietnam War, which brought many Americans to see their country as an imperialist nation bent on colonizing the "third world." So, when many Mexican-Americans, Puerto Ricans, and Asian-Americans began to identify themselves as third world people, they gained a new perspective on the schools: the schools' attempts to assimilate their children was an attempt to colonize them. In consequence, they rejected the traditional claim that by becoming Americanized their children would become equal to others. As they now saw it, by Americanizing their children, the schools treated them unfairly, depriving them of their cultural identity.

Like blacks and like women, these ethnic minority groups criticized the textbooks and the curricular materials and brought about the inclusion of minority authors and the insertion into the curriculum of relevant descriptions of the minority experience. But these minority groups faced an educational obstacle not encountered by blacks and women: language. Their children's lack of facility in English made them educationally handicapped. Frequently, non-English-speaking students were "tracked" into classes for the mentally retarded.

To remedy these social injustices, Congress passed the Bilingual Education Act in 1968, which provided funds for new educational approaches to meet the needs of limited-English-speaking ability. The Department of Health, Education and Welfare followed up with guidelines requiring districts to "take affirmative steps" to rectify their language deficiency in order to open the instructional program to these students. By 1980 thirteen states had mandated bilingual education, and the federal courts in other states had ordered some districts to provide such programs for non-English-speaking students.

The ostensible purpose of bilingual education was to provide instruction to students in their native language. By 1977 the U.S. Office of Education reported that it had funded the preparation of teaching materials in sixty-eight different languages. Yet the bilingual education movement actually went beyond the issue of language to culture itself, promoting what came to be called bicultural, or sometimes multicultural, education. This included ethnic studies programs that informed children about their own native cultural heritage, about the contributions their groups had made to civilization, and about the current problems and difficulties their groups faced in the United States. The Ethnic Heritage Studies Program Act of 1972 provided federal grants to promote such programs in American schools.

To carry out such programs, schools had to hire more minority teachers and, in some cases, retrain the teachers they already had so that they would understand the contributions and life styles of their minority students, become sensitized to dehumanizing biases and prejudices, and learn how to create learning environments that contribute to the self-esteem of all students. This bicultural or multicultural education would, its advocates promised, create a more egalitarian society.

Bilingual/bicultural education, like the assimilationist or Americanization education given to earlier immigrant groups, was still a form of socialization. But now, instead of socializing newcomers to some "ideal American" stereo-

type, the school set out to socialize children to their ethnic heritage: to cultivate pride and esteem in their ethnic identity, to ensure a heightened sense of
being, respect, cohesiveness, and survival—a belief that the ethnic group is
good.

Is this what schools are for?

VI

Racism, sexism, and cultural imperialism did not exhaust the complaints made
against American schools in the 1960s and 1970s. Many also accused the
schools of being "elitist." This charge grew out of attempts to help the poor.

In the 1960s Americans discovered (or rediscovered) poverty in this supposedly affluent society. The explanation usually given is that this came about
through the medium of print. Books like *The Other Americans: Poverty in the
United States* (1962), by Michael Harrington, and articles like Dwight Mac-
Donald's "Our Invisible Poor" (*New Yorker,* January 19, 1963), are said to have
influenced President John Kennedy, who then proceeded to work out a new
federal program that ultimately became, under President Lyndon Johnson, the
war on poverty.

Now it may be that the writings of intellectuals did help to launch the war
on poverty, yet one cannot ignore that in the sixties people became conscious
of the poor through the medium of television. More important, television
helped the poor to become conscious of themselves. Once the poor saw the
reality of their situation, once they saw their position in the society, they
became outspokenly critical of the economic arrangements of the society. Thus,
it is not so much that other people discovered that poor people lived in America in the sixties as it is that poor people in the sixties made public their presence—and their discontent.

As happened in the case of blacks and women, television helped people
see that poverty was a national, not a local, problem, and that being poor
meant being a member of a systematically victimized group of people. Television shattered the isolation of the poor. Living in Appalachia or in the ghettos of large cities, the poor had heretofore interacted only with others like
themselves, having little or no contact with the rest of America. With the coming of television, the poor could observe how people with money lived—the
quality of their lives, their standards of living, their attitudes, their options.
Inevitably, the poor became aware of how deprived they were. In absolute
terms, of course, the poor in America were better off than the poor in other
nations. Moreover, the number of the poor had markedly decreased during
the twentieth century. But by comparing themselves to the rest of the nation—
a comparison television made possible—these people saw themselves as *relatively* deprived. Moreover, the poor could see that they not only had less
money than other people in the society, they were living in a different culture—a culture of poverty. They lived lives different from the lives of the rest

of Americans. Most devastating of all, it now seemed that to be poor was to belong to an entity, a group, with more or less stable membership—not a social class, but a racial or ethnic group. In America, it seemed to many, to be black was to be poor, to be Hispanic was to be poor, to be an Appalachian was to be poor. Television brought about this realization. There were no blacks who appeared on television in the mainstream American culture, no Hispanics, no people from Appalachia. There were, of course, "The Real McCoys," and later, "The Beverly Hillbillies," but these shows simply strengthened the notion that the rural poor were living in a different culture, a culture of poverty out of which they could never really escape, even if they miraculously became rich. For poor people seemed to be trapped in a culture, or a cycle, from which they could not, on their own, escape: the unemployed poor had a low standard of living that included scant medical care, inadequate housing, insufficient education, all of which led to low employment opportunities, which led to being poor . . . and so it went.

The one link in the cycle that appeared susceptible to change was education. As the January 1964 Economics Report of the President put it: "Universal education has been the greatest single force contributing both to social mobility and to general economic growth." If the children of the poor were given "skills and motivation," the Report went on, "they will not be poor adults." When, later that year, President Johnson declared war on poverty, the battle plan consisted primarily of programs to educate the poor.

In this war on poverty, the federal government launched attacks on three fronts of education. First, there were federally funded programs, planned and managed at the local level, destined to teach basic cognitive skills. These included a preschool program for children of the poor, called Head Start; compensatory education for poor children in elementary and secondary schools; and adult education programs to teach reading and writing skills to persons over eighteen years of age. The second frontal attack focused on the retention of poor children in schools. Here the federal government funded a host of different programs including: (1) Upward Bound programs to locate underachieving high school students from low-income families and prepare them for entry into postsecondary education; (2) financial aid to local schools for programs to reduce dropouts; (3) the Neighborhood Youth Corps, to encourage teenagers to continue or resume school by providing part-time employment in useful local projects; (4) Educational Opportunity Grants to institutions of higher learning for scholarships to full-time students of "exceptional financial need;" (5) work-study programs that provided financial aid to colleges to pay students from low-income families to work part time. The third frontal attack on poverty consisted of programs to teach specific job skills. These included increased expenditures for vocational education, which rose from $156 million to more than $400 million by 1974; the Job Corps, which set up centers where high school dropouts could receive job training; work-experience programs "for people unable to support or care for themselves or their families." Also included were the Manpower Development Training Act, which in 1966 was amended to serve primarily the poor; and, finally, the JOBS program provided government subsidies to private employers to hire and train the hard-core unemployed.

All of this, of course, was nothing more than another application of the socialization concept of education: an attempt to eliminate poverty and create a more egalitarian society by socializing the poor—teaching them the skills, attitudes, beliefs, values, and understandings that would enable them to get and keep jobs. Unfortunately, the educational programs did not work; the federal government lost the war on poverty.

Evaluations of compensatory education in the late sixties revealed little or no improvement in educational achievement, while the Head Start programs provided only short-term advantages. (Later evaluation studies, however, did indicate that the programs may have been more effective than originally estimated.) The second line of attack, that designed to retain children of the poor in school, had no significant impact on increasing the educational attainments of disadvantaged youngsters, and those programs that appeared to be successful, such as Upward Bound, tended to concentrate on the least disadvantaged of the poverty group. The third line of attack, teaching specific job skills, did have a slight effect on removing persons from poverty, but this did not hold for the vocational education programs or for the Job Corps. Under the Nixon administration, most of the educational programs of the war on poverty were cut back or scrapped, and the emphasis shifted to what was called career education, which allowed children to explore the world of work—sometimes by leaving school for half-time employment.

Educators trotted out many and varied excuses to explain this spectacular education failure of the war against poverty. A few followed Arthur Jensen to argue that blacks, who comprised most of the target population of the war on poverty, failed to profit from the educational programs because they were genetically inferior: they had lower IQs. Most educators rejected this and instead explained the education failure by claiming that schools simply could not offset the influence of the environment—the influence of family and neighborhood background was too strong for the school to make a difference. This is how many educators interpreted the findings of the Coleman Report on racial inequality. Additional support for this theme that schools could not make a difference came from books by Christopher Jencks (*Inequality*, 1972) and Kenneth Keniston (*All Our Children*, 1977).

Those educators who kept their faith in the power of education to solve all social problems shored up that faith by insisting that the educational programs of the war on poverty had failed because they had employed inadequate methods, or followed the wrong curricula, or relied on a faulty organization—the usual ad hoc arguments Americans have continually employed to immunize their faith in the power of education to cure all social ills. Marxists, predictably, explained the failure by telling us, once again, that the schools of a capitalist society serve the interests of the capitalists. So, since it is in the interests of the capitalists that there always be a class of (relatively) poor people, the war against poverty had never been more than a rhetorical war, intended to ward off criticism of the capitalist system, which, the Marxists tell us, is the real root of poverty.

It was only much later that social scientists like William Julian Wilson explained the failure of the war on poverty by the high levels of employment during this period. Yet this explains only why the poor were unable to get jobs; it does not explain the failures in educational achievement and school retention. To explain this, we must, I think, take account of the widespread student rebellion against schools and schooling in the late sixties and seventies—a rebellion against socialization that led not to the abandonment of socialization but only to a new kind of socialization.

VII

Student resistance in the 1960s took many different forms, including the flouting of school rules and regulations, absenteeism, disruptive behavior, and assaults against teachers. Between 1970 and 1973 such assaults increased by 85 percent. National concern about school discipline surfaced in the annual Gallop polls on the attitudes of the public toward education: beginning in 1969 and every year thereafter, save one, until 1986, the public cited the number one problem of the schools as discipline. (In 1986, discipline dropped to second place, behind the use of drugs.) Children of the affluent, as well as children of the poor, rejected socialization. Among the former, this rebellion took milder forms: the wearing of jeans and army clothes, longer hair, changes in the language of discourse, and protest meetings to demand student rights. When school people tried to combat student resistance to socialization, the students took them to court. In 1969 the U.S. Supreme Court in *Tinker v. Des Moines* ruled that students do not "shed their constitutional rights to freedom of speech and expression at the schoolhouse gate." The specific issue in this case was about the students' right to wear black armbands to protest the Vietnam War. But in its decision, the court not only recognized the constitutional right of students to express their opinions, it legitimated vigorous expression of that opinion, declaring that some degree of disorder in schools is acceptable and positively educational because the world itself is "disputatious." Subsequent court decisions on dress codes, hair length, and underground newspapers compelled schools to make fewer personal demands on students. Another Court case *(Goss v. Lopez)* granted students due process in the matter of suspension. Other court cases prohibited schools from "preventing" illicit behavior, restricting them to "punishing" such behavior. The courts have also guaranteed students the right to be free from unreasonable searches of themselves, their school lockers, and their personal property. And students have the right to file a grievance and the right to appeal a decision made by school officials when a question arises concerning the scope of their rights.

In addition to establishing their rights, students marshaled massive resistance to the schools' efforts to get them to learn what they were supposed to learn. Across the nation, students rejected the curriculum as irrelevant, meaningless, and lacking in significance. They refused to study or to "apply themselves." Students have always, to some extent, resisted the efforts of the school to socialize them. But in the sixties and seventies this resistance became a moral resistance that was part of the general rejection of the inegalitarian American society: a rejection of its racism, its militarism, its imperialism, its materialism. Students pointed out that schools were simply "credential mills" bent on processing people into personnel. The students rebelled against being turned into functionaries who were supposed to maintain the unjust, unequal "system."

Where did such an outlook come from? Why did the young now perceive the schools as authoritarian agencies of socialization? It is true that radical social critics like Paul Goodman and Edgar Friedenberg had written books and articles about the way schools were "universal traps" that attacked the "dignity of youth," but few of the young ever read this heady stuff. Yet almost all subscribed to the outlook this radical literature promulgated.

What has to be noted, I think, is that the sixties' generation was the first television generation—the first to be raised on, and by, and perhaps for, television. Television, I have argued, helps make people more morally sensitive to social injustice—to racism, sexism, cultural imperialism, in short, to all forms of elitism. The young simply by being young were less attached to the existing arrangements, hence, more ready to criticize the society they saw presented on television. "We grew up old," wrote Joyce Maynard; "we are the cynics who see the trap door at the magic show, the pillow stuffing in the Salvation Army Santa Clauses, the common tricks in the TV commercials." ("That isn't really a genie's hand coming out of the washing machine . . . it's just an actor with gloves on.") More readily, perhaps, than their parents, the sixties generation "saw through" the relationships encoded on television. Television provided the distance that enabled them to become critical of how men treated women, how whites related to blacks, how cops handled criminals, how teachers responded to students; critical of the position in society of the poor, the handicapped, the mentally ill, the "off beat," and the eccentric. In short, television helped the young perceive the moral inadequacies, the social injustices, the inequalities current in the society.

Take the vapid and innocuous sitcoms of the late fifties ("I Love Lucy," "My Little Margie"). These presented weekly episodes that built upon lies and hypocrisy: if Ricky Ricardo or Vern Albright brought an Important Person home to dinner, everyone in the family would lie about life styles, wealth, or tastes. Lucy would lie about buying a new dress or burning the roast. To critical young viewers, domestic life as presented was full of pretense and sham. While adults seemed to accept the TV portrayal of relations between husband and wife, workers and employers, parents and children, many young viewers became critical of those relationships.

Then there were the quiz show scandals, where contestants on shows like "The $64,000 Question" and "Twenty-One" were supplied with answers and coached on how they should "play" the role of the contestant. There, on television, young people saw that even college professors, like Charles Van Doren, would cheat and lie for money.

On the dramatic shows of the early sixties, young people watched how the idealistic young rebel was socialized to the existing system. In all of these dramatic series, one usually found an older, wiser colleague who weekly worked to help the young neophyte to understand and accept the traditional arrangements. On "The Defenders," a young defense attorney was initiated into the legal system by a wise and understanding father. On "Dr. Kildare," an impetuous, idealistic intern, who put principle before tradition, was counseled by an older mentor, Dr. Gillespie, who weekly preached patience and understanding. On "Ben Casey," viewers saw a more rugged, unbuttoned character than Kildare, a young physician more angry with the system but who also was guided by a mentor into an understanding and appreciation of the existing medical arrangements. "The Nurses" had the same format of a continual socialization of an idealistic student nurse by a crusty, but understanding, older guide. In the field of education, there was "Mr. Novak," a young teacher who was the Dr. Kildare of the classroom, while Dean Jaggar played his Dr. Gillespie. All of these shows dealt with real problems—on the medical shows, for example, there were cases of syphilis, thalidomide babies, drug abuse, abortion, teenage pregnancy. But these problems were always dealt with, in the end, according to the rules. And the story line always, in the end, endorsed the wisdom and rightness of the traditional, established arrangements.

Yet by raising these issues and presenting them in dramatic form on the screen, television allowed many people to begin to question the moral rightness of the established order. The system of relationships embedded in the existing institutions was not perfect, most everyone would admit, even though everyone was expected to adjust to and accept those relationships. But the first television generation became increasingly critical and restless.

As the young saw it, schools socialized them to accept the existing network of relationships within the system. In the system, everyone played a role—professionals, like lawyers, doctors, and teachers, as well as policemen, nurses, salesmen, secretaries, and factory workers—all were imprisoned by the roles the system imposed on them, enclosed by the relationships prescribed and proscribed by their occupations. Had not the young witnessed the imposed relationships in television shows like "Dr. Kildare," "The Doctors," "Medic," "The Defenders," "Perry Mason," "Dragnet," "Naked City," "The Nurses," "The Ann Southern Show"? The role constraints of every occupation, it seemed to the young, made people's lives sterile, empty of experience. All people had to be mechanical, never expressing their own feelings, doing only what was dictated by the functional requirements of the job. Not only work time, but all of life, seemed to be prescribed by the system.

The young also watched news and documentary shows that informed them about what was going on in the society: the black protest movement, the women's movement, the Vietnam War. As a result of watching television, they came to see that, in this land of inequality, this land of social injustice, they were only one more group among many others who were victimized. The society, as they perceived it, was racist, sexist, imperialistic, militaristic, and elitist.

Active student protest against the system began in colleges and universities but soon filtered down to the high schools, often promoted and fostered by college students and recent college graduates who had entered the teaching profession intending to use the schools to launch the revolution to create a better society. Most teachers, of course, did not want to start a revolution, yet many did sympathize with the complaints of the students. For the first time in educational history, radical proposals for educational change received serious and widespread attention. Best-selling books, articles in scholarly journals and popular magazines, television shows, lecture tours, and college classrooms all served as vehicles to promote the proposals for radical change—and to promote the names of the radical critics who proposed them. The proposals for radical reform came in three waves, each succeeding wave signaling deeper disillusion with existing educational arrangements.

The initial band of radical critics sought to eliminate those features of the established educational system that oppressed the young. John Holt denounced the prescribed curriculum; Neil Postman and Charles Weingartner ridiculed the passive, subject-centered methods teachers used; Herbert Kohl and Jonathan Kozol excoriated the customarly unfriendly, depersonalized, even lethal atmosphere and ambiance in most classrooms and schools.

In time, some of these critics saw the inadequacy of their own radical proposals. A smorgasbord curriculum, or an inquiry method of teaching, or open classrooms, just did not go far enough. Some, like Kohl and Kozol, joined others, like Dennison, Rossman, and Graubard, who argued that it was not possible to reform the existing schools. The established schools reflect the existing society, their argument went, so to change the schools, one must first change the society. And to change the society, one had to create new, different schools—free schools. Such schools would be free from the constraints society had imposed on them in order to preserve the status quo.

Finally, some critics announced that free or alternate schools were not enough either. A more radical revolution was needed. So John Holt and others joined with Ivan Illich and Everett Reimer in pronouncing that reformed schools, even radically reformed schools, were not the solution; schools were the "problem." We must de-school society, they said; expunge the school from society. Only then will a different, better civilization emerge—a peaceful, egalitarian, sharing civilization.

With this last wave of radical critics, we reach the edge of educational nihilism. At this juncture, many educators got off the bandwagon of radical educational reform.

But by this time, most of the schools had changed. Not that they had abandoned the notion that education is a process of socialization. It was just that socialization had become "softer." Students now were to be socialized to become the kind of person the sixties generation held to be ideal: open, tolerant, self-centered, egalitarian, and committed. In keeping with this soft socialization, the methods in most classrooms during the seventies became more student centered as teachers tried to follow the interests, concerns, and needs of the students. The classroom and school atmosphere became more informal:

students and teachers dressed more casually, discourse was more relaxed, discipline less evident. And students enjoyed more freedom to choose what they wanted to study from an ever-increasing array of courses and programs.

Is this what schools are for?

VIII

Television raised the consciousness of yet another group during the 1960s: the disabled. Through television, the disabled came to see how thoroughly society had excluded them, shunting them off to asylums or keeping them at home. They had, of course, always known they were excluded, but they had never known what they were being excluded from. Television became a window onto that world, the world they had never been allowed to enter or participate in. Television disclosed to them what went on in schools and factories, in offices and shops; it showed people playing games and sports and traveling on planes and trains. On television, the disabled saw the able-bodied engaging in activities barred to them, but at the same time they realized that they could perform many of these tasks, participate in these goings-on—at least they felt they should have the opportunity to do so.

As a consequence of watching television, many of the disabled became increasingly aware and resentful of the many barriers that excluded them: architectural barriers, legal barriers, and above all, attitudinal barriers. The attitude of most people toward the disabled was not hostile; indeed, most able-bodied people gave little or no thought to the disabled unless they happened to have a disabled relative or friend. But when they did think about them, they thought of the disabled as handicapped: dependent, ineffectual, unable to function in the world without the help of the able-bodied.

Television not only raised the hopes of the disabled by providing them with a picture of a world that they felt they could participate in, at least to some degree; television also educed from them feelings of anger and resentment, because the world it presented contained no disabled. Although one-fifth of all adults in America are disabled, television showed them not at all in the sitcoms, or on the news teams, or in television movies, or in the commercials. Television, of course, simply reflected the exclusionary character of the society. Seeing this exclusivity displayed on the television screen provided the distance that enabled the disabled to become critical of it in a way never possible before. Moreover, when the disabled did appear on television in the telethons for muscular dystrophy, for example, their appearances reinforced the attitudes of the able-bodied: the disabled were handicapped. And on the hugely popular "Gunsmoke," the gimpy-legged Chester added further support to the handicapped conception of the disabled: Chester was ineffectual, unable to function without the help of Marshall Matt Dillon.

With the coming of television, then, the disabled came increasingly to view themselves as a persecuted minority, victims of social injustice. Like blacks, women, and other groups who saw themselves as victims in the 1960s, the disabled and their relatives formed organizations, coalitions, councils, and associations to fight for equality and social justice. These included the American Coalition of Citizens with Disabilities, the National Center for a Barrier-Free Environment, the Paralyzed Veterans of America, the Consortium Concerned with Developmental Disabilities, the National Council for Independent Living, and the American Disabled for Accessible Public Transportation. At the same time, the newly aroused disabled and their relatives breathed militant activism into older organizations like the Council for Exceptional Children and the National Association for Retarded Citizens.

All these groups launched public information campaigns, sponsored programs, held seminars and conferences, and became lobbying groups at the local, state, and federal levels. They helped to establish presidential advisory groups, such as President Kennedy's Committee on Mental Retardation and President Johnson's Committee on Employment of the Handicapped. Like those groups who represented blacks or women, the advocate organizations for the disabled also turned to the courts to challenge discriminatory practices and to secure equal rights. They fought statutes depriving the disabled of the right to vote, to own property, to bear children, to speak for themselves, to obtain occupational licenses, or to be eligible for insurance.

In response to the protests from these advocates for the disabled, television's portrayals of them began to change by the 1970s. In "Ironside," Raymond Burr played the role of Chief of Detectives of the San Francisco Police Department Robert Ironside, who was paralyzed from the waist down. In "Longstreet," James Franciscus appeared as a blind insurance investigator. Neither character displayed the dependency, the ineffectuality, the severely limited capacities common to the stereotypical concept of the "handicapped." At the same time, prominent people from different fields who had disabled children appeared on television talk shows to inform the public about the capacities and the needs of this forgotten minority. Pearl Buck, Roy Rogers, Dale Evans, and members of the Kennedy family gave stature and respectability to this movement to secure social justice.

Inevitably, the advocates for the disabled came to the conclusion that education was the key to overcoming the barriers against them. "The Miracle Worker" (a television play before it became a smash Broadway hit and later a movie) reminded everyone how education had helped the blind and deaf Helen Keller. If they received adequate and appropriate education, the argument went, all or most of the disabled would be able to participate equally in the world—as workers, citizens, consumers, spectators, professionals, clients, and customers.

But to become educated, they had first to demonstrate that they were educable. And to do this, the disabled had to gain access to the public schools, which, in many localities, simply denied them admission. In many school systems, the deaf, the blind, the orthopedically impaired, the mentally ill and emotionally disturbed, and the retarded were not considered "teachable" in the traditional sense and were, therefore, excluded from the schools.

Yet simply getting into the public schools was not enough. For once inside the schools, the disabled usually found themselves in another restrictive environment—a special school, or a special class with special teachers—separated from the rest of the students. Moreover, much of the special education they received aimed at correcting the disabilities, socializing them to the "normal" world. Special education was not concerned with upgrading the life of the disabled or with changing the attitudes of the able-bodied toward the disabled. Until now, special education consisted of socializing the disabled to accommodate to the world created and run by and for the able-bodied.

The advocates for the disabled wanted to turn all this around. Instead of restriction and exclusion, the disabled wanted in. Instead of being socialized to the existing arrangements, they wanted those arrangements to change, to accommodate to them, to their disabilities. To pull this off, they had to change the attitudes of the able-bodied, and the best time to do this was while they were growing up. Inevitably then, they focused on what came to be called *mainstreaming*, the integration of disabled children into regular classrooms. This served two purposes: first, the disabled children could learn how to participate in the "normal" world by participating in it; second, the able-bodied children could learn about the capacities and the needs of the disabled from daily interaction with them. Mainstreaming, the argument went, would create a more egalitarian society.

Another aspect of how the schools treated disabled children also had to change: the professional arrogance of the educators. For a long time educators had cavalierly labeled children as retarded or handicapped without consultation with the parents. Then they went ahead to provide a "special" education for these children, one different from that given to other students, once again, without consultation with the parents about the appropriateness of the special education. Parents wanted to curtail these arbitrary acts of the educators, all the more so since, in some instances, schools were "overlabeling:" classifying black and non-English-speaking students as mentally retarded and emotionally disturbed and placing them in separate, restricted, special classes, thus perpetuating racial segregation in a new guise.

In 1971 the advocates for the disabled won their most significant court case: *PARC v. State of Pennsylvania*. Here, parents affiliated with the Pennsylvania Association for Retarded Children successfully sued the state for failing to provide an education for retarded children, thus establishing that education for the disabled is a right, not a privilege. More than this, the court also endorsed the principle of mainstreaming, insisting that disabled students be placed in the "least restrictive" educational environment: "placement in a regular class is preferred to placement in a special class, and placement in a special class is preferable to placement in any other program, whether homebound, itinerant, or institutional." The PARC decision also affirmed the principle of due process, insisting that parents be involved in any decision related to their child. Prior to assessment, program change, or service implementation, schools had to inform parents, who had to agree, in writing. Moreover, the court required schools to create a formal system for dealing with any disagreements should they arise.

Following this, advocates for the disabled across the land brought similar cases to the courts, all of which followed the precedents set in the *PARC* case, guaranteeing disabled children the right to public education, the right to a "least restrictive" environment, and the right to procedural due process. In some of these cases, the courts went on to develop the concept of an "appropriate" education for the disabled. They directed schools to individualize their programs or to tailor each child's educational program to his or her specific needs, to teach the child, not the handicap.

Following these judicial decisions, most state legislatures and state departments of education passed laws and issued regulations mandating education of the disabled. By 1974 twenty-five states required schools to provide parents with procedures for due process. States such as Illinois and Massachusetts required schools to draw up individualized educational plans (IEPs) for each disabled child. By 1975 twenty-two states required mainstreaming of disabled children, at least part of the time.

Yet in spite of the favorable court rulings and the enabling state legislation, the schools could educate only a fraction of the disabled children in the nation. Education of the disabled was simply too costly. Local communities and individual states had limited funds to spend on education, so to spend it on educating the disabled meant diverting it from the general education programs, a politically unpopular course of action. Federal financing became the obvious solution.

The advocates for the disabled had already positioned themselves to exert pressure on the federal government. In 1966 they had successfully engineered an amendment to the 1965 Elementary and Secondary Education Act (ESEA), securing authorization for funds for "the initiation, expansion, and improvement of programs and projects . . . for the education of handicapped children at the pre-school, elementary and secondary education levels." In the very same year, they persuaded Congress to establish within the Federal Office of Education a Bureau of Education for the Handicapped (BEH) along with a National Advisory Committee on Education and Training of the Handicapped. These governmental advocates worked closely with the staff of sympathetic members of Congress to prepare legislation. In 1975 Congress passed PL 92-142, the "Education for All Handicapped Children Act," which assured that all handicapped children receive "a free, appropriate public education which emphasizes special education and related services designed to meet their unique needs." The federal government was to pay a portion—up to 40 percent—of the "excess costs" of special education beyond the cost of the regular school program.

Federal funding for the education of the disabled never reached the levels expected, or promised. Yet by 1980, 98 percent of all students in need of special education were receiving it. And the schools had mainstreamed almost 70 percent of these 4 million students. And for each disabled student, the school district had to convene a team consisting of the special-needs teacher, a counselor, a psychologist or social worker, an administrator, and sometimes health-care professionals. With the parents, the team works out an appropriate course of study. Special-needs teachers also communicate with classroom teachers about their students who are mainstreamed. In many regular classrooms, schools supply additional special services, such as someone to present the lessons in sign language for a mainstreamed deaf student. By the end of the decade, television was presenting this new attitude toward the disabled in shows like "Life Goes On" and "L.A. Law," both of which sensitively, but sometimes simplistically, described how the able-bodied and their world has accommodated to the mentally retarded.

IX

The attempts of all these various groups—blacks, women, the non-English-speaking, the disabled—to resist the traditional socialization schools imposed on them created serious problems for teachers, who now found themselves criticized from all sides for the role they played in the socialization process. Parents criticized their teaching methods, the course materials they used, their practices, their procedures, and their attitudes. Not only the parents of the minority students, but other parents as well joined in on the teacher bashing that took place in the sixties. Everybody wanted to tell the teachers what to do and how to do it. Articles in national magazines and popular books complained that teachers did not know how to teach . . . which maybe was all right, since the critics pointed out that teachers did not know their subject matter, either.

This national outpouring of complaints and criticisms made clear to teachers that the public simply did not view them as professionals, like physicians and lawyers. No one told physicians or lawyers how to do their jobs. Teachers, of course, had never commanded the prestige and status of physicians, or their salaries either. Yet most teachers had persisted in believing that, even though the public did not pay them lavish salaries, most people, nevertheless, did respect them, did view teaching as an important occupation and teachers as special people. Television destroyed that illusion.

Popular television shows of the late 1950s like "Our Miss Brooks" and "Mr. Peepers" revealed the contempt and disdain most Americans had for teachers. Teachers appeared on TV only as buffoons in comedy shows, which was never the case with physicians or lawyers. What truly humiliated teachers was the knowledge that many of their students watched, and enjoyed, these demeaning portrayals of teachers.

Increasingly, teachers came to regard themselves as victims: victims of a system that accorded them low pay, low prestige, and very little autonomy to carry out the awesome task of educating the nation's children. Like other groups who had become conscious of their victimization during this period, teachers now began to recognize the need to organize in order to protect themselves. Professional educational organizations already existed—The National Education Association (NEA), founded in 1857; and the American Federation of Teachers (AFT), founded in 1916—but neither had done much to protect teachers or to further their interests.

The average salaries of teachers in the fifties remained very close to the national average for all employed persons, while the average income for most other professions exceeded this by at least 50 percent. As late as 1957–1958, 25 percent of all classroom teachers received an annual salary of less than $3500, and some 46,000 teachers were paid less than $2500—a figure that was $1690 less than the average for all employed persons, including those employed only part time. Teachers had no control over entry into teaching at the state level and were unable to bargain collectively at the local level. They had no say with regard to the conditions of employment or any say about changes made in those conditions. As one commentator wrote in 1960: "The foremost fact about teachers organizations is their irrelevance on the national scene. Their futility in protecting the public interest and the legitimate vocational aspirations of teachers is a national tragedy. . . . Because their organizations are weak, teachers are without power; because they are without power, power is exercised on them to weaken and to corrupt public education."

Then, in the sixties, a dramatic transformation took place. It began in 1961 when the United Federation of Teachers (UFT), an affiliate of the AFT, sought and won the right to become the collective bargaining agent for the teachers of New York City. Within a few years, affiliates of the AFT won bargaining rights in Detroit, Chicago, Milwaukee, Baltimore, Newark, Boston, Philadelphia, Washington, D.C., and a number of smaller cities. Once the AFT had demonstrated how collective bargaining protected teachers and furthered their interests, the NEA followed its lead, fighting for and winning the first statewide bargaining statute in Michigan in 1965. By the 1980s thirty-four states had mandated collective bargaining, and de facto bargaining rights existed in most of the cities of the remaining states, so that 73 percent of the nation's public school teachers are now covered by collective bargaining arrangements.

Collective bargaining is a process for establishing the terms and conditions of employment. This includes wages, and here teacher unions have made dramatic changes. In 1967–1968, for example, there was a 15-percent increase in salary in all school districts in New York State. Nationally, the average annual salary of instructional staff more than doubled between 1960 and 1975, rising to $12,070. By 1981 the average salary was $20,114, reaching $28,044 by 1988. Perhaps more important than the actual salary figures was the emergence, through collective bargaining, of a single salary schedule for all teachers, pegged to years of service and academic credits. With this, teachers with a master's degree are paid more than teachers with only a bachelor's degree, and teachers with academic credits beyond the master's degree are paid more than teachers with a master's degree. Under the single salary schedule, the teachers' union, at the time they negotiate their contracts with the local school board, simply demands a rise in the entire salary schedule so that all teachers will benefit. This approach to wages eliminated differential salaries for teachers of specific subjects—like science and mathematics—as well as differential salaries based on superior teaching performance (merit pay). The unions' success in obtaining salary increases for public school teachers rests largely on the state tenure laws and guarantees of due process that the unions have also won for teachers. Tenure and guaranteed due process prevent school boards from firing, replacing, or transferring teachers when they strike. With job security far beyond that enjoyed by employees in the private sector, teachers have understandably become more militant and more ready to strike. In 1960 there were 3 teacher strikes in the United States, in 1966 there were 30, and 183 in 1969. In 1975 the number of teacher strikes rose to 218, and in 1979 to 242.

In addition to wages and hours, teacher unions have bargained about other conditions of employment including assignments, transfers, adjunct duties, leaves, evaluation procedures, and many other personnel matters. Inevitably, collective bargaining encroached upon educational policy issues, such as the curriculum, textbook selection, testing, grading, consultation with parents, and other aspects of school policy insofar as these impacted on work loads and working conditions. If a school board, for example, sought to add new courses, or to drop old courses, this would affect the work loads and working conditions of those teachers presently employed. The union will demand retraining and continued employment of the teachers of the courses being dropped. Or it will discourage dropping the courses by demanding severance pay and continuation of benefits; and it will help in finding employment for those teachers to be laid off.

In addition to securing substantial salary increases, job protection, and increased autonomy for teachers, the unions have actively engaged in political activity at the local, state, and national levels. With almost 2 million members, the NEA is the largest union in the world. It represents almost 60 percent of American public school teachers, while the AFT, with 700,000 members, represents another 20 percent. Teacher unions have endorsed and campaigned for school board candidates who support teachers; they have lobbied for state laws and regulations that benefit teachers and against those that adversely affect them. At the national level, teacher unions have helped obtain and shape federal school aid policies and have blocked proposals they opposed. In 1976 and again in 1980 the NEA endorsed Jimmy Carter for President, in return for which Carter in 1979 made the secretary of education an officer in the Cabinet.

The most recent thrust of teacher unions to secure professional autonomy has taken place in the area of teacher certification. In an effort to control entry into the profession, the NEA has tried to create "teacher-dominated" state standard boards—commissions with the authority to set statewide standards for educating and certifying teachers. Beginning in the late 1960s California, Minnesota, Oregon, and a few other states established professional standards boards, and in 1987 Nevada created the first state board that gave teachers a controlling voice. The AFT has thrown its support behind the Carnegie Forum's National Board for Professional Teaching Standards. Lacking the power to impose national standards, this board expects to award teaching certificates all states will accept. One of the consequences of the teachers' union control over entry into the profession will be a reduction in the supply of teachers, which will thereby drive up teacher salaries. But what is good for teachers, the unions tell us, is good for public education.

X

Television continued and continues to educe moral criticism from those who watch it, criticism of the unfair, unjust relationships depicted on the screen. But during the 1980s that criticism began to take a decidedly conservative tilt. Now people complained about such social injustices as reverse discrimination against white people and the unfair treatment of males through affirmative action, and sometimes they complained about the unjustifiable demands made upon the rest of society by the non-English-speaking and the disabled. Minorities—blacks, Hispanics, women, the disabled—the argument went, were receiving *unfair* favorable treatment in the society—in hiring practices, in salary increments, in college admissions policies, in scholarship aid, in political appointments, in the allocation of public monies.

Much of this resentment, envy, and blame marked a resurgence of the ideology of individualism. Individualists complained that the egalitarians had abandoned the traditional notions of merit, individual responsibility, and self-reliance in the pursuit of jobs, wages, appointments, and prizes. Concern with equality of results rather than equality of opportunity had resulted in quotas and special privileges for blacks, women, the disabled, and the non-English-speaking. Moreover, the individualists pointed out, the egalitarians continued to complain even though the society had changed and inequalities had been eliminated. Here, the individualists relied on television as their source of reference.

What had happened was that, instead of depicting the actual relationships that existed in the society, television had begun to present myths. Largely in response to demands made by the minority groups themselves, television producers had consciously and deliberately moved away from stereotypical relationships and instead begun presenting blacks, and women, and Hispanics, and the disabled in positions of power and prestige, working and playing in harmony with others. These myths were encoded in dramatic shows, in sitcoms, in TV movies, on talk shows, on news shows, and in commercials. Since most people now relied on television as their reference source for what was going on in society, these mythical depictions of an egalitarian, harmonious, pluralist society "demonstrated" to the individualist critics that "enough had been done" for the minorities. As a result, they rejected the continuing complaints and demands from blacks, women, Hispanics, and the disabled as unfounded and unfair.

During this decade, the actions of the government, at all levels and in all branches, clearly reflected this conservative, or individualist, reaction. Thus, we find the federal government severely reducing all financial aid and support for the programs created in the sixties and seventies to help the minority groups. At the same time, the Supreme Court, in a series of cases, sharply narrowed earlier civil rights decisions, making it more difficult for blacks to secure redress against racist practices. It was during this period, too, much to the amazement and dismay of most women, that the Equal Rights Amendment failed to win support in a sufficient number of states—some state legislatures

actually reversed earlier endorsement of the amendment. The eighties also saw
the emergence of the "English only" movement, a moral crusade against bilin-
gualism. In the 1988 election voters in two states decided that English was the
official language of their states. And for the first time, court decisions began
to go against the disabled: the Supreme Court in 1979 ruled against a deaf
woman who had been denied admission to a nursing program in Southeast-
ern Community College, North Carolina; again in 1982 the Court ruled against
requests for a sign-language interpreter for a deaf child: Congress had
intended, the Court declared, "more to open the door of public education to
handicapped children on appropriate terms than to guarantee any particular
level of education once inside."

During the eighties, then, television helped to apply the brakes to the egalitarian changes it had helped to launch in the sixties and seventies: the civil
rights movement, the women's movement, and the movements among the
non-English-speaking minorities and the disabled. Moreover, since whatever
victories these movements had won came about in large part through the help
of the government acting on their behalf, the individualist reaction against
social reform spilled over to create a current of ideological resistance to government interference in the lives of people.

Yet the eighties was not just a reactionary decade, not merely a period
spent solely dismantling the educational reforms of the sixties and seventies.
It was also a decade that witnessed the birth of a new education reform movement, a movement created by another electronic medium: the computer.

XI

The computer created the postindustrial world of the 1980s. First, computers
enabled national companies to become worldwide multinational corporations
that produced goods in one part of the world (where labor was cheaper), while
management teams resided elsewhere, and marketing operations spread all
over the globe. Such dispersal and decentralization of activities were possible
only because electronic computers could overcome the obstacles of both time
and space, transmitting information (data) around the world instantaneously.
Second, computers created the postindustrial world by taking the procedures
workers followed—in offices, on the factory floor, in salesrooms, and in warehouses—and transforming them into programmed processes. Computers took
over the work formerly done by people as companies installed computer-inte-
grated manufacturing (CIM), computer-assisted design (CAD), computer-
assisted manufacturing (CAM), and flexible manufacturing systems (FMS).

On the face of it, the arrival of the postindustrial world was a time for cel-
ebration. A worldwide economy, unhindered by national barriers, could
increase the production and equalize the distribution of goods so that all could
live lives without want. Moreover, with the computers taking over the repet-
itive, boring tasks of many jobs, the drudgery of work would disappear. But
instead of a time of happiness, the 1980s became a time of fear, a time of worry.

People fretted endlessly about risks heretofore unrecognized or ignored: social risks, political risks, economic risks, health risks, environmental risks. In the eighties, America became a risk-aversive nation.

This heightened aversion to risk came about, I think, because of the computer. The computer vastly increased the amount of information we have about the world we live in. But in doing this, it converted all information into (statistical) data. Suddenly, statistics were everywhere; the world was being mathematized. In the economic realm alone, the U.S. Bureau of the Census publishes a monthly report that includes twenty-eight economic "indicators," comprising fourteen "leading indicators," eight "coincidental indicators," and six "lagging indicators," plus sixty other economic indicators predictive of "turning points." In addition, there is the Gross National Product, the Growth Rate, the Dow Jones, the Balance of Payments, the Cost of Living Index, and the Industrial Production Index. In the political realm, the president became the object of statistical ratings, while politicians everywhere increasingly relied upon public opinion polls. In magazine advertisements, the use of statistics rose by 75 percent between 1965 and 1970. No magazine article, no book, no television announcement about social, political, or economic matters was without statistics, or explanations of statistics. These computer-generated statistics reveal trends, directions, patterns, and probabilities about what is going on in the world that previously went unnoticed. Through computer-generated statistical data about health, for example, we found during the seventies that America was thirteenth among the nations for infant mortality and twenty-second in the life-expectancy table for a boy of ten. We learned that, in America, there are forty-eight times as many gun murders a year as in the roughly equivalent combined populations of West Germany, England, and Japan; that almost one in every five young men is rejected for military service on health grounds; that there are 5000 small towns without a doctor.

Most of the trends and patterns generated by the computer revealed goings-on that were unwanted. Thus, the computer helped businessmen uncover practices in their operations that were uneconomical; it helped politicians spot decisions that were impolitic; and with the help of the computer, social critics discovered conditions that were unsafe and dangerous. As a result, we became a risk-aversive nation. Businessmen became less entrepreneurial and tried to avoid risk through mergers or through the manipulation of the stock market; politicians became more circumspect, avoiding dicey decisions and comporting themselves more and more in accord with the opinions of the electorate as revealed through continuous polls; and throughout the society, people became more cautious about what they ate, where they walked, what they said. At the same time, litigation, and insurance against litigation, mushroomed as many sought to make others liable for any adversity they suffered, because the others, you see, had not done enough to prevent risk.

Understandably, then, in this age of the computer, Americans also gathered, processed, and dispersed censuslike statistics about the condition of American education. The most recent barrage of computer-compiled statistical data came from the New Jersey State Department of Education when it initially distributed in November 1989 reports on each of the state's 2174 elementary, junior, and senior high schools. These reports included statistics on the academic performance of students in each school, standardized test scores, staff-to-student ratios, attendance rates, instructional time, and the amount of money spent on each pupil. In addition the reports included the dropout rates for each school, basic skills test results, passing rates for the High School Proficiency Test, and how well students have scored on the Scholastic Aptitude Test (SAT). Not only states but the federal government, too, published computer-generated data about the schools.

Inevitably, all these statistics revealed unwanted patterns and trends that drew widespread criticism. In 1974 Congress created the National Center for Educational Statistics as part of the U.S. Department of Education and mandated an annual statistical report on the condition of education in the United States. One of the first acts of the center was to sponsor biennial tests of American school children, called the National Assessment of Education Progress (NAEP). Focusing on specific learning areas (science, math, citizenship, writing, reading, literature, music and social studies), the NAEP found that, between 1973 and 1980, the average score in mathematics earned by seventeen year old declined 3.6 percentage points. In science, too, the scores continually dropped from 1970 to 1980. Overall, there was a "growing weakness" in U.S. students' attainment of "higher-order skills"; that is, students could neither solve problems, nor read with understanding long, complicated passages, nor interpret the tone and mood of an author.

The most shocking revelations about the decline in academic achievement came in 1975, when the College Board announced that SAT scores had sharply declined since 1970. The decline had actually begun in 1963, but this was thought to be due to the entry of the baby boomers into the educational pipeline at that point. But in 1970 no dramatic demographic changes occurred; the SAT scores simply declined. Over a fourteen-year period, the verbal scores dropped forty-nine points and the mathematical scores declined thirty-two points. Studies of other standardized tests of verbal skills also described the same pattern of falling scores over the same period.

Those who recognized that America had entered the postindustrial age found such statistics disquieting. In the early 1980s the Bureau of Labor Statistics projected that 58.6 million job positions would become available between 1982 and 1995, and that 46 percent of them would require high levels of academic preparation. If the American educational system could not produce workers with the knowledge, learning, information, and skilled intelligence necessary to keep the postindustrial society going, the nation would lose its economic hegemony. Already, the Japanese had pushed past the United States in some fields, while the South Koreans and West Germans were gaining in others. Once again, Americans looked to their schools as a panacea: this time, the schools were expected to help America keep and improve on its slim competitive edge in the world markets.

At least, this was the message of the more than two dozen national commissions, committees, and task forces on education that now suddenly sprang up. These included the National Commission on Education, appointed by the U.S. Secretary of Education; the Task Force on Education for Economic Growth; the Task Force on Federal Elementary and Secondary Educational Policy; the Commission on Pre-College Education in Mathematics, Science and Technology; the Committee for Economic Development; the Carnegie Fund for the Achievement of Teaching; and the Business-Higher Education Forum.

The first and most influential report came from the National Commission on Excellence in Education in 1983. Appropriately entitled *A Nation at Risk*, this government document announced that American schools were awash in a "rising tide of mediocrity." After quoting statistics about the decline in SAT scores, along with the depressing results of the National Assessment of Educational Programs, the commission went on to provide additional statistics to further demonstrate how much the nation was at risk:

- International comparisons of student achievement, completed a decade ago, reveal that, on nineteen academic tests, American students were never first or second and, in comparison with other industrialized nations, were last seven times.
- Some 23 million American adults were functionally illiterate by the simple tests of everyday reading, writing, and comprehension.
- About 13 percent of all seventeen-year-olds in the United States can be considered functionally illiterate. Functional illiteracy among minority youth may run as high as 40 percent.
- Average achievement of high school students on most standardized tests is now lower than twenty-six years ago, when *Sputnik* was launched.
- Over half the population of gifted students do not match their tested abilities with comparable achievement in school.
- College Board achievement tests also reveal consistent declines in recent years in such subjects as physics and English.

During the spring of 1983 three more national reports on the sorry condition of American schools followed, with more coming out the next year. All the reports found the same four problems: an inadequate emphasis on academic studies, a lack of standards, poor teaching, and an absence of leadership. All these problems had come about as the unanticipated consequences of the transformations made in the schools in the sixties and seventies—transformations sparked by television. At that time, I have argued, television raised the nation's consciousness about the unjust and unequal relationships in the society between the races, between the sexes, between the generations, between ethnic groups, and between the fit and the disabled. To help the victims overcome their disadvantages, the schools had changed and added programs, courses, textbooks, and curriculum materials. The result, especially in secondary schools, was the emergence of what one group of critics called "the shopping mall high school"—an academic institution that offered something for everyone, a place where each self-constituted group could find programs, courses, activities, and services that were meaningful, significant, and relevant—to that group. The number of different courses offered in American high schools in 1972–1973 almost doubled those offered in 1960–1961, increasing from 1,100 to 2,100. With such fragmentation came a deemphasis on academic work. As the U.S. Department of Education noted: "courses of a practical nature proliferated." In addition, some career education programs allowed students to take paid jobs outside of school and gave credit for occasional reporting on their work. Other career education programs permitted students to leave school early each day if they had a job. As the critics of the eighties saw it, the schools lacked academic rigor, common standards, and educational coherence.

The television-induced consciousness of the unequal and unjust relationships within the society during the sixties and seventies had brought a core of teachers into the schools who wanted to make the education of the young a more humane transaction. They were more student oriented, more empathetic, more accepting, less impositional, and less demanding. Concerned with the affective side of education, many such teachers deemphasized cognition and down-played academic skills—complained the critics of the eighties. One high school teacher one of these critics talked to, declared: "I think it's very unfair if a child comes and really puts forth an effort and is doing his very best and is there every day trying; and yet you defeat him with an F. . . . I'm not going to give him F's just because he's not capable of doing what the average student in the room is doing."

These changes in school practices, policies, and programs had taken a toll in educational leadership. For the changes had come about as the result of student and parent protests, state and federal regulations, and court orders, all of which not only disrupted the normal operations of the school but also put school principals and superintendents in thrall to multiple, often conflicting, authorities. Coupled with this, school administrators now confronted teacher union militancy and the student rights movement, which further eroded their authority. The critics of the eighties found the schools in disarray with no one in charge: the schools lacked leadership.

One measure of the lack of school leadership was the increase in school violence. A national survey conducted by the National School Boards Association released early in 1994 disclosed a collection of shocking statistics generated by the computer: Eighty-two percent of the 729 districts responding to the survey said that violence had increased in their schools over the past five years. Sixty-one percent of the districts reported weapons incidents, 39 percent said there had been a shooting or knifing at school, 23 percent reported a drive-by shooting in their district and 15 percent reported at least one rape. Seventy-eight percent reported student assaults on students; 60 percent reported student assaults on teachers.

XII

The national school reports on the sorry state of education served as the wellspring for what U.S. Secretary of Education Terrel H. Bell called "a tidal wave of reform." Actually, the educational reform movement of the eighties consolidated two earlier attempted reforms. In the fifties, when Americans believed that the schools constituted the main line of defense in the cold war with the U.S.S.R., reformers had called for the schools to cultivate excellence. In the sixties and seventies, when people believed that the schools could overcome the social injustices rampant in the society, educational reformers had emphasized equity. Now, in the eighties, when reformers demanded that the schools produce the educated workers needed by the postindustrial society, they insisted upon both excellence and equity: *all* students were going to receive an excellent academic education.

How could these proposed reforms be implemented? Not by the federal government. For although the Reagan administration had launched this educational reform movement with the publication of *A Nation at Risk*, the president found himself in an awkward position. Elected in 1980 on the promise to "get the government off the people's backs," Ronald Reagan had vowed to abolish the Department of Education, only just made a cabinet-level position by his predecessor, Jimmy Carter. (Carter had created the U.S. Department of Education just before the election, hoping thereby to woo the support of the NEA, whose members accounted for 10 percent of the delegates at the 1980 Democratic convention.) But when *A Nation at Risk* became a best seller—3 million copies sold—and educational reform sat, in the words of Secretary of Education Bell, "on everyone's front burner," it seemed unwise to abolish the U.S. Department of Education. Instead, the strategy became one of having the federal department encourage the states to carry out the necessary reforms: raise standards, increase testing, establish accountability, strengthen requirements, and secure better teachers and better teaching. By 1985 *Education Week* could report that all fifty states had fashioned an "unprecedented" number of laws and rules for the nation's schools: forty-three states had raised high school graduation requirements, with fifteen of them requiring an exit test for graduation; thirty-seven states had instituted statewide assessments of students; twenty-nine states had upgraded teacher education requirements to include a mandatory competency test; and eighteen states had increased teachers' salaries. Moreover, the governors of many states, eager to keep or attract high-tech corporations to their states, rigorously championed these reforms.

Yet the "unprecedented" activity on behalf of education had brought no significant changes in student achievement by the end of the decade. The statistics on student achievement spewed out of the computer continued to depict us as a nation at risk: "The impact of educational reform does not appear in national data," the National Center for Educational Statistics soberly announced in its 1988 report, *The Condition of Education*. In its judgment, "the academic performance of students, as measured by standardized tests, shows that students cannot perform many ordinary tasks." The condition of education in the United States was not good: "Only a small portion of seventeen year olds perform at the highest proficiency levels. Where trend data are available, overall performance of U.S. students is not changing significantly. . . . While the gap between white and black and Hispanic student performance has been reduced, it still remains significant. In the most fundamental area, reading, few students even in the eleventh grade can defend their judgments and interpretations about what they read. Similar deficiencies show up in mathematics and science, where performance has been low for more than ten years and has improved very little. In the areas of U.S. history and literature, results are mixed. While students are familiar with early American history and the Bible, they show little familiarity with either recent U.S. history or literature."

That same year, the NAEP had reported that seventeen year olds' science achievement as measured in 1986 remained well below the levels achieved in 1969. The report concluded that "more than half of the nation's seventeen year olds appear to be inadequately prepared either to perform competently jobs that require technical skills, or to benefit substantially from specialized on-the-job training." The following year, the results of the first International Assessment of Educational Programs disclosed that American thirteen year olds had the lowest average mathematics proficiency among all the nations studied. American students scored below students from Korea, Canada, Spain, the United Kingdom, and Ireland. In Korea, 78 percent of the thirteen year olds could use intermediate mathematical skills to solve two-step problems, compared to only 40 percent of their counterparts in the United States. The same international assessment found that, in science proficiency, American students scored slightly higher than the students of Ireland and the French-speaking students of Ontario and New Brunswick but were below students from the rest of Canada, Korea, the United Kingdom, and Spain.

A study of the state of humanities and arts education in the nation's public schools conducted in 1987 by the National Endowment for the Humanities (NEH) and by the National Endowment for the Arts (NEA) found that more than two-thirds of the nation's seventeen year olds were unable to locate the Civil War within the correct half-century; that more than two-thirds could not identify the Reformation or *Magna Carta;* that vast majorities demonstrated unfamiliarity with: Dante, Dostoevski, Chaucer, Austin, Whitman, Hawthorne, Melville, and Cather. Here, too, the nation was at risk, or, as Lynn Cheney, Head of NEH put it, "our sense of nationhood is at risk when we fail to teach the young the ideas that have molded us and the ideals that have mattered to us."

The nation's schools had not attained the hoped-for excellence, nor had they attained equity, either. The 1989 report from the Committee on Policy for Racial Justice declared that, although "economically successful black parents today can send their children to good desegregated schools, public or private, poor black children still do not have such options. They remain, thirty-four years after *Brown,* racially isolated, largely segregated, and subjected to inferior schooling."

Even the teachers found little to celebrate. In its 1988 *Report Card on School Reform,* the Carnegie Foundation disclosed that, in a survey of more than 13,500 teachers, the vast majority—nearly 70 percent—said that the national push for school reform deserves a C or less. One teacher out of five gave the reform movement a D or an F.

When Lauro Cavazos took office in 1989 as secretary of education in the new Bush administration, his "progress report" revealed that, despite a 46 percent jump in the average amount that local, state, and federal governments spent per pupil since 1983, the percentage of high school students who graduated actually had dropped. Moreover, 13 percent of America's seventeen-year-olds—and perhaps 40 percent of minority youths of the same age—were functionally illiterate. And combined scores on the SAT have only risen slightly, from 893 to 904. "We are standing still," Secretary Cavazos lamented.

A few years later, in September 1993, the Education Department of the Federal Government released what the *New York Times* called "a bleak statistical portrait" of educational failure. According to the report, nearly half of the nation's 191 million adult citizens are not proficient enough in English to write a letter about a billing error, or able to calculate the length of a bus trip from a published schedule.

XIII

In the waning years of the twentieth century, educational reformers remained undaunted: their faith perdured. New, different plans and schemes for educational reform sprang from the word processors of educational theorists. Theodore Sizer *(Horace's Compromise)*, John Goodlad *(A Place Called School)*, Ernest Boyer *(High School)*, and Mortimer Adler *(The Paideia Proposal)* all focused on the restructuring and reorganization of the local school. Theodore Sizer was quoted as saying, "I don't think we've gotten to the heart of the problem yet. The problem *is* the existing system. And until we face up to that fact—that the existing system has to change—we're not going to get the kinds of changes everybody wants"

What "everybody wanted" was: a greater emphasis on the intellectual purpose of schooling, less diversity in the curriculum, better teaching, and more effective leadership. But as this group of educational reformers saw it, these changes had to come from the bottom up, not from the top down. These reformers viewed federal and state-imposed standards as part of the problem, since such regulation curtailed the autonomy of teachers and school administrators by laying detailed prescriptions and propositions on them.

The solution to educational reform, they argued, was "teacher empowerment." This had great appeal to those teachers who had long chafed under the restraints that prevented them from becoming "true" professionals—"like physicians and lawyers." Many teachers and their professional organizations, like the AFT, took up the slogan of teacher empowerment as the key to educational reform. The Carnegie Task Force on Teaching as a Profession concurred. In its 1986 report *(A Nation Prepared: Teachers for the 21st Century)*, this task force called for more autonomy for educators: "If the schools are to compete successfully with medicine, architecture, and accounting for staff, then teachers will have to have comparable authority in making the key decisions about the services they render."

In the late 1980s, a new proposal for reform appeared—a top-down approach. To get education moving again, George Bush, who claimed he wanted to be the "education president," convened an unprecedented "education summit" with the governors of all the states in September 1989. The conference resulted in what they called "a Jeffersonian compact to enlighten our children and the children of generations to come." Declaring that "the time for rhetoric is past," the conference created a task force to establish clear national goals, "goals that will make us internationally competitive."

Two years later, in April 1991, President Bush released *America 2000: An Educational Strategy*, a plan to move American education toward six ambitous goals. These grandiose goals promised that, in addition to all students becoming competent in English, mathematics, science, history and geography, (1) all children will start school ready to learn, (2) American students will be first in the world in science and math achievement, (3) the high school graduation rate will increase to at least 90 percent, (4) schools will be totally free of drugs and violence, and (5) there will be universal adult literacy,

George Bush left office before much was done to implement this plan, but his successor, Bill Clinton, who played a leading role in the governors group that adopted these goals, promised to carry the ball forward—to establish "world class" standards for schools, voluntary national tests for students, new American schools for local communities, and a private sector research and development fund. The Education Act, passed in Spring 1994, defined a radically expanded role for the federal government. It establishes a National Educational Goals Panel to set goals for all American schools, and it sets up a National Education Standards and Improvement Council to certify the standards to measure progress toward the goals. Participation by each state is voluntary, but only by producing plans that conform to the content and performance standards set out by the national panels can a state have access to the over $400-million pot of funds offered by the federal government. The Bill empowers the U.S. Secretary of Education to oversee state and local community planning processes to reach the goals.

XIV

While most wished the reformers well, not everyone shared their confidence that the public schools could be reformed—evident in the dramatic increase in the number of children attending private schools, and in the number of children being schooled at home. Since 1980, 28 states have adopted home-school statutes that exempt homeschooling from compulsory attendance laws. There are currently about 300,000 children educated at home in the United States. At the same time, private school enrollments have increased—an increase about equal to the decline in public school enrollments. Worthy of note here is that many public school teachers send their own children to private schools. In 1986, 30 percent of the public school teachers in both Albuquerque and Nashville did, while in Los Angeles, 29 percent did, and in San Francisco, the figure was 25 percent, and in Seattle, 23 percent.

There are two reasons for this withdrawal from public schools. First, more and more people have concluded that public schools no longer provide a quality education. Second, even more have concluded that the public schools are not society's problem solver: indeed, as they see it, public schools have become the source of many of society's social conflicts. These parents do not want their children involved in, or affected by, such conflicts.

The public schools, as we have seen, have always functioned in a political context. They worked so long as individualism and hierarchy were the dominant ideologies in America. When these ideologies reigned, the political control over schools rested with influential, middle-class, white males, who used the schools to socialize the young into the kind of people they wanted them to be. But the coming of television changed all that by making various groups—women, blacks, ethnic minorities, and the disabled—aware of oppressive inequalities in the society. These groups demanded, and secured, enough control over the schools to begin to use them to socialize their children as *they* desired. In doing this, these groups set afoot a vast increase in federal and state statutes, bureaucratic rules, and judicial decisions, all of which imposed severe political restraints on local school administrators. In this transformed political landscape, local school administrators could exercise no leadership—not because they lacked will or commitment, but simply because American public schools are now controlled by a pluralist democracy increasingly dominated by the ideology of egalitarianism.

In this situation, no local school administrator can impose a single-minded, agreed-upon purpose. Local schools can have no direction or goal. The only task is to stay afloat. The local administrator's job is to ensure order and stability, trying to satisfy at the same time the different demands of all the competing groups while seeing to it that no other groups are adversely affected.

Not only special-interest groups and their advocates, but teachers, too, have secured sufficient political power to prevent local administrators from exercising leadership. In most local school districts, administrators have little or no power to change textbooks, abolish courses of study, adjust class size, dismiss incompetent teachers, conduct evaluations of teachers, lengthen their work day, or change their work loads. Quite simply, local school administrators can do little or nothing to improve the performance of teachers. Teacher unions have tenure agreements, single-salary schedules, and collective bargaining rights that have effectively removed all control over incentives and punishments that administrators in the past could employ to extort more work from their teachers. In addition, any "legal" but unpopular demands an administrator might make of teachers face the possibility of grievance arbitration and extended impasse procedures to resolve conflict. The upshot of teacher militancy is that administrators now make few, if any, demands on their teachers.

Nor can teachers push students. Although all the educational reformers demand that teachers must make students work harder, today's students have legally recognized rights that deprive teachers of many of the incentives and punishments they used in the past to extort work from students. "Student resistance" and "performance strikes" are facts of life in many schools. Moreover, most schools cannot expell students, and to suspend them requires strict adherence to time-consuming, and enervating, due-process procedures. Theodore Sizer has described how students "played the game adult educators asked them to play only when and how they wanted to." In this sense, he adds, "kids run schools. Their apparent acquiescence to what their elders want them to do is always provisional." Moreover, teachers and students know that, if pressed, students may drop out of school, which automatically reduces the amount of state aid the school receives. Teachers, therefore, are loath to antagonize students. Instead, teachers and students negotiate tacit treaties not to expect or demand too much of each other.

The rise of egalitarianism has not only debilitated the quality of education in public schools, it has also created social conflicts—interminable and irresolvable social conflicts. Anyone who can read—or anyone who watches television—knows that public schools have become battlegrounds for serious social conflicts in matters like sex education, multicultural education, affirmative action, Afrocentrism, tracking, and creationism. These conflicts are politically undecidable, because they stem from strongly held values that many are unwilling to compromise. So any solution proposed to satisfy one group inevitably harms, or threatens, the values of some other politically conscious group. Since these conflicts cannot be resolved through the political process of negotiation and compromise, they often wind up in the courts, where judges impose solutions. These judicially imposed solutions usually satisfy the minority group that had complained about victimization, but the solution often infuriates members of the majority, who now declare that it is they who are being victimized.

These conflicts are interminable because so many people—teachers, administrators, lawyers, government officials, activist group leaders—make their living off these issues. Rather than go out of business, they endeavor to uncover new forms of oppression. In short, social conflict has been institutionalized in the public schools.

Few people want to return to the paternalistic, authoritarian policies, practices, and procedures that characterized public schools when they were under the sway of the ideologies of individualism and hierarchy. But on the other hand, most people want schools that provide a quality education, as well as schools that accept the pluralist society we now have and foster cooperation and interaction—not conflict—between persons who disagree on basic values. We can no longer use the public schools to impose elitist solutions—or majority solutions, or minority solutions—on the population as a whole. This is why so many parents are moving beyond public education.

In 1981 James Coleman released the findings of his study of public and private schools that showed that the structure, organization, and policies of private schools resulted in higher student achievement than in public schools, as well as more disciplined and orderly conduct. In these private schools, Coleman found that administrators and teachers had more autonomy, that the emphasis was on the intellectual purpose of schooling, and that rigorous academic standards were enforced.

The reason for this success of the private schools is that they operate in the market place, not in the political order. According to this argument, in a free market, schools compete for students. Only schools that provide customers with what they want will survive. Private schools are subject to none of the political obstacles that prevent public schools from promoting quality education. To attract customers, administrators in private schools set forth clear goals and purposes, hire only teachers who subscribe to these goals, and expect teachers to push students to pursue those stated goals.

Free from the court decisions, the laws, and the regulations that cripple the public schools, private schools remain autonomous institutions: decisions are made quickly, and changes are readily implemented. If teachers or students or parents are unhappy with the goings-on in a private school, they withdraw and go someplace else; whereas in a public school, they stay and become politically active in order to combat what displeases them.

Those who endorse a free market system of education favor parental-choice plans like tuition tax-credits and vouchers, which would give parents money to pay for the tuition of their children at any school of their choice, public or private. Some favor entrepreneurial schools—schools run for profit by private enterprise, independently or under contract to school boards. This approach to educational reform, its proponents point out, accepts the pluralism and diversity of American society and allows parents to seek out those schools that provide the kind of education they want to buy; and it allows schools to offer any kind of education there is a demand for in the market place.

Here are some examples of problems that plague the public schools that would be readily resolved or disappear in a market system of education.

- In New York City, Chancellor Joseph Fernandez issued a model teaching guide, *Children of the Rainbow,* that included the recommendation that teachers provide classroom experiences that "view lesbians/gays as real people to be respected and appreciated." One local school board refused to change the curriculum "to promote the acceptance of sodomy." The furious social conflict that ensued resulted in the central board voting not to renew the chancellor's contract.
- California requires that textbooks issued in public schools emphasize healthful food. When a publisher decided to include in one of its texts a story called "A Perfect Day for Ice Cream," which had first appeared in *Seventeen* magazine, it had to change the title because of its perceived glorification of fatty foods. So it appeared as "A Perfect Day," and references within the story to pizza and chiliburgers were also deleted.
- Earlier in California, the Standing Committee to Review Textbooks from a Multicultural Perspective detected racism in such phrases as "the afternoon turned black," "it's going to be a black winter," and "the deputy's face darkened."
- The District of Columbia refused to purchase any songbook that contained the word *darky* in Stephen Foster lyrics (and Georgia refused to buy any book that changed the lyric to *brother*).

- In Duval County, Florida, Planned Parenthood sued the school board for accepting an abstinence-based curriculum for its sex-education program.
- In New York City, after months of conflict, a state appellate court, in a 3 to 2 decision, decided that parents have the right to prevent their children from receiving condoms in high school health programs. A lawyer with the New York Civil Liberties Union denounced the decision: "It is putting obstacles in the way of young people who are sexually active."
- In New Jersey, the State Department of Education issued a family life curriculum for pupils from kindergarten through the third grade that includes information on intercourse, masturbation, reproduction, and fetal growth. It provoked bitter controversies between state officials and groups of parents.
- In Cincinnati, in response to parental complaints about the disparate impact of the school discipline code on white and black students, a court ruled that race and gender records be kept of the teachers referring a student for disciplinary action, and also the race and gender of the student.

In a market system of education, parents would seek out schools that offered the kind of curriculum and the kind of programs, discipline codes, and textbooks they preferred. They would withdraw from schools if they disapproved of what the school offered. Moreover, in an open market, new schools would appear to supply the kinds of education consumers demand. No one person, or group, has ever been wise enough, and today no one is politically powerful enough, to impose a common education on all. Nor is there any need to do this in a democratic, pluralist, society.

- Recently, the California State Board of Education banned an Alice Walker story from a statewide English test because it was "anti-meat eating."

In a market system of education, there would be no statewide examinations.

- In 1994, fully half the states had public school financing lawsuits pending. According to the Equity Center, the rich 5 percent of the nation's school districts spend an average $11,801 per pupil, while the poorest 5 percent spend $3,190.

In a market system of education, there would be no rich or poor districts. There would be expensive and less expensive schools. Parents would decide how much to spend on their own children's education and select the school accordingly. All parents would receive the same school vouchers, but could, if they wished, add additional money of their own to spend for schools of their choice.

- In Houston, schools have jettisoned the traditional grading system. To the consternation of many parents, instead of getting A's or B's on the report cards, students in the early grades are pegged into one of eight progressive stages: discovery, exploration, developing, expanding, connecting, independent, application, and synthesis.

Because some parents complain that standard grading systematically discriminates against their children, some schools have adopted outcome-based objectives (OBE) like these. In a market system of education, where parents pay the school tuition, they would be likely to demand an honest and objective assessment of their children's academic progress.

- In Ohio, all teenage mothers and pregnant women under 20 who attend school get an additional $62 in their monthly welfare checks.

Such bribery would not exist in a market system of education, where schooling is privately paid for. In public schools, producers (educators) create the demand for education; in a market system, consumers create the demand.

Not surprisingly, since the transaction costs fall heavily on them, most educators oppose a market system of education. Schools of education, too, oppose it, because they construe their role as the preparation of educators for what exists. But the signs are clear that this is the direction American education is taking. Witness the growth of contracting out of teaching in a number of urban school districts, as well as the increase in the number of open enrollment plans.

In 1988, Minnesota became the first state in the nation to enact a comprehensive open-enrollment plan. Within two years, Arkansas, Iowa, and Nebraska adopted similar plans, and some twenty other states were considering proposals for open enrollment.

A Gallup Poll in 1989 found that "the public favors by a two to one margin allowing students and their parents to choose which public schools in their communities the student will attend." The poll reported that nonwhites and younger adults especially favored the idea of parental choice. In spite of such polls, however, Californians in 1993 voted two to one against a voucher plan—perhaps as a result of the $16 million the National Education Association (NEA) had spent to defeat it. Earlier, the NEA voted at its 1989 convention to oppose any state or federal plan for school-choice programs that gives parents the right to select the school their children attend. The main argument of the NEA is that such programs will destroy the public school system, because it is the first step toward providing public financial aid to private schools.

The NEA may be correct. But in the twenty-first century, perhaps the only way Americans can shore up their lagging faith in education is to move beyond the public schools.

Bibliographic Note

A great number of historical analyses of education have appeared since the first edition of *The Imperfect Panacea*. Here are some of the most noteworthy: Robert L. Church, *Education in the United States* (New York: Free Press, 1976); Lawrence A. Cremin, *American Education* 3 volumes (New York: Harper and Row, 1970–1988); Robert L. Hampel, *The Last Little Citadel: American High Schools Since 1940* (Boston: Houghton-Mifflin, 1986); Walter Feinberg, *Reason and Rhetoric: The Intellectual Foundations of 20th Century Liberal Educational Policy* (New York: John Wiley and Sons, 1975); Clarence J. Karier, *The Individual, Society, and Education* (Urbana: University of Illinois Press, 1986); Michael B. Katz, *Reconstructing American Education* (Cambridge: Harvard University Press, 1987); David S. Nasaw, *Schooled to Order* (New York: Oxford University Press, 1979); Paul E. Peterson, *The Politics of School Reform, 1870–1940* (Chicago: University of Chicago Press, 1985). Diane Ravitch, *The Schools We Deserve* (New York: Basic Books, 1985); Diane Ravitch, *The Troubled Crusade: American Education 1945–1980* (New York: Basic Books, 1983); Stanley Schultz, *The Culture Factory: Boston Public Schools, 1789–1860* (New York: Oxford University Press, 1973) and Joel Spring, *The American School: Varieties of Historical Interpretations of the Foundations and Development of American Education*, 2nd Edition (New York: Longman, 1990); Selwyn K. Troen, *The Public and the Schools: Shaping the St. Louis System, 1838–1920* (Columbia: University of Missouri Press, 1975).

Two helpful guides to the history of American education are: Francisco Cordasco and William W. Brickman, *A Bibliography of American Educational History* (New York: AMS Press, 1975); and Sol Cohen's monumental *Education in the United States: A Documentary History* (New York: Random House, 1974, 5 volumes.)

ONE: THE AMERICANS AND THEIR SCHOOLS

In this rapid survey of the pre-Civil War functions of the American school I have drawn freely on the work of Daniel Boorstin, *The Americans, The Colonial*

Experience (New York: Random House, 1958), Rush Welter, *Popular Education and Democratic Thought in America* (New York: Columbia University Press, 1962), and Bernard Bailyn, *Education in the Forming of American Society* (Chapel Hill: University of North Carolina Press, 1960). I have also used the interpretations of the role of higher education given by Frederick Rudolph, *The American College and University* (New York: Alfred A. Knopf, 1962) and Richard Hofstadter and Walter P. Metzger, *The Development of Academic Freedom in the United States* (New York: Columbia University Press, 1955).

The basic texts on the influence of the printing press are Elizabeth L. Eisenstein, *The Printing Press as an Agent of Change*, vols. I & II (New York: Cambridge University Press, 1979) and Lucien Febvre and Henri-Jean Martin, *The Coming of the Book* (London: Verso Books, 1984).

TWO: THE EVOLUTION OF THE PUBLIC SCHOOL

In my analysis of the moral reformers, I relied heavily on Paul Boyer, *Urban Masses and Moral Order in America* (Cambridge: Harvard University Press, 1978) and Clifford S. Griffin, *Their Brothers' Keepers: Moral Stewardship in the United States, 1800–1865* (New Brunswick: Rutgers University Press, 1960).

In my analysis of schools in the antebellum period, I am indebted to the work of Carl Kaestle, *Pillars of the Republic: Common Schools and American Society, 1780–1860* (New York: Hill and Wang, 1983); *The Evolution of an Urban School System: New York City, 1750–1850* (Cambridge: Harvard University Press, 1973), and *Education and Social Change in Nineteenth Century Massachusetts* (New York: Cambridge University Press, 1980), which he wrote with Maris A. Vinovskis. I am deeply indebted to the analyses of this period in Lawrence A. Cremin's monumental *American Education: The National Experience, 1783–1876* (New York: Harper and Row, 1980) and Rush Welter's *Popular Education and Democratic Thought in America* (New York: Columbia University Press, 1962).

Other educational histories I found useful include: Frederick M. Binder, *The Age of the Common School, 1830–1865* (New York: John Wiley and Sons, 1974); Frank Tracy Carlton, *Economic Influence upon Educational Progress in the United States* (1908) (New York: Teachers College Press, 1965); Robert L. Church, *Education in the United States: An Interpretive History* (New York: The Free Press, 1976); Lawrence A. Cremin, *The American Common School: An Historic Conception* (New York: Teachers College Press, 1951); Ellwood P. Cubberly, *Public Education in the United States* (Cambridge: Houghton-Mifflin Company, 1919); Michael B. Katz, *Reconstructing American Education* (Cambridge: Harvard University Press, 1987); Joel Spring, *The American School, 1642–1990* (New York: Longman, 1990); and David Tyack and Elizabeth Hansot, *Managers of Virtue: Public School Leadership in America, 1920–1980* (New York: Basic Books, 1982).

A number of excellent collections of original sources relevant to this period is available. These include: Daniel Calhoun, *The Educating of Americans: A Documentary History* (Boston: Houghton-Mifflin, 1969); Michael B. Katz, *School Reform: Past and Present* (Boston: Little, Brown and Company, 1971); Rush Welter, *American Writings on Popular Education in the Nineteenth Century* (Indianapolis: The Bobbs-Merrill Company, 1971); and Wilson Smith, *Theories of Education in Early America, 1655–1819* (Indianapolis: The Bobbs-Merrill Company, 1973).

Paul Mattingly provides an excellent study of the "friends of education" in *The Classless Profession: American Schoolmen in the Nineteenth Century* (New York: New York University Press, 1975). Theodore R. Sizer's *The Age of the Academies* (New York: Teachers College, 1964) is an excellent source. Carl Kaestle's *Joseph Lancaster and the Monitorial Movement* (New York: Teachers College Press, 1973) contains useful information. Jonathan Messerli has written a very readable biography of Mann, *Horace Mann: A Biography* (New York: Alfred A. Knopf, 1972). Warren Burton's reminiscences are in *The District School as it Was* (1833) (Boston: Lee and Shepherd, 1897).

Culture Theory is described in Mary Douglas, *Natural Symbols: Explorations in Cosmology* (London: Barrie and Rockliff, 1970). Also see Michael Thompson, Richard Ellis and Aaron Wildavsky, *Cultural Theory* (Boulder: Westview Press, 1990); and Richard Ellis, *American Political Cultures* (New York: Oxford University Press, 1993).

In my analysis of anti-Catholicism, I relied heavily on Ray Billington, *The Protestant Crusade: 1800–1860* (New York: The Macmillan Company, 1938). Lloyd P. Jorgenson's *The State and the Non-Public School* is an excellent history of the conflicts between Protestants and Catholics over schooling. An excellent study of the Catholic attempts to secure public funding for their schools is Vincent P. Lannie, *Public Money and Parochial Education: Bishop Hughes, Governor Seward and the New York School Controversy* (Cleveland: The Press of Case Western Reserve University, 1968). Diane Ravitch, *The Great School Wars: New York City, 1805–1973* (New York: Basic Books, 1974) is also helpful. General information on religion and education can be found in Leo Pfeffer, *Church, State and Freedom* (Boston: The Beacon Press, 1954) and Charles Leslie Glenn, Jr., *The Myth of the Common School* (Amherst: The University of Massachusetts Press, 1987). Ruth Elson's analysis of schoolbooks is *Guardians of Tradition: American Schoolbooks of the Nineteenth Century* (Lincoln: University of Nebraska Press, 1964).

THREE: RACIAL INEQUALITY AND THE SCHOOLS

My account of the Yankee teachers in the South is based on the work of Henry Lee Swint, *The Northern Teacher in the South* (Nashville: Vanderbilt University Press, 1941).

The attempt of the Southern states to set up a system of education is treated by Edgar W. Knight in *Public Education in the South* (Boston: Ginn, 1922) and Charles W. Dabney, *Universal Education in the South* (Chapel Hill: University of North Carolina Press, 1932). For the battle against the Freedmen's Bureau, I have relied upon John Hope Franklin's *Reconstruction: After the Civil War* (Chicago: University of Chicago Press, 1961). I have leaned heavily on this work as well as his monumental, *From Slavery to Freedom* (New York: Alfred

A. Knopf, 1937). Much of my discussion of this period was also influenced by C. Vann Woodward's *Origins of the New South 1877–1913* (Baton Rouge: Louisiana State University Press, 1951). I have also consulted Walter L. Fleming's *Documentary History of Reconstruction* (New York: Peter Smith, 1950). Chapter IX of the second volume contains documents pertaining to "Educational Problems of Reconstruction."

I have based most of my discussion of the Peabody Fund on the history written by J. L. M. Curry, *A Brief Sketch of George Peabody, and a History of the Peabody Education Fund* (Cambridge: J. Wilson & Son, 1898). An excellent study is Earle H. West, "The Peabody Education Fund and Negro Education," *History of Education Quarterly*, vol. VI, no. 2 (Summer 1966).

The picture of Negro education during the eighties and nineties is based on Woodward *(op. cit.)* and Horace Mann Bond, *The Education of the Negro in the American Social Order* (New York: Prentice-Hall, 1934). C. Vann Woodward's *The Strange Career of Jim Crow* (New York: Oxford University Press, 1957) supplied the data for my discussion of the Populist movement in the South.

For the career of Booker T. Washington I used his autobiography, *Up from Slavery* (New York: Doubleday, Page, 1901). I quoted from this and also from his *Selected Speeches* (Garden City: Doubleday, 1932). I also found Rayford W. Logan, *The Negro in American Life and Thought: The Nadir, 1877–1890* (New York: Dial, 1954) helpful.

For the career of William E. B. Du Bois I used the biography by Francis L. Broderick, *W. E. B. Du Bois: Negro Leader in Time of Crisis* (Stanford: Stanford University Press, 1959). The quote from Du Bois is from his *The Souls of Black Folks* (Chicago: A. C. McClurg, 1903).

My interpretation of recent developments has been influenced by Louis Lomax, *The Negro Revolt* (New York: Harper & Row, 1962), Howard Brotz, *The Black Jews of Harlem* (New York: Free Press, 1964), Charles E. Silberman, *Crisis in Black and White* (New York: Random House, 1964), and Nathan Glazer, "Negroes and Jews: The New Challenge to Pluralism," *Commentary*, vol. 38, no. VI (December 1964).

Important recent studies include: Henry A. Bullock, *A History of Negro Education in the South, from 1619 to the Present,* (New York: Praeger, 1970); Ronald K. Goodenow and Arthur D. White, eds., *Education and the Rise of the New South* (Boston: G. K. Hall & Company, 1981); Louis R. Harlan, *Booker T. Washington,* 2 volumes (New York: Oxford University Press, 1972–1983); Louis R. Harlan, *Booker T. Washington: The Wizard of Tuskegee, 1901–1915,* (New York: Oxford University Press, 1983), Robert C. Morris, *Reading 'Riting, and Reconstruction: The Education of Freedmen in the South, 1861–1870,* (Chicago: University of Chicago Press, 1981).

FOUR: THE CITY AND THE SCHOOLS

For the growth of the city I have used Arthur M. Schlesinger, *The Rise of the City, 1878–1898* (New York: Macmillan, 1933), Blake McKelvey, *The Urbanization of America* (New Brunswick: Rutgers University Press, 1963), Constance

McLaughlin Green, *The Rise of Urban America* (New York: Harper & Row, 1965), and Charles N. Glaab, *The American City, A Documentary History* (Homewood, IL: Dorsey Press, 1963), especially Chapter III. Maldwyn Jones, *American Immigration* (Chicago: University of Chicago Press, 1960) supplied much of the information on immigrants.

For my description of the impact of the city on the immigrant families I have relied on Oscar Handlin, *The Uprooted* (Boston: Little, Brown, 1951) and the essays in a volume he edited, *The Historian and the City* (Cambridge: M.I.T. Press, 1963). I have also been influenced by Mary Antin's *The Promised Land* (Boston: Houghton Mifflin, 1912).

The reaction to the immigrants is best described in the words of Jacob Riis. I consulted *How the Other Half Lives* (New York: Scribner's, 1903) and *The Battle with the Slums* (New York: Macmillan, 1902). The Americanization movement is treated in Edward G. Hartmann, *The Movement to Americanize the Immigrant* (New York: Columbia University Press, 1948), and John Higham, *Strangers in the Land: Patterns of American Nativism 1860–1925* (New Brunswick: Rutgers University Press, 1955).

The data on compulsory education was obtained from Forest C. Ensign, *Compulsory School Attendance and Child Labor* (Iowa City: Athens Press, 1921) and John L. Lawing, *Standards for State and Local Compulsory School Attendance Service* (Maryville, MO: Forum Print Shop, 1934).

A good summary of the growth of the educational enterprise during this period can be found in Ernest Carroll Moore, *Fifty Years of American Education: A Sketch of the Progress of Education in the United States for 1867–1917* (Boston: Ginn, 1917). More detailed information is found in Nicholas M. Butler, ed., *Education in the United States* (New York: American Book Company, 1910), Douglas E. Lawson, *Curriculum Development in City School Systems* (Chicago: University of Chicago Press, 1940), and Arthur Henry Chamberlain, *The Growth of Responsibility and Enlargement of Power of the City School Superintendent* (Berkeley: University of California Press, 1913). The sorry plight of the urban schools of the period is depicted in Joseph Mayer Rice's *The Public School System of the United States* (New York: The Century Company, 1893) and a brief introduction to the beginnings of school administration is Elwood P. Cubberly, *Public School Administration* (Boston: Houghton Mifflin, 1916).

William T. Harris lavished praise on the graded school in numerous writings. I quoted from one of them, "Elementary Education," in *Monographs on Education in the United States*, No. 3 (Albany: J. B. Lyon Company, 1904).

I found some helpful material on specialization in W. S. Deffenbaugh, "Public Education in the Cities of the U.S.," U.S. Bureau of Education, Bulletin 1918, No. 48 (Washington, D.C.: Government Printing Office, 1919).

John D. Philbrick describes the new city normal schools in *City School Systems in the United States* (Washington, D.C.: Government Printing Office, 1885). The work of Edward Sheldon at Oswego is discussed by Andrew P. Hollis, *The Contributions of the Oswego Normal School to Educational Progress in the United States* (Boston: Heath, 1898). I found the quote from Elizabeth Mayo's *Manual* in Lois C. Mossman's *Changing Conceptions Relative to the Planning of Lessons* (New York: Teachers College, Columbia University, 1924).

The study of dropouts in St. Louis appeared in the U.S. Commissioner of Education Report for 1899–1900. For the Herbartians I found helpful Charles De Garmo's *Herbart and the Herbartians* (New York: Scribner's Sons, 1895). The *Yearbooks* of the National Herbart Society for the Scientific Study of Teaching were published from 1895 to 1898. Its successor, the National Society for the Scientific Study of Education (later, the National Society for the Study of Education) began to publish yearbooks in 1901.

I based my description of John Dewey's Laboratory School on the account in Katherine Camp Mayhew and Anna Camp Edwards, *The Dewey School* (New York: Appleton-Century, 1936). The quote from Edward Ward about social centers appears in Clarence A. Perry, *Wider Use of the School Plant* (New York: Charities Publication Committee, Russell Sage Foundation, 1910). The quote from Lord Bryce is from *Modern Democracies* (New York: Macmillan, 1921). The description of the "community school" of the thirties is based on the volume edited by Samuel Everett, *The Community School* (New York: Appleton-Century, 1938). The quotes from Arthur Bestor are from his *Educational Wastelands* (Urbana, IL: University of Illinois Press, 1953). The quote from Richard Hofstadter about intellectuals in the 1950's is from his *Anti-Intellectualism in American Life* (New York: Alfred A. Knopf, 1963). I obtained the statistics for the fifties and sixties from Oscar Handlin's *The Newcomers* (Cambridge: Harvard University Press, 1954) and from the collection of articles in *The Schools and the Urban Crisis*, edited by August Kerker and Barbara Bonmarito (New York: Holt, Rinehart and Winston, 1965); the quote from James B. Conant is also in this volume. Most of the material on the urban black is from Charles E. Silberman, *Crisis in Black and White* (New York: Random House, 1964).

Recent important studies include: George Dykhuizen, *The Life and Mind of John Dewey* (Carbondale: Southern Illinois University Press, 1971); Michael Katz, *Class, Bureaucracy and Schools: The Illusion of Educational Change in America* (New York: Praeger Publishers, 1971); Herbert M. Kliebard, *The Struggle for the American Curriculum, 1893–1958* (Boston: Routledge & Kegan Paul, 1986); Ellen Candliffe Lagemann, ed., *Jane Addams on Education* (New York: Teachers College Press, 1985); William J. Reese, *Power and the Promise of School Reform* (Boston: Routledge and Kegan Paul, 1986); David B. Tyack, *The One Best System: A History of American Urban Education* (Cambridge: Harvard University Press, 1974); Bernard J. Weiss, ed., *American Education and the American Immigrant* (Champaign: University of Illinois Press, 1982).

FIVE: ECONOMIC OPPORTUNITY AND THE SCHOOLS

For the history of the labor movement I used John R. Commons *(et al.)*, *History of Labor in the United States* (New York: Macmillan, 1926), Henry Pelling, *American Labor* (Chicago: University of Chicago Press, 1961), and Philip S. Foner, *History of the Labor Movement in the United States* (New York: International Publishers, 1955).

The material on the American businessmen is based on Sigmund Diamond, *The Reputation of American Businessmen* (Cambridge: Harvard University Press, 1955), Matthew Josephson, *The Robber Barons* (New York: Harcourt, Brace, 1934), Stewart H. Holbrook, *The Age of the Moguls* (New York: Doubleday, 1953), and Edward C. Kirkland, *Dream and Thought in the Business Community 1860–1900* (Chicago: Quadrangle Books, 1964).

Most of what I say about the American success literature is based on Irwin G. Wyllie, *The Self-Made Man in America* (New Brunswick: Rutgers University Press, 1954). I also used Robert D. Mosier, *Making the American Mind* (New York: King's Crown Press, 1941) for this genre of literature as well as for his analysis of the *McGuffey's Readers.* Louis B. Wright, "Franklin's Legacy to the Gilded Age," *Virginia Quarterly Review,* vol. XXII, no. 2 (Spring 1946), was useful. I also found helpful Charles Carpenter, *History of American Schoolbooks* (Philadelphia: University of Pennsylvania Press, 1963). John Tebbel has a brief, informative study of Horatio Alger, *From Rags to Riches* (New York: Macmillan, 1963). I also found helpful John Cawelti, *Apostles of the Self-Made Man* (Chicago: University of Chicago Press, 1965).

William Miller's analyses of the business elite appear in a book he edited, *Men in Business* (New York: Harper Torchbooks, 1962) and in an essay in *The Reconstruction of American History* (New York: Harper Torchbooks, 1963), edited by John Higham. The disenchantment of Americans during the eighties is sketched briefly in Samuel P. Hays, *The Response to Industrialism* (Chicago: University of Chicago Press, 1957) and Eric Goldman, *Rendezvous with Destiny* (New York: Alfred A. Knopf, 1952) and more fully in Chester A. Destler, *American Radicalism* (New London: Octagon, 1946). For the commentary of one who personally experienced that disenchantment, see Richard T. Ely, *Social Aspects of Christianity* (New York: T. Y. Crowell & Company, 1889). In addition to Andrew Carnegie's *Triumphant Democracy* (New York: Scribner's, 1886), I have quoted from two collections of his essays: *Empire of Business* (New York: Doubleday, Page, 1902) and the *Gospel of Wealth and Other Timely Essays,* edited by Edward C. Kirkland (Cambridge: Belknap Press of Harvard University, 1962). For what I say about Carnegie I am indebted to Robert G. McCloskey, *American Conservatism in the Age of Enterprise* (New York: Harper Torchbooks, 1964). The *Report* of the Mosely Education Commission was published by the Commission in London, 1904.

For the development of vocationalism in higher education I am heavily indebted to the brilliant study by Laurence R. Veysey, *The Emergence of the American University* (Chicago: University of Chicago Press, 1965) and to Frederick Rudolph, *American College and University* (New York: Alfred A. Knopf, 1962).

I. L. Kandel's statistics for the number of high schools in 1860 appear in his *History of Secondary Education* (Boston: Houghton Mifflin, 1930). The comparative study of high school programs in the nineteenth century is John E. Stout's famous *The Development of High School Curricula in the North Central States from 1860 to 1918* (Chicago: University of Chicago Press, 1921).

In discussing the work of the Committee of Ten, I have profited greatly from Theodore Sizer, *Secondary Schools at the Turn of the Century* (New Haven: Yale University Press, 1964) and from Edward King, *The Shaping of the American High School* (New York: Harper & Row, 1964). I also used the study of the Carnegie Unit made by E. Tompkins and W. Gaumnitz, published as "The Carnegie Unit: Its Origin, Status and Trends" (United States Department of Health, Education and Welfare Bulletin No. 7, 1954).

For the beginnings of vocational education in the schools, I used Charles A. Bennett, *History of Manual and Industrial Education 1870 to 1917* (Peoria, IL: Manual Arts Press, 1937), Grant Venn, *Man, Education and Work* (Washington, D.C., American Council on Education, 1964), and Edward King *(op. cit.). The Report of the Massachusetts Commission on Industrial and Technical Education* (The Douglas Commission) was published by the Commission in Boston in 1906. The proceedings of the meetings of the National Society for the Promotion of Industrial Education were published in New York by the Society as *Bulletins,* beginning in 1907. All talks delivered at NEA conventions are published yearly by the association as *Proceedings.*

The report of the Commission on the Reorganization of Secondary Schools was published as a Bulletin (No. 35) of the Bureau of Education as "Cardinal Principles of Secondary Education" (Washington, D.C.: Government Printing Office, 1918).

The studies by Robert and Helen Lynd are *Middletown* (New York: Harcourt, Brace, 1929), and *Middletown in Transition* (New York: Harcourt, Brace, 1937). The study conducted by Warner, Havinghurst, and Loeb is *Who Shall Be Educated?* (New York: Harper, 1944). The book I refer to by Patricia C. Sexton is *Education and Income* (New York: Viking, 1961).

The term "The Expert Society" is taken from the valuable book by Burton R. Clark, *Educating the Expert Society* (San Francisco: Chandler, 1962). I also used *Education and Manpower* (New York: Columbia University Press, 1960), edited by Henry David.

The essay by David Bazelon is "The New Class," *Commentary,* vol. 42, no. II (August 1966). Paul Goodman uses the phrase "The Universal Trap" in *Compulsory Mis-Education* (New York: Horizon, 1964).

Recent important studies include: C. A. Bowers, *The Progressive Educator and the Depression* (New York: Random House, 1969); Hugh Hawkins, *Between Harvard and America: The Educational Leadership of Charles W. Eliot* (Chicago: The University of Chicago Press, 1972); Edward A. Krug, *The Shaping of the American High School,* Volume 2 (Madison: The University of Wisconsin Press, 1972); Ellen Candliffe Lagemann, *Private Power for the Public Good: A History of the Carnegie Foundation for the Advancement of Teaching* (Middletown: Wesleyan University Press, 1983), and *The Politics of Knowledge: The Carnegie Corporation, Philanthropy and Public Policy* (Middletown: Wesleyan University Press, 1989); Marvin Lazerson and W. Norton Grubb, *American Education and Vocationalism: A Documentary History* (New York: Teachers College Press, 1974); Marvin Lazerson, *Origins of the Urban School: Public Education in Massachusetts, 1870–1915* (Cambridge: Harvard University Press, 1971); David Tyack, Robert Lowe, and Elizabeth Hansot, *Public Schools in Hard Times: The Great Depression and Recent*

Years (Cambridge: Harvard University Press, 1984); Paul C. Violas, *The Training of the Working Class* (Chicago: Rand McNally, 1978); Arthur Zilversmit, *Changing Schools: Progressive Education, Theory and Practice, 1930–1960* (Chicago: The University of Chicago Press, 1993).

SIX: THE GOVERNMENT AND THE SCHOOLS

For information about the political situation after the Civil War, I used Thomas C. Cochran and William Miller, *The Age of Enterprise* (New York: Harper & Row, 1961; revised edition), Richard Hofstadter, *The American Political Tradition* (New York: Alfred A. Knopf, 1948), Samuel P. Hays, *The Response to Industrialism* (Chicago: University of Chicago Press, 1957), and Eric Goldman, *Rendezvous with Destiny* (New York: Vintage Books, 1956; revised edition).

My interpretation of the response of the liberal reformers leans heavily on Rush Welter, *Popular Education and Democratic Thought in America* (New York: Columbia University Press, 1962). I also found Goldman *(op. cit.)* helpful.

For the work and thought of William T. Harris I found invaluable Merle Curti, *The Social Ideas of American Educators* (Paterson, NJ: Littlefield, Adams, 1963; revised edition) and Lawrence A. Cremin, *The Transformation of the School* (New York: Alfred A. Knopf, 1961). I also consulted John R. Anscott, "Moral Freedom and the Educative Process, A Study in the Educational Philosophy of William Torrey Harris" (Unpublished Ph.D. dissertation, New York University, 1948), John S. Roberts, *William T. Harris, A Critical Study of his Educational and Related Philosophical Views* (Washington, D.C.: National Education Association, 1924), and *William Torrey Harris, 1835–1935,* edited by Edward L. Schaub (Chicago: Open Court, 1936).

For my discussion on Charles W. Eliot I used the work of Frederick Rudolph, *The American College and University* (New York: Alfred A. Knopf, 1962), Laurence R. Veysey, *The Emergence of the American University* (Chicago: University of Chicago Press, 1965), and above all Samuel Eliot Morrison, *Three Centuries of Harvard* (Cambridge: Harvard University Press, 1936). I made extensive use of Eliot's essays collected in *American Contributions to Civilization* (New York: Century, 1898) and those collected and edited by Edward Krug, *Charles W. Eliot and Popular Education* (New York: Teachers College, Columbia University, 1961).

In my treatment of progressive politics I used all the works cited earlier (in the first two paragraphs) plus Richard Hofstadter, *The Age of Reform* (New York: Alfred A. Knopf, 1955). (Recently, in "Woodrow Wilson's Prediction to Frank Cobb: Words Historians Should Doubt Ever Got Spoken," *The Journal of American History,* vol. LVI, no. 3 (December 1967), Jerold S. Auerbach raised considerable doubt concerning the authenticity of the oft-quoted remarks Woodrow Wilson supposedly made to Frank Cobb.)

For my remarks on G. Stanley Hall and Edward Lee Thorndike I made use of *Psychology and the Science of Education,* edited by Geraldine M. Joncich (New York: Teachers College, Columbia University, 1962) and *Health, Growth, and*

Heredity, edited by Charles E. Strickland and Charles Burgess (New York: Teachers College, Columbia University, 1965). I also found Cremin *(op. cit.)* helpful.

My discussion of John Dewey is based on my reading of his *Reconstruction in Philosophy* (Boston: Beacon, 1948), *The Quest for Certainty* (New York: Minton, Balch, 1929), *The School and Society* (Chicago: University of Chicago Press, 1943), *Democracy and Education* (New York: Macmillan, 1916), *How We Think* (New York: Henry Holt, 1922), and *Experience and Education* (New York: Macmillan, 1938).

My remarks on the University of Wisconsin were based, in part, on Frederick C. Howe, *Wisconsin: An Experiment in Democracy* (New York: Scribner's, 1912), Merle Curti and Vernon Curstensen, *The University of Wisconsin: A History,* Volume II (Madison: University of Wisconsin Press, 1949), and Charles McCarthy, *The Wisconsin Idea* (New York: Macmillan, 1912).

For the description of the post-progressive period I used Hofstadter, *The Age of Reform,* Goldman *(op. cit.),* and Arthur M. Schlesinger, Jr., *The Crisis of the Old Order* (Boston: Houghton Mifflin, 1957). I also found helpful John Chamberlain's *Farewell to Reform* (New York: Liveright, 1932).

In addition to Harold O. Rugg and Ann Shumaker's *The Child-Centered School* (Yonkers: World Book, 1928), I used Rugg's *Foundations for American Education* (Yonkers: World Book, 1947).

The section on the New Deal rests heavily on the interpretation of Richard Hofstadter. I also found helpful Sidney Fine, *Laissez Faire and the General-Welfare State* (Ann Arbor: University of Michigan Press, 1956).

For the work of the American Youth Commission I consulted *Youth and the Future* (Washington, D.C.: American Council on Education, 1942), and Homer P. Rainey, *How Fare American Youth?* (New York: Appleton-Century, 1938).

For my discussion of the group at Teachers College I used Cremin *(op. cit.).* *The Educational Frontier,* edited by William H. Kilpatrick (New York: The Century Co., 1933), was also published as *Yearbook XXI* of the National Society of College Teachers of Education. *Reorganizing Secondary Education* (New York: Appleton-Century, 1939) was prepared by V. T. Thayer, Caroline B. Zachary and Ruth Kotinsky for the Commission on Secondary School Curriculum. K. L. Heaton and G. R. Koopman authored *A College Curriculum Based on Functional Needs of Students* (Chicago: University of Chicago Press, 1936). I profited from Thayer's description of the whole period in *Formative Ideas in American Education* (New York: Dodd, Mead, 1965). John F. Latimer's book is *What's Happened to Our High Schools?* (Washington, D.C.: Public Affairs Press, 1938). B. Paul Komisar's " 'Need' and the Needs-Curriculum" is in B. O. Smith and R. H. Emnis, *Language and Concepts in Education* (Chicago: Rand McNally, 1961).

I found parts of Daniel Bell's *The Reforming of General Education* (New York: Columbia University Press, 1966) helpful for understanding what is happening today. I also found Cremin *(op. cit.)* of value here. The 1958 quote from the Chancellor of the University of Kansas came from *Federal Educational Policies,*

Programs and Proposals (Washington, D.C.: U.S. Government Printing Office, 1960). Admiral Hyman Rickover's best seller was *Education and Freedom* (New York: Dutton, 1959).

In addition to Clark Kerr's *The Uses of the University* (New York: Harper Torchbooks, 1966), I profited from Hal Draper's essay, "The Mind of Clark Kerr" in *Revolution at Berkeley* (New York: Dell, 1965), edited by Michael V. Miller and Susan Gilmore.

Important recent studies include: Hugh Davis Graham, *The Uncertain Triumph: Federal Education Policy in the Kennedy and Johnson Years* (Chapel Hill: University of North Carolina Press, 1984); Patricia A. Graham, *Progressive Education: From Arcady to Academe* (New York: Teachers College Press, 1967); Geraldine Jonich, *The Sane Positivist: A Biography of Edward L. Thorndike* (Middletown: Wesleyan University Press, 1968); Ira Katznelson and Margaret Weir, *Schooling for All: Class, Race, and the Decline of the Democratic Ideal* (New York: Basic Books, 1985); Dorothy Ross, *G. Stanley Ross: The Psychologist as Prophet* (Chicago: The University of Chicago Press, 1972); Robert B. Westbrook, *John Dewey and American Democracy* (Ithaca: Cornell University Press, 1991).

SEVEN: THE DECLINE OF THE PUBLIC SCHOOL

A great number of historical analyses of the last twenty-five years of education have appeared since the first edition of *The Imperfect Panacea*. Here are some of the most noteworthy: Fred and Grace Hechinger, *Growing up in America* (New York: McGraw-Hill, 1975); Geraldine Joncich Clifford, *The Shape of American Education* (Englewood Cliffs, NJ: Prentice-Hall, 1975); W. Norton Grubb and Marvin Lazerson, *Broken Promises: How Americans Fail their Children* (Chicago: The University of Chicago Press, 1988); and Charles E. Silberman, *Crisis in the Classroom* (New York: Random House, 1970). A brief, sprightly, overview of some of the issues and many of the figures active during this period can be found in *The School Book* by Neil Postman and Charles Weingartner (New York: Delacorte, 1973).

The Gallup polls on American attitudes toward education appear yearly in the September edition of *Phi Delta Kappan*; the first ten polls appear in *A Decade of Gallup Polls of Attitudes toward Education, 1969–1979*, edited by Stanley M. Elam (Bloomington, IN: Phi Delta Kappan, 1979). A valuable reference source for the period is *A Digest of Supreme Court Decisions Affecting Education*, edited by Perry A. Zirkel and Sharon N. Richardson (Bloomington, IN: Phi Delta Kappan Educational Foundation, 1988). The literature on the influence of television is enormous. Three of the most helpful are: Erik Barnouw, *Tube of Plenty: The Evolution of American Television* (New York: Oxford University Press, 1982); Joshua Meyrowitz, *No Sense of Place: The Impact of Electronic Media on Social Behavior* (New York: Oxford University Press, 1985); and Neil Postman, *Amusing Ourselves to Death* (New York: Viking Books, 1985). Also see my *Getting Better Television and Moral Progress* (New Brunswick, NJ: Transaction Books, 1991).

Of the many books on the black struggle, I have found the following the most helpful: Clayborne Carson, *In Struggle: SNCC and the Black Awakening of the 1960s* (Cambridge: Harvard University Press, 1981); David C. Garrow, *Bearing the Cross: Martin Luther King Jr. and the Southern Christian Leadership Conference* (New York: William Morrow and Co., 1986); James A. Geschwender, ed., *The Black Revolt* (Englewood Cliffs, NJ: Prentice-Hall, 1971); Jennifer L. Hochschild, *The New American Dilemma: Liberal Democracy and School Desegregation* (New Haven: Yale University Press, 1984); and Juan Williams, *Eye on the Prize: America's Civil Rights Years 1954–1965* (New York: Viking Books, 1987).

Responses to the Coleman Report (James S. Coleman et al., "Equality of Educational Opportunity, Report of the Office of Education to Congress and the President" [U.S. Printing Office, July 1966]) are contained in Frederick Mosteller and Daniel P. Moynihan, eds., *On Equality of Educational Opportunity* (New York: Random House, 1972) and in *The Harvard Educational Review* 37 (Winter 1968). A helpful bibliography is Francisco Cordasco, *The Equality of Educational Opportunity* (Totowa, NJ: Littlefield, Adams and Co., 1973). Responses to the Jencks Report (Christopher Jencks and Associates, *Inequality: A Reassessment of the Effects of Family and Schooling in America* [New York: Basic Books, 1972]) are in *The Harvard Educational Review* 43 (February 1973).

On the women's movement and sexism in the schools, I consulted Nancy Frazier and Myra Sadker, *Sexism in School and Society* (New York: Harper and Row, 1973); Jo Freeman, *The Politics of Women's Liberation* (New York: David McKay, 1975); Steven D. McLaughlin et al., *The Changing Lives of American Women* (Chapel Hill: University of North Carolina Press, 1988); Judith Stacey et al., eds., *And Jill Came Tumbling After: Sexism in American Education* (New York: Dell Publishing Co., 1974); and Winifred D. Wandersee, *On the Move: America's Women in the 1970s* (Boston: Wayne Publishers, 1988). Also, see: Myra and David Sadker, *Failing at Fairness: How America's Schools Cheat Girls* (New York: Charles Scribner's Sons, 1994); David Tyack and Elizabeth Hansot, *Learning Together: A History of Coeducation in American Public Schools* (New Haven: Yale University Press, 1990).

Good introductions to ethnicity and bilingual education are Joshua A. Fishman et al., *Language Loyalty in the United States* (The Hague: Mouton, 1966); Michael Novak, *The Rise of the Unmeltable Ethnics* (New York: Macmillan Co., 1971); Thomas Sowell, *Ethnic America: A History* (New York: Basic Books, 1981); and Abigail M. Thernstrom, "E Pluribus Plura—Congress and Bilingual Education" (*The Public Interest* 60 [Summer 1980]). Also, see: Theodore Anderson and Mildred Boyer, *Bilingual Schooling in the United States* 2 volumes (Washington, D.C.: U.S. Superintendent of Documents, 1970).

An excellent study of poverty in America is James T. Patterson, *America's Struggle against Poverty: 1900–1980* (Cambridge: Harvard University Press, 1981), while an evaluation of the war on poverty can be found in Robert H. Haveman, ed., *A Decade of Federal Anti-Poverty Programs: Achievements, Failures, and Lessons* (New York: Academic Press, 1979). More recent assessments of the battle against poverty are Lisbeth B. Schorr, *Within Our Reach: Breaking the Cycle of Disadvantage* (New York: Doubleday, 1988) and William Julius Wilson, *The*

Truly Disadvantaged (Chicago: University of Chicago Press, 1987). An assessment of the 1965 Elementary and Secondary Education Act (ESEA) is Stephen K. Bailey and Edith K. Mosher, *ESEA: The Office of Education Administers a Law* (Syracuse: Syracuse University Press, 1968). Education of vocational education programs are in John T. Grasso and John R. Shea, *Vocational Education and Training: Impact on Youth* (New York: The Carnegie Foundation, 1979) and Marvin Lazerson and W. Morton Grubb, *American Education and Vocationalism* (New York: Teachers College Press, 1974). Information on students' rights is contained in Beatrice Gross and Ronald Gross, *The Children's Rights Movement* (Garden City, NY: Anchor Books, 1977) and Allen H. Levine et al., *The Rights of Students* (New York: Avon Books, 1973).

The most important works of those I have called the radical school critics of the late sixties and early seventies are John Holt, *How Children Fail* (New York: Pitman, 1967); Neil Postman and Charles Weingartner, *Teaching as a Subversive Activity* (New York: Delacorte, 1969); Herbert Kohl, *36 Children* (New York: New American Library, 1967); and Jonathan Kozol, *Death at an Early Age: The Destruction of the Hearts and Minds of Negro Children in the Boston Public Schools* (Boston: Houghton Mifflin, 1967). Three books that chart the course of the free school movement are George Dennison, *The Lives of Children* (New York: Random House, 1969); Jonathan Kozol, *Free Schools* (Boston: Houghton Mifflin, 1972); and Allen Graubard, *Free the Children: Radical Reform and the Free School Movement* (New York: Random House, 1973). The theories put forth in *Deschooling Society* (New York: Harper and Row, 1970), by Ivan Illich, and in *School Is Dead* (New York: Doubleday, 1971), by Everett Reimer, are critically assessed in *After Deschooling: What?* (New York: Harper and Row, 1973), edited by Alan Gartner, Colin Greer, and Frenk Riessman. Excerpts from many of the radical educational critics are anthologized in *Radical School Reform* (New York: Simon and Schuster, 1969), edited by Ronald Gross and Beatrice Gross; and in *Innovations in Education: Reformers and Their Critics* (Boston: Allyn and Bacon, 1975), edited by John Martin Rich. There are critiques of the movement in *Radical School Reform: Critiques and Alternatives* (Boston: Little, Brown and Co., 1973), edited by Cornelius J. Troost, and in Henry J. Perkinson, *Two Hundred Years of American Educational Thought* (New York: David McKay, 1976).

Some of the "revisionist" histories published in the 1970's include: Samuel Bowles and Herbert Gintis, *Schooling in Capitalist America: Educational Reform and the Contradictions of Economic Life* (New York: Basic Books, 1976); Colin Greer, *The Great School Legend: A Revisionist Interpretation of American Education* (New York: Basic Books, 1972); Edgar B. Gumbert and Joel Spring, *The Super School and the Super State: American Education in the Twentieth Century* (New York: John Wiley and Sons, 1974); Clarence J. Karier, Paul Violas, and Joel Spring, *Roots of Crisis: American Education in the Twentieth Century* (Chicago: Rand McNally, 1973); Michael Katz, *Class, Bureaucracy and Schools: The Illusion of Educational Change in America* (New York: Praeger Publishers, 1971); and Joel Spring, *The Sorting Machine: National Educational Policy Since 1945* (New York: David McKay, 1976). Also, see Ira Shor, *Culture Wars: School and Society in the Conservative Restoration, 1969–1984* (Boston: Routledge & Kegan Paul, 1986).

The struggle of the disabled for social justice is covered in Frank Bowe, *Handicapping America: Barriers to Disabled People* (New York: Harper and Row, 1978); John Gliedman and William Roth, *The Unexpected Minority: Handicapped Children in America* (New York: Harcourt Brace Jovanovich, 1980); Susan E. Hasazi et al., *Mainstreaming* (Bloomington, IN: Phi Delta Kappa Educational Foundation, 1979); and Erwin L. Levine and Elizabeth M. Wexler, *PL 94-142: An Act of Congress* (New York: Macmillan Co., 1981). Also see: Reed Martin, *Educating Handicapped Children: The Legal Mandate* (Champaign, IL: Research Press, 1979).

An insightful analysis of the status of teachers in 1960 is Myron Lieberman, *The Future of Public Education* (Chicago: The University of Chicago Press, 1960). Descriptions of the teacher unionization movement are in Charles W. Cheng, *Teacher Unions and the Power Structure* (Bloomington, IN: Phi Delta Kappa Foundation, 1981); Anthony M. Cresswell et al., *Teacher Unions and Collective Bargaining in Public Education* (Berkeley: McCutcheon Publishing, 1980); Marshall O. Donley, Jr., *The Future of Teacher Power in America* (Bloomington, IN: Phi Delta Kappa Educational Foundation, 1977); and Thomas J. Flygare, *Collective Bargaining in the Public Schools* (Bloomington, IN: Phi Delta Kappa Educational Foundation, 1977).

The central document of the educational reform movement is the National Commission on Excellence Report: *A Nation at Risk* (Washington, D.C.: U.S. Superintendent of Documents, 1983). A helpful collection of articles on this report is Beatrice Gross and Ronald Gross, *The Great School Debate* (New York: Simon and Schuster, 1985); also see "Reform in the 1980s," *Teacher* 1, no. 1 (September 1989). For a critique of the reform movement, see Christine M. Shea et al., eds., *The New Servants of Power: A Critique of the 1980s School Reform Movement* (New York: Greenwood Press, 1989); also see The Carnegie Foundation on the Advancement of Teaching, *Report Card on School Reform: The Teachers Speak* (New York: The Carnegie Foundation, 1988). A brilliant analysis of American high schools in the eighties is Arthur Powell et al., *The Shopping Mall High School* (Boston: Houghton Mifflin Co., 1985). Some of the many assessments and appraisals of education made in the eighties are: Lynn V. Cheney, *American Memory: A Report on the Humanities in the Nation's Public Schools* (Washington, D.C.: National Endowment for the Humanities, 1988); Committee on Policy for Racial Justice, *Visions of a Better Way: A Black Appraisal of Public Schooling* (Washington, D.C.: Joint Center for Political Studies, 1989); Linda Darling-Hammond, *Equality and Excellence: The Educational Status of Black Americans* (New York: College Entrance Examination Board, 1985); Archie E. Lapointe et al., *A World of Difference: An International Assessment of Mathematics and Science* (Princeton: Educational Testing Services, 1988); Ina V. S. Mullis and Lynn B. Jenkins, *The Science Report Card, Elements of Risk and Recovery: Trends and Achievement Based on the 1986 National Assessment* (Princeton: Educational Testing Services, 1988); and Diane Ravitch and Chester E. Finn, Jr. *What Do Our 17-Year-Olds Know?: A Report on the First National Assessment of History and Literature* (New York: Harper and Row, 1987). Specific proposals for the reform of the schools were made by Ernest L. Boyer, *High School: A*

Report on Secondary Education in America (New York: Harper and Row, 1983); John I. Goodlad, *A Place Called School* (New York: McGraw-Hill, 1984); and Theodore R. Sizer, *Horace's Compromise: The Dilemma of the American High School* (Boston: Houghton Mifflin Co., 1985). Analyses of the impact of collective bargaining on teachers and schools are contained in Maurice R. Berube, *Teacher Politics: The Influence of Unions* (New York: Greenwood Press, 1988) and Joseph W. Nieman, *America's Teachers* (New York: Longman, 1989). The claim that American education must move beyond public schooling is forcefully argued in Myron Lieberman, *Beyond Public Education* (New York: Praeger, 1986), and in *Public Education: An Autopsy* (Cambridge: Harvard University Press, 1993. Also, see John E. Chubb and Terry Moe, *Politics, Markets and America's Schools* (Washington, D.C.: The Brookings Institution, 1990).

I have elaborated my views about what schools are for in *The Possibilities of Error* (New York: David McKay, 1971), *Learning from Our Mistakes* (Westport, CT: Greenwood Press, 1984), and *Teachers Without Goals/Students Without Purposes* (New York: McGraw-Hill, 1993).

Name Index

Subject Index